CW01465474

Visions of Ted Bundy

The Psychic and the Chi Omega Murders

Susan Waller Lehmann

The people, places, and events described in this book are real. However, the author has changed the names and identifying characteristics of some of the people referenced in this story to protect their privacy. The author has relied on the memories of those who shared their experiences to make this story as accurate as possible. Events, conversations and timelines have been recreated from interviews, personal notes, conflicting newspaper and media accounts, police reports and, of course, psychics. Any errors are the sole responsibility of the author.

Cover design by Peter Lehmann.

Edited by Vince Font.

ISBN 978-0-9992300-0-8 (Soft cover)
ISBN 978-0-9992300-1-5 (Hard cover)
ISBN 978-0-9992300-4-6 (Ebook)

Library of Congress Control Number: 2017905291

White Rhino Press, Pleasant View, UT.
https://www.whiterhinopress.com.

Publisher's note: If you have any questions or comments, please contact us at white.rhino.press@gmail.com.

For George Cravey Brand
1940 – 2007

Contents

Foreword

At 3:15 in the morning of January 15th, 1978, I was awakened from a deep sleep by the ringing of my telephone. I had been a homicide investigator for the Leon County Sheriff's Department and had recently been promoted to the rank of lieutenant.

When that phone rang, I had no idea that my life for the next several months was going to lead me down many paths that I had never dreamed of walking. I certainly never would have chosen to spend, what I now recall as the most troubled time of my life, solving one of the most tragic and gruesome murders, which completely rocked the sleepy town of Tallahassee, Florida.

Known to many as the Chi Omega murders, investigating the brutal slaying of two Florida State University coeds and the savage attacks suffered by three other young women that early morning, was the hardest job I have ever experienced. After 20 years of investigating and solving hundreds of homicides with the sheriff's department, State Attorney's Office, and other law enforcement agencies, this was the first experience I had with a serial killer.

In the wake of the discovery of the five victims, we investigators faced a perplexing and frightening realization: a lone man had entered a fully occupied sorority house and attacked four young women, leaving two dead and two others unconscious and badly wounded. The attacker was able to flee the house, undetected and unseen, except by a lone woman who saw his profile in the shadows of the dark house. Later that same morning, he entered a duplex blocks away and attacked another young woman. What baffled investigators more than anything else was the fact that this assailant left virtually no clues to his identity. He left scant traces of himself behind, and the little evidence he did leave, we were unaccustomed to using. We can now look back to the Chi Omega murders and realize, with great sadness, that Ted Bundy ushered in a new age of homicide investigation. He created a whole new category of homicide, that of serial murders.

The sleepy town of Tallahassee entered a period of grave fear; in fact, even the most hard-boiled of police were afraid that the killer, who was so bold to have killed in a sorority house filled with women, would strike again, catching us off guard. On the evening when I faced the shocked and grieving families of the victims, I promised I would do anything and everything to catch the man who damaged all of our lives.

And I meant it.

Two days after the murders, I received a phone call from a young man who claimed to have knowledge of the killer. He said he could help us. In talking with this man, who identified himself only as Joseph, I learned that he knew many details of the slayings that were not known to many people, and certainly unknown outside of the investigative task force.

Joseph called himself a mystic, although most people would refer to people like him as psychic. I certainly had no previous experience dealing with people who had dreams or visions, but in fact, he frightened me with the information he had. I was unsure, during the phone conversation, whether he was someone who could help, or in fact, was the killer we were seeking.

As it turned out, Joseph's information became an integral part of the Chi Omega investigation. He was able to convey details of things he had dreamed would happen in the future, as well as clues and enough insight into the killer, that we were nearly able to catch Ted Bundy in Tallahassee. He certainly was able to assist us with information necessary so that Pensacola Patrolman David Lee was able to apprehend Bundy in Pensacola as he was preparing to leave Florida.

The arrest and conviction of Ted Bundy was not the result conclusively of Joseph's information, but he provided much that was necessary and integral to finding the man responsible for the deaths of the Chi Omega girls and 12-year-old Kimberly Leach. Perhaps the single most important thing that I can say about Joseph is that he truly opened my eyes to issues that are not easily explained or visible in black and white, and the role the intangibles must play in solving complex serial crimes.

When Susan Waller approached me in 1979 about Joseph's involvement with the Chi Omega murders, I was willing to go on record with her newspaper. At that time, however, I was thwarted in my attempts to tell the story. The sheriff, Ken Katsaris, was up for reelection, and had suffered much critical press since the Chi Omega murders had happened 18 months earlier. It was the opinion of the sheriff and his closest advisors that many details of the investigation needed to be kept quiet. I did not want to release any information that might have assisted Ted Bundy with his appeals.

In light of this, I asked Susan to wait. I promised I would one day give her the true story of the capture of Ted Bundy. Neither one of us even suspected that it would take over 10 years.

I have worked closely with Ms. Waller in the writing of this book. It has been very important to us both that the story be told as factually as possible. She has been very diligent in capturing the emotions and the bizarre conversations experienced by those of us who were unfortunate enough to become the players in a tragedy cast by Theodore Robert Bundy. There is truly more to this world than we can ever explain.

George C. Brand, Jr.
February 29th, 1991

Preface

When people ask me what this book is about, I say it is about two things. It is the story about what happened to Tallahassee, Florida, in the aftermath of the Chi Omega murders, and it is also the story of three men: a Southern cop, a psychic, and a well-known serial killer. This narrative is just as timely now as it was 20 years ago. The phenomenon of serial killings is no longer an infrequent and random fact of life, but has become a perplexing and frighteningly common aspect of homicide investigations throughout the country.

As bizarre as this story may seem, it is absolutely true. Some dialogue has been recreated from the memories of the people involved, as many of the conversations were never recorded. This book is an accurate depiction of the many frustrations that may be encountered during the hunt for serial murderers.

Life sometimes gets in the way of our best laid plans, and this book took a long time to be born. But, like a child, this story has followed me through the years, and it's time now to tell it.

Crimes continue, mistakes are made... and psychics are used.

Susan Waller Lehmann
March 31st, 2017

Part I: A Place Where We Used to Live

Chapter 1: Lady Writer

In late October of 1979, Helen Baxter was the only female reporter working on the staff of the *Independent Florida Flambeau,* Florida State University's independent student newspaper. It received no financial support from the university. Helen was a paid reporter, and a full-time student.

At the time, Helen was 21 years old, thin, with short blonde hair. One of the staff photographers often asked her to be a model in advertising shoots, but she only agreed to do that once. Blue-eyed and tanned even in the winter months, Helen looked like the Miami girl she was.

Florida State University (FSU) is located in Tallahassee, Florida, the capitol city. In 1979, Tallahassee was a mid-sized town with two daily papers. The main city paper is the *Tallahassee Democrat*, which at the time was owned by one of the largest newspaper chains in the country, Knight Ridder. The other newspaper was the *Independent Florida Flambeau.*

Helen walked up the circular driveway to an old FSU maintenance building where the *Flambeau* was housed. Laurie Jones, the paper's business manager, came out of the advertising office and greeted her. The young women were good friends. Laurie looked worried as she handed Helen a note, as if she were delivering bad news.

"This is a pretty strange message," Laurie said. "This guy just wouldn't shut up. He said he worked with the police as a psychic to catch Bundy, and he's claiming the reward money. He said his name was Joseph, and something else rather weird. He wants you to call him. He made me promise to give you this message." She looked toward the windows of the newsroom.

"What did he say that was weird?"

"He said he also goes by the name 'Two Skins.'"

Helen snorted. "Really? Is he an Indian, like a Seminole or something?" She began laughing at her joke.

"I don't know," Laurie said, placing her hands on her hips, a sure sign she was becoming annoyed. "Ask him yourself. But I wouldn't tell anyone if you just threw the message in the trash."

"Yes, I could do that, but then he'd just call and bug you to death for the rest of your life. Unless," Helen said with a smile. "Oh, hell. Did Nichols put you up to this? It's a joke, right?"

Laurie didn't laugh. "I'd tell you if it was one of Nichols' jokes."

Bruce Nichols was the arts and features editor of the newspaper and shared an office with Helen. He was a tall, reedy blond man in his early 20s.

"You sure it's not Nichols?" Helen asked, looking into Laurie's eyes searching for a hint of a tease. "You know this is just the kind of shit he likes to pull to give me a hard time."

Laurie shook her head.

"Then it has to be some stoner kid playing a joke, trying to grab a headline," Helen said and read the note.

There were many activists on campus with causes ranging from opposition to the U.S. government and its support of OPEC, U.S. imperialism, the Greek system at FSU, and the death penalty, to support for the ideals of Socialism, women's equality—especially in sports funding—and a perennial favorite, legalizing marijuana. Additional color was provided by a crusading evangelical minister who often took center stage at the outdoor student union each Friday. Jeering crowds would taunt his suggestions to give up "drinking and whoring." There was quite a buzz around campus when the minister showed up with a girlfriend. She became part of his act, shaking a tambourine and singing hymns, her body swaying seductively under her peasant dresses to the delight of those watching. It's impossible to say if he picked up any converts, but his act was pure entertainment for many. Everyone, it seemed, had a cause and the student union provided an enthusiastic audience.

The leading news at the moment was the continuous, daily protests of the Iranian students in the student union area demanding the removal of the U.S.-supported Shah, Mohammad Reza Shah Pahlavi. Days earlier, on October 22nd, 1979, the Shah fled Iran to the relative safety of the United States to undergo cancer treatment. Tensions were rising both domestically and abroad.[1]

Iranians in the U.S. had had their assets frozen; they couldn't go back to Iran, even if they wanted to. The campus swarmed with FBI and, it was suspected, CIA agents. Helen knew two people who she thought were CIA operatives. Primarily, though, it was the American students who got into jams, and young men from fraternities were those most likely to find themselves in hot water with the campus administration. Their capers were often reported in the papers, and Helen believed the letter to be a fraternity prank.

"Why do I always get this stupid crap?" Helen asked. "You direct it all to me, don't you?"

"You handle the crime beat. That's where all the crazy stuff comes from." Laurie shrugged. "I don't think this is a joke, though. This guy was... different."

"Really? I'm going to talk with Wilson."

Helen walked across the circular drive to the stairs leading up to the newsroom. James "Jamie" Wilson, the editor of the *Flambeau*, shouted her name as she entered the newsroom with the note in hand.

In his mid-20s, Wilson had a thick mustache and brown hair parted down the middle. He was the best-looking guy at the newspaper, and Helen had a huge crush on him for the first several months they had worked together. He had a lot on his hands managing the writers in his office, and none of them liked to meet the nightly deadlines. He was the enforcer of rules to a group of gifted and highly undisciplined writers. He was known for doing the "Wilson stomp," an angry, foot-stamping jig that was often accompanied by the pounding of his right fist into his left hand.

Helen doubted Jamie trusted any of his writers to meet a deadline or to act responsibly on their own, and he didn't mind letting everyone know where he stood on any subject, especially on the behavior of his reporters. As the executive editor, he had a paper to run with as few legal problems as possible. He was held

---

[1] On November 4th, 1979, the U.S. Embassy would be occupied by a group of Iranian students in support of the Iranian Revolution. 52 Americans were held hostage for 444 days until their release after the inauguration of President Ronald Reagan.

directly responsible by the publishers for all mistakes.

Jamie kept his small office clean. He had a photograph of a beautiful woman on his wall that Helen had never summoned the courage to ask him about. The rest of the newsroom was usually littered with trash, newspapers, magazines, and empty beer cans. Nearly every night, after the deadline was met, Wilson would lighten up. Sometimes, he would even have a beer with the writers, but he rarely went with them to the bars they frequented after the paper was put to bed.

"Have you heard about this Joseph guy?" Helen asked as she stepped into Jamie's office and handed him the note.

"Who?" he said as he read the note. "Oh, yeah. Listen, Baxter, sometimes reporters have to cover the crappy stories as well as the good ones. It comes with the territory. I've talked with this guy myself. He needs to be checked out."

"What's his story?"

"Call him and find out. Maybe something usable." He handed her the note and gave her a dismissive look. "You asked for the crime beat, and you're likely to find some crazies out there. If you don't want to cover this, we'll just have to send you to charm school so you can learn to run the advice column. But until then," he pointed toward the back room, "find your desk and make some calls. We get paid to report the news, not talk about it."

He began his dance, directing his voice to everyone within earshot. "Move! Write some news! Deadline's coming!"

Helen rolled her eyes as she turned on her heels and headed back to her desk. The newsroom was a small, cramped, four-room office space in the shape of a square. Jamie's private office was next to the office Helen shared with Nichols and the occasional part-time arts and features writers. The front door separated the main editing room from the sports office. Each desk had a phone and a typewriter. Every room was staffed with talented personalities.

Helen sat down at her desk, unfolded the note, and read it again.

> *A man named Joseph called. He wants to talk to you about his claim for the reward money on Bundy. Call him today. Try until you reach him. He also goes by the name "Two Skins." You must keep his name secret.*

There was a telephone number.

She dialed it slowly and let the phone ring. No one answered. A strange feeling came over her as she hung up. Her stomach was upset from too much coffee. She hadn't eaten breakfast or lunch. She hadn't done well on an exam earlier in the day. She suddenly felt irritable and pissy. She'd had too much alcohol the night before, like she did almost every night. Each day, she smoked at least one pack of cigarettes. She needed sleep, decent food, and exercise. This note referring to Bundy didn't help her mood, either.

As a young woman who had lived in Tallahassee at the time of the murders, anything with Bundy's name on it piqued her interest. The Chi Omega murders and the manhunt for Ted Bundy had generated the biggest news stories in Tallahassee, but she wasn't certain she could muster much enthusiasm for someone seeking reward money.

She recalled that immediately after the deaths of the FSU coeds, people in the community put up thousands of dollars to encourage anyone who may have had information that led to the arrest and conviction of the killer to come forward. Helen vaguely remembered something about a man who'd put in a claim for the reward money because he owned the Volkswagen that Bundy had stolen and was driving when he was apprehended in Pensacola.

Now, some new guy—this Joseph—was claiming the reward money too. It was stuff for the *National Enquirer*.

Just as long as I don't have to see Bundy again. Helen remembered how an ex-boyfriend had snuck her into the Leon County Jail just before Bundy's Chi Omega trial. He'd had help from his cousin, who worked in the sheriff's office. This was the second time she'd seen the notorious killer. "You're not the one,"

Bundy had said to her from his jail cell. "I wanted the other girl."

The fact that he remembered her terrified Helen. She wasn't able to speak, and left the jail immediately. *So much for a scoop*, she thought.

Embarrassed at the memory, she reached for the phone again to begin making her daily calls to her police contacts. Her first call was to the FSU police spokesperson to learn what kinds of mischief students had gotten into the night before. Although it was still early, she needed to gather the crime reports for the day. Normally, she was still gathering stories right up to the daily deadline.

Jim Sewell, the FSU police spokesman, said he'd call her back when he was ready. She looked at her typewriter, an old Royal manual, and realized that somebody had swiped its ribbon. The guys liked to rile her, so finding a usable typewriter ribbon was a daily mission she usually undertook in good humor. But today, she was in no mood to pander to her coworkers' pranks.

"Alright, assholes, who took my ribbon?" she yelled.

Several guys in the editing room turned to look at her. No one acted like a hoax was in progress; there were none of the usual smiles or giggles. That bothered her. The guys always snickered when they were up to something.

She sighed and tossed the note into the wastebasket and decided to forget about it. If it was real, this Joseph guy would call back. She was not going to mess with him unless he called again.

In those days, the newsroom was a tough place for young women. The male reporters often told crude jokes and made blatantly sexist comments about females. The two bathrooms were disgusting, and Helen had gotten into the habit of using the women's room in the business office next door.

Most aspiring Lois Lanes would get an assignment or two and never return to the office. Women were scared off by the guys. But Helen so genuinely wanted to be a reporter that she ignored the guys or laughed them off. Some were even her friends. The guys never stopped teasing her, though.

It helps to be pretty, she thought as she got up to search for a replacement ribbon. Thoughts of Joseph faded as she fell into the familiar march to the all-important newspaper deadline.

◆❖◆

The days passed. By Thursday, Helen had completely forgotten about Joseph and his claim for the Bundy reward money. It was a typical Thursday. All of the phone lines were ringing and reporters were yelling to each other or to people on the other end of the phones. The heater was finally working now that the weather had warmed up to 70 degrees, and Helen was sweaty and running on deadline. The ribbon broke on the Royal.

Right on schedule, she groused to herself, then laughed. *Why the fuck can't they buy us a box of brand-new ribbons?*

As she moved the battered Royal around to remove the broken ribbon, its "specially designed" line space lever fell onto the desk. She heard the screw roll off the desk and clatter somewhere onto the filthy floor.

She knew she could fix it, but reconsidered. *I am not going to crawl around on all fours to find that damn screw. The guys would love that.*

Sunlight poured in through the open window behind her and made the day seem hotter. Nichols, seated across from her, was already halfway through a bottle of tequila and it was only 2 in the afternoon. It was payday and everyone had money for food, booze, and cigarettes—at least for a day or two.

She picked up the Royal and walked to another desk where a potential replacement sat forlornly. This one was missing its "H" key, which meant that she would have to hand-write the missing letter into all of her copy. She examined the unclaimed typewriter and reluctantly swapped it out with hers. It had a ribbon. *Maybe it will make it through the rest of the day.*

She was at her desk with a cigarette hanging out of her mouth, squinting through the smoke and talking on the phone with Dick Simpson, the public relations officer for the Leon County Sheriff's Department, when the door to the newsroom opened.

She looked up and watched a man walk in. He was in his mid-20s and of average height, with long, wavy brown hair and a ragged beard. He was thin and resembled John Lennon. As he stepped through the doorway, she noticed the dark-tinted wire-rimmed glasses that hid his eyes.

He carried a large leather bag that bulged with books and papers. It hung by a wide leather band on his left shoulder that crossed his body. Its bulky weight rested on his right hip. He looked like a lot of guys on college campuses in the late 1970s. He looked like a hippie.

The man leaned over and said something to Mike McCarty, a skinny, perpetually unshaven rookie news reporter who edited wire service copy next to the front door. Mike turned around and pointed to Helen. Her eyes locked with the bearded guy for a second, then her heart began to race, thumping in her ears.

"Shit," she muttered.

She completely lost her train of thought on the story Dick Simpson was relaying to her over the phone. She mumbled something about calling him back and hung up. She cast a glance over her shoulder and seriously considered climbing out the window before things went any further. Something told her to *run*.

"Hey, Baxter," Mike yelled. "This guy's here to see you."

Everyone in the room froze for a second. They had all heard about the "psychic" note. There are no secrets in a newspaper office. Even Jamie Wilson stepped out of the sports room to look at the guy.

Hesitantly, she took a breath, looked out the window again, then picked up her notepad and pen, cigarettes, and a lighter. She walked over to the young man, put her hand out, and smiled. He had a firm handshake that lasted longer than Helen wanted it to. She had to pull her hand away.

"My name is Joseph," he said, looking into her eyes.

"I'm Helen Baxter," she replied, rather sternly. "We can talk back there if you'd like." She turned and pointed to her office area, where Nichols was making faces at her.

"I'd rather go outside, it's a nice day. If you don't mind?" Joseph asked quietly.

"Fine."

He sat down on the steps in front of the newsroom. Helen joined him, sitting to his left so she could see into the newsroom window. He looked at her out of the corner of his left eye and raised his eyebrows.

"Well?" Helen asked. She lit a cigarette.

She knew without looking that all of the newsroom boys were watching them. Nothing she did, it seemed, went unnoticed.

Cars drove by. Students on foot and students on bikes walked along the roadway. The *Flambeau* office was located on Woodward Avenue, across from the FSU Student Union building and swimming pool, the only street that cut straight through the campus. Next to them stood a large tree that was beginning to lose its leaves. A few pears up near the top of the tree were dried up and rotted, somehow still clinging to the limbs.

"What kind of tree is that?" Joseph asked.

"A pear tree," she answered. "Earlier in the fall, Laurie Jones and I picked the fruit and made some pies. Laurie works in the business office. They're not the kind of pears you can pick and eat, but they make good pies. I think they're called sandstone pears."

Out of the corner of her eye, she saw Wilson watching them. He had begun pacing by the window while ostensibly guiding McCarty's editing.

Joseph pulled a Bible out of his leather bag, opened it, and handed it to her. "Would you please read Genesis, chapter six, verses one through four? Aloud?"

"Really?" Helen said, annoyed. She stood up. "I don't have time for this. I have a story to do, and an early deadline as I ride with the city cops tonight."

"Please." Joseph reached out as if to touch her, then lowered his arm. "Please, I don't mean to offend you. I just need a little help from you."

Helen realized she wasn't going to be done with this guy until she let his tale play out, so she began to read, pausing occasionally to take a drag from her cigarette.

"And it came to pass, when men began to multiply on the face of the earth, and daughters were born unto them,

That the sons of God saw the daughters of men that they were fair; and they took them wives of all which they chose.

And the LORD said, My spirit shall not always strive with man, for that he also is flesh: yet his days shall be a hundred and twenty years.

There were giants in the earth in those days; and also after that, when the sons of God came in unto the daughters of men, and they bear children to them, the same became mighty men which were of old, men of renown.

She closed the Bible and handed it back to him. "Okay, fine. I read it for you." She stubbed out the cigarette. "What does 'sons of God' and 'daughters of men' mean? And why is this important to you?"

"Not everything you hear and see is as it seems," he said. "So, we have a man who could not drink alcohol because he made a vow to God. And this man was in a restaurant or at a party and by accident, he was served wine. Now, he thought it was a soft drink and he took a sip. Is he guilty of breaking his vows to God?"

"Really? Are you serious?" She wondered where this was going. She glanced at the newsroom, but no one was watching anymore, so maybe they weren't playing a joke on her. "Yes. Yes, the guy broke his vow, I guess."

Joseph smiled at her and laughed lightly. "No. If the man didn't know he was being served wine, and trusted the person serving him to give him a soft drink, then how could he be guilty, unless he took a second sip, on purpose?"

"Okay, I see your point, but I'm not much interested in vows to God and all that." She looked at her watch. "What does this have to do with Bundy? As I've said, I have an early deadline and no stories yet today, so if you have something to tell me, please get to it."

She looked closely at Joseph. Scraggly beard aside, he was actually kind of attractive, in a John Lennon-Beatles sort of way, and he didn't *seem* dangerous. His clothes looked clean, and while not new, they weren't raggedy. He didn't smell badly, either. His dark-brown hair, although long, looked freshly washed and was neat. He didn't look like a street person. Helen wondered if he had a girlfriend.

"Don't worry about it," he said with a smile. "Wisdom is different to you. You wonder what all of this has to do with Bundy, and I know you're busy. You're probably wondering what kind of women like me." He stopped and waited for her reaction. She sat still. "Women like you, actually."

How the fuck did he know what I was thinking?

She lit another cigarette to hide her discomfort.

Crap. I'll smoke this whole pack if I stay out here much longer.

Her hand trembled.

Then Joseph leaned forward, placed his elbows on his knees, and told Helen a story. Now that his attention had shifted away from her, she settled in and listened to what he had to say. He explained that shortly after the winter semester had begun in 1978, he started to have dreams about someone evil coming to Tallahassee. This was "just about a week prior" to the Chi Omega murders that occurred on January 15th. He said that after the murders, he'd had frequent and worrisome dreams about evil forces and a corrupt and immoral man.

"What kind of 'evil forces' are you talking about?"

"A very powerful, very evil person. Or persons," he said. "Like the one the police were looking for. He was looking for me, too, in my dreams."

"So, are you saying that when you got these visions about the Chi Omega murders that Ted Bundy was looking at *you* in your dreams?"

"Something like that."

"How does that work? You dream about him and he dreams about you?" She stared at Joseph. He did not answer. "Were you involved with the killings?"

Her question was a valid one. Some people were skeptical that Ted Bundy had been the sole assailant on that cold January 1978 night when two girls were murdered in a busy sorority house and two other women were brutally beaten. A fifth young woman, who lived just blocks away, had been severely and permanently injured that night as well. "Had Bundy acted alone?" was a popular topic of conversation on those long nights Helen spent riding with police officers and sheriff's deputies.

"Let me tell you my story," Joseph said.

He spoke for over an hour and Helen listened. She did not make any notes, but she did write down one important name: Lieutenant George Brand of the Leon County Sheriff's Department. Joseph mentioned Brand's name repeatedly during his narrative.

"George Brand was the only one I dealt with, except maybe for the woman who answered the phones at the command post and took the notes I'd call in to Brand. I don't recall her name to save my life. She's real pretty, though. I saw her again the other day. I'm really bad with names. You'll find that out about me. I don't forget faces, but I'm bad with names."

"So, you'd get these visions and then call them in to the task force? Seriously?" She couldn't wait to make that call. If what he said was true, it would make a pretty interesting story.

Joseph wanted Helen to write about him so that he could claim a portion of the reward money that had been raised after the Chi Omega murders. He thought he deserved at least some of it because of his "work" in assisting the task force.

"I don't want the money myself," he assured Helen. "I would give it to the families of the victims."

"What are we talking about here? It's like $10,000, right?"

He nodded. "And when you write the article, you can never use my last name."

"I don't know your last name," she said. "But when I write stories, I use last names. That's my policy and that's the policy of this paper. Jamie Wilson, my editor, would have to make that decision. It's not mine to make."

"Okay, please ask him. People don't need to know what I'm capable of doing. It would frighten them and some would come after me, to use me... or hurt me. I just want to be left alone and go to my classes and work on my music. I don't want to be a target or a freak."

Helen stood up and reached out to shake his hand. "I'll need to talk with my editor, but I'll see what I can do." She didn't want to agree to anything at this point. She wanted to say no. She thought for a moment. "Hey, didn't the *Democrat* run stories about the people claiming the reward money?"

"As a matter of fact, they did."

"Did they run one on you?"

He seemed to grow uncomfortable. "No, they wouldn't write about me. They wanted my last name and I wouldn't give them that. They also wanted to run a picture of me with the article."

"Oh. So that's why you're here, because you think the rules are different at the *Flambeau*?" Helen felt indignant that Joseph had come to her newspaper because the *Democrat* had turned him down.

"I came to see you because I was told to," he replied.

"How were you told? Because I do the crime beat, right?"

"I had a dream."

Helen froze, her pen in midair. Joseph's statement set her nerves on edge again. This was a bizarre conversation, and she felt a headache coming on.

"Can you read minds, or do you have X-ray vision or anything like that?" she asked.

She had seen the *Superman* movie with Christopher Reeve the past winter, and had been quite impressed when Superman had known the color of Lois Lane's panties because he could see through most anything. She had looked at her date during the movie and wished he was Superman. He wasn't even close, but he was a nice guy.

I think that was probably the last date I went on.

She sighed. Now she was giving this Joseph guy some crap.

"No, not really," he replied with a slightly sinister smile. "But if you have a mole on your hip, it would be only a coincidence." He reached over and touched her right hip lightly with his index finger.

Oh, my God! She jumped nearly three feet into the air.

"Don't touch me!" she barked, and moved beyond his reach.

The hairs on her head and neck stood on end, and goosebumps crawled her arms and legs. Her face tingled and flushed, and her heart raced. She did, indeed, have a small mole right where he had touched her—but it was visible only when she was completely naked.

How did he know about that?

Just then, Wilson stuck his head out the window. "Baxter, Dickie Simpson keeps calling. He says he's got some crime info for you."

"I, uh, I'll be inside in a minute, we're about done now," she said in a tightly controlled voice. Her heart was pounding. She felt breathless. She tried not to betray her terror. She didn't want Joseph to touch her again, not even to shake hands. She backed up the stairs to the newsroom door.

"Helen, you need to get to know me better," Joseph said. "Please? Maybe dinner at my place tomorrow night? I live in a house just above Lake Ella. I have football practice with my boys. I help coach 10-year-old kids. But after that, maybe?" He walked backward toward Woodward Avenue. "I'm really a nice guy, you'll see."

"Maybe," she said, although she meant "Hell no." She desperately wanted to get back inside to safety.

Joseph turned and walked toward the university pool. She waited until he was out of sight. When he was gone, she went next door to the business department and entered Laurie's office. She closed the door behind her and leaned against it.

"You look like a mess," Laurie said.

"I feel like I'm going to pass out." Helen sat down on the chair next to Laurie's desk. "Oh, my God, Laurie, I just spoke with a pretty scary dude."

She told Laurie about Joseph's story, her mole, and reading Bible verses as she dragged hard on a cigarette.

"Do you think he's dangerous?" Laurie said. She opened the window behind her to let in some fresh air. She hated cigarette smoke, but she tolerated Helen's smoking.

"I think he may be stalking me," Helen said. "You know how the *Democrat* ran articles about unanswered questions concerning the Bundy case?"

"Yes, I've read them. We've run some letters to the editor about that too. Do you think this guy could be an accomplice to Bundy, or if he was involved with the Chi Omega murders?"

"I don't know."

They speculated about Joseph to the point of hysteria. Laurie picked up the phone receiver and dialed a number. She handed the phone to Helen.

"Sheriff's office," a woman answered.

"Lieutenant Brand, please."

"We don't have a Lieutenant Brand here, ma'am."

Helen heard a strange buzzing in her ear and had to consciously remain seated in her chair. "Are you sure there's no Lieutenant Brand?" She spoke steadily, but she fought panic.

"No, ma'am, not that I know of. But hold on, let me ask someone."

Helen placed her hand over the mouthpiece on the receiver and turned to Laurie with the phone still to her ear. "Oh, my God, he's a psycho and he's after me. The lady said there's no Lieutenant Brand. What the hell am I going to do? Who can I talk to?"

"Ask for someone to protect you, maybe have him arrested," Laurie said. She stared at Helen worriedly. "Talk to Dickie Simpson. He'll know what to do."

"Ma'am?" The sheriff's receptionist was back. "Ma'am, I'm new here, I'm sorry, I've been told we do have a Captain George Brand.

Could he possibly be the person you want to talk to?"

"I'll try him," Helen said quickly, then exhaled, her lungs burned. She hadn't realized she'd been holding her breath. She looked at Laurie and winked.

"This is Captain Brand," a man with a deeply timbered Southern growl said. It was a big voice.

Helen sputtered something about being a reporter and meeting a guy who claimed to be the psychic who caught Ted Bundy.

"Joseph?" Brand laughed heartily. "That boy came to see you?"

"Yes, he did."

"And he told you about his ability, about what he did for us?"

"Yes." Helen was unnerved by this man's candor. She thought getting verification of Joseph's story was going to be a lot more difficult than this.

"Yeah, well he's a little different. I'm surprised he told you about it."

"He asked me to speak with you, to verify his claims."

"He did, did he?" Brand cleared his throat. "Well then, let's have a chat. Come on down to my office at the courthouse tomorrow morning and we'll talk."

Brand hung up. Still shaking, Helen handed the receiver back to Laurie.

"Okay, Brand's real and he knows Joseph. I guess that means I'm doing the story."

"I heard him loud and clear," Laurie said. She shrugged her shoulders and raised her eyebrows as Helen left to go back to the newsroom.

Helen was dazed and worried. She knew she should have felt relieved when Brand agreed to meet her, and seemed to *like* Joseph, but she still had an uneasy feeling about the situation.

Jamie was in her face before she'd gotten two steps through the door. "Who was that guy? Was that the psycho guy?"

"Yeah, that was him," she said slowly.

"Well, have you written some copy? It's two hours to deadline and I want to see your stuff. You were with him for over an hour on my time." He tapped his watch. "Did you get a scoop out of him?"

"I think so," Helen said, walking to her desk.

"Today?"

"No, not today, next week."

The "H"-less typewriter she'd snatched earlier had been stolen from her desk. Two hours to deadline and no typewriter. Of course, she still didn't have her daily copy, either.

"I need a typewriter, damn it!"

All of the guys laughed.

"And I need a story."

She grabbed a typewriter from the desk of a younger sportswriter who reached up and grabbed his copy. She ignored his protests and carried it back to her own desk. The typewriter had a ribbon and all keys were present, so she was in business. She sat down, feeling spacey until her reporting and writing instincts kicked in. She knew she had to find out more about Joseph.

She did not realize then how quickly her life was about to change.

Chapter 2: Tomorrow's News

During late October 1979, Helen was the staff crime reporter for the *Flambeau.* She also worked on several headline stories for the paper. One of these articles was about the Tallahassee chapter of the Police Benevolent Association (PBA), the union that represented police officers. The PBA and the sheriff's department were involved in contract negotiations over a lawsuit that had been filed against the sheriff's department. Deputies wanted job security, and the PBA wanted to be allowed to represent deputies in personnel matters.

It was a volatile issue. Several law enforcement officers involved with the negotiations came forward to the press and expressed concern. The elections were less than a year away. Sheriff Ken Katsaris had good community support because of the Bundy convictions, but the members of the PBA weren't openly campaigning for him. The deputies wanted job security, and the right to strike if unfair working conditions existed.

Katsaris refused to allow the union into the department, citing the Chi Omega case and concerns over public safety. The sheriff's deputies wanted to work as employees of the county and not at the whim of the sheriff, who could hire and fire without cause.

Over the previous year, Helen had developed very good sources of information through the police officers and deputies she routinely worked with. Two nights a week, she rode along with officers from the City of Tallahassee Police Department, and one night a week she would ride with sheriff's deputies. Helen not only reported on the stories she witnessed, but she gained the trust and respect of many in law enforcement. It was no secret among the officers that many deputies feared working under Sheriff Katsaris, but they knew they'd lose their jobs if they openly supported another candidate or spoke out against him.

◆❖◆

The day after Helen met Joseph, she went to meet Captain George Brand. His office was located in the Leon County

Courthouse. Helen was accustomed to meeting Dick Simpson, the sheriff's spokesperson, in the lobby. When she rode with the deputies, she usually met them in the squad room or in the parking garage. Today, she was meeting someone with a private office.

She told the receptionist she was there to meet Captain Brand, then sat down to wait.

Sheriff Katsaris came through the lobby. He paid Helen just enough attention to acknowledge he knew who she was from the recent PBA meetings and a handful of news conferences. She smiled and shook his hand.

A woman came out and asked Helen to follow her. She was Brand's secretary. As Helen turned the corner, the secretary motioned to the first doorway on the right. The nameplate on the door read Captain George Brand.

"Please come in. Thank you, Carol," said a gravelly Southern voice, a sure sign of a heavy smoker.

When Helen stepped into the room and saw the big burly man, the first thing she noticed was that he looked like the actor Joe Don Baker who had played Sheriff Buford Pusser in the 1970s movie *Walking Tall.*

George Brand walked around his desk, offered Helen his hand, and introduced himself.

"Hi there, I'm Captain Brand. Please have a seat."

They settled into their chairs.

"Captain Brand," Helen said, "I'd like to ask you something."

"What's that?"

"Is Joseph someone dangerous?"

Brand laughed and slapped his hand down on his desk.

"No, no. That boy's alright."

"What do you mean?" She thought about Joseph touching the mole on her hip.

"He's about as safe a person to be around as anybody I know. Hell, he's probably safer. You can trust him. Why, what did he do?"

"Oh, nothing," she said dismissively. "But I don't meet people like him every day."

"Neither do I," Brand said.

She cleared her throat.

"I've been with the *Flambeau* for about a year or so, and as you may know, I've been riding with deputies from your department for many months now."

"The mullet wrapper?" Brand teased. "Actually, I know who you are. I always read your stories." He lit a cigarette and blew the smoke toward the ceiling.

"So, in all of my dealings with the police and sheriff's department, I've never heard about Joseph before. Who is he?"

"Well, now," Brand began. "Joseph's different. He's always polite, but he has strange thoughts about things. But I can assure you, Joseph is not a killer, and you don't need to be afraid of him. He's just... how should I say this? *Unusual.*"

Helen relaxed a bit at Brand's description of Joseph. Now she wanted the story.

"Captain Brand, I would say that calling Joseph *unusual* is an understatement."

They shared a laugh.

Their conversation, while friendly, quickly turned into a cat-and-mouse game.

"How did you come to work with Joseph?" Helen asked.

"What did he tell you?"

"He said that he called you on the telephone and gave you some information. When he came to meet you for the first time, you sent someone else to meet him, and that the officer was rude to him."

Brand laughed.

The conversation continued this way for several minutes, with Helen relaying to Brand the story Joseph had told her. Brand provided no additional details, nor did he comment on what Helen said. The conversation was one sided, and Helen grew frustrated. She stopped talking for a moment and waited to see if Brand would begin to tell his version of the story. He remained quiet.

"What can you tell me about the psychic file?" Helen asked.

Brand stared at her for a few seconds, his face a brick wall. Helen's palms were sweating. She was nervous.

He leaned back in his chair and placed his folded hands over his chin, with his index fingers pointing up over his lips. He squinted. "How do you know about that file?" he asked.

"Joseph told me about it."

Brand sighed deeply and lit a cigarette.

"Joseph said that some of the stuff in that file is pretty scary. Is that true?"

"Lady, what's in that file will scare you to death." He glanced at the door. "There are things in there that I never dreamed of, ever, and I've been in law enforcement for many years. I thought I'd seen it all, until those letters and drawings came along."

Helen noticed Brand had lowered his voice to just above a whisper.

"Is there anything about Joseph, maybe some notes in the file?"

"Yeah, some of his notes are in there. Some are in other places." Brand glanced at the door again. "I'm not sure what's still in the file anymore. I haven't seen it for a while. It's always been kept under lock and key."

"May I see the file and some of Joseph's notes? Will it prove Joseph's story?"

"Miss Baxter," Brand said. "It is Miss, isn't it?"

"Yes, but please, call me Helen."

"Well, Helen, why would you want to open up something that might be better off left alone?"

"Joseph wants to put in a claim for the reward. He said he wants the money to go to the victims, all of it. He said you'd help." She chewed on the top of her pen.

"Joseph is a surprising person," Brand answered. "He deserves the reward. But no one in this town is going to give it to him."

"Even if it's for the victims? That's who he said he'd give it to."

Brand rubbed his forehead.

"If he wants to give the money to the victims, I'll see what I can do to help. As long as he doesn't want the money for himself." He stood up. "I'm surprised Joseph wants publicity."

"Would you believe I still don't know his last name?"

"That's Joseph. Just ask him. He'll tell a pretty young lady like you."

They shook hands again.

"I'll see what I can do," Brand said. "You can call me later today, or on Monday. But don't leave any messages." His last words sounded like a warning.

Helen left the sheriff's department and headed back to the office. She drove down College Avenue, past the Oak Apartments. Bundy had lived there just prior to the Chi Omega murders and the place still felt spooky to her. She turned a couple of corners and found herself driving past the Chi Omega sorority house, where two girls were brutally murdered, and two others barely managed to survive savage beatings.

Helen approached Woodward Avenue, then passed the Dorman Hall dormitory. She began to get a strange, fluttering feeling in her stomach. The story made her feel very uncomfortable. She tried to switch her thoughts to something more pleasant, but couldn't.

As Helen entered the *Flambeau* office, Jamie Wilson came out and wanted to know if she'd learned anything about the "psycho."

"It's a real story, Jamie, but I don't have anyone on record yet. I might be getting some secret psychic file from the sheriff's department. Supposedly, there is documented proof that he worked with the investigation. Once I see it, do I write the story?"

"You bet. That one might make AP or UPI." He rubbed his chin and smiled at her. "Watch yourself with this guy, though. Psychic really means psycho."

"Thank you, Jamie." She opened the door to leave. "Have a

good weekend. See you Sunday."

When Helen approached her car, she noticed that someone had left a note on her windshield. She pulled out the piece of paper and read it.

> *Please come to my house for dinner tonight. I will make a nice meal for you. I would like to also take you to the fair this evening. I want to thank you for trying to help me. Please call me and let me know if you'll join me. I'll be home from 2-5 today, then I have to help coach football.*
>
> *Joseph*

She crumpled the note and looked for a trash can. She didn't see one, so she stuffed the note into her purse. She drove over to Brenda's house to hang out with her that afternoon. They shared several classes and liked to tackle some of their writing projects together.

When she arrived at Brenda's, they discussed going out but couldn't come up with anything other than grabbing a burger and hanging out at one of the bars on Tennessee Street. Neither could muster up much interest in those activities.

Helen pulled the crumpled note from her purse and handed it to Brenda.

"This guy's kind of creepy," Helen said. "But he's also sort of interesting, too."

"What are you saying?" Brenda asked. "Do you want to go out with him tonight?"

"No, I really can't go out with this guy. I might be writing a story about him, and Jamie would lose his mind if I went out with Joseph," Helen said.

"What kind of story?"

"He said that he helped catch Bundy. He calls himself a psychic, and someone at the sheriff's department actually verified Joseph's story today."

"A psychic?" Brenda was immediately fascinated. "Like, can he tell our fortunes and stuff like that?"

"Oh, Brenda, I don't know. But it could be an interesting night, right?" Helen lit a cigarette. "For both of us? How about we go together?"

◆❖◆

Helen was very nervous as she drove to Joseph's house with Brenda. Common sense told her not to go; she knew better than to spend time with someone who, more than likely, was crazy.

Helen was surprised when she pulled into Joseph's driveway. The home was lovely, and sat right above Lake Ella in the heart of downtown Tallahassee. In her experience, college students didn't live that well, as both she and Brenda could attest.

"What a nice place!" Brenda whispered as they approached the front door. "What's this guy do again?"

"I think he's in school," Helen said as Joseph opened the front door.

He led them inside and gave them a tour of the house. It had to be one of the nicest rental houses Helen had ever seen. Joseph lived with three other people, two guys and a young woman, all grad school students. Joseph, who was three years older than Helen, had taken several years off from school before he came to FSU to finish his Bachelor's degree.

"Come out to the kitchen," he said. "I'm cooking some chicken and I don't want to burn it."

Brenda grinned from ear to ear as they followed Joseph to the kitchen. "He cooks?" she mouthed to Helen.

Joseph pulled a bottle of white wine out of the refrigerator. As Helen and Brenda drank enthusiastically, they noticed Joseph wasn't drinking.

"Aren't you having any?" Helen asked him.

"No. I can't drink any alcohol right now."

"Why not?" Brenda was intrigued. "Are you sick?"

"No, nothing like that. I've taken a vow."

"Oh, like an AA vow?" Brenda asked. "Sometimes I think that I need to go to AA."

They laughed.

"Yes," Joseph said, "something like that. I haven't had a drink or a haircut in over a year."

Helen regarded his long, brown ponytail. "Did you also take a vow not to cut your hair?" she asked jokingly.

Joseph simply replied, "Yes, exactly."

Odd, Helen thought, but asked no more.

She said very little during dinner. She was uneasy about Joseph and wondered what she was doing at his house. She knew she needed to keep herself at a professional distance. But as the evening went on, she realized Joseph was neither weird nor creepy.

She was glad for Brenda's company; she kept the conversation lively, asking Joseph a million questions about his background and his classes. He answered them all, and Helen learned he was from Miami as well, but North Miami, while she had grown up in South Miami.

When Brenda stopped talking to sample Joseph's chicken, he seized the opportunity to ask Helen about her upbringing.

"Well, I went to Southwest High School and graduated in '76," Helen began. "And then I worked that summer at a library and came to FSU in the fall."

"Do you have brothers or sisters?"

"Yes, one sister, but she's older than I am. She's married with two little boys."

"I have six brothers and sisters," he said. "I'm right in the middle."

"Goodness," Brenda said. "That's a lot of kids."

Helen had difficulty imagining seven siblings.

"What kind of hobbies do you have, Helen?"

She had to think for a minute. She didn't know if she had any hobbies, at least not lately. All she seemed to do was work and go to school. She took a long sip of wine, trying to come up with an answer.

"Drinking and dancing and smoking," Brenda blurted out. She hooted and slapped her hand on the table. "That's her major."

Helen snorted and wine came out her nose. Ruefully, she had to admit that Brenda was right.

"Helen, do you have a boyfriend?" Joseph asked.

She took another sip of wine while both Brenda and Joseph watched her expectantly.

"I do," she lied.

Brenda stayed quiet.

Joseph's roommates came into the dining room and introduced themselves. Marty was a paramedic and was in law school. He had not been on duty during the Chi Omega murders, but many of his coworkers had been. The other guy, Mike, was getting a Master's degree in forestry. Helen was amazed that Joseph's house and roommates seemed so *normal.*

After dinner, the three went to the county fair. They walked through the 4-H exhibits and the local craft displays. Then they each bought a wristband and rode the carnival rides for hours, until the fair closed for the evening. The three of them laughed and talked like old friends.

"I think I'm in love," Brenda cooed after they had dropped Joseph off at home.

Helen was amused by Brenda's infatuation. She could see why her friend liked Joseph, but she did not share Brenda's sentiments; however, she had to admit to herself that she hadn't had so much fun in years.

As Helen drove home after dropping Brenda off, she thought about her friend's crush on the "psychic." Helen was tickled because there could not be two people more dissimilar than Brenda and Joseph.

She thought about the time she had gone with Brenda to visit her family. Brenda had grown up in a Florida Panhandle town so small that it no longer existed. Her father raised fighting roosters and kept them staked in front of his mobile home. Helen remembered driving up to the front of Brenda's father's house and seeing at least 30 birds, each with a leg chained and staked to the bare dirt yard. While they could not attack each other, they were close enough to constantly antagonize each other. Helen sat in the car and watched the roosters squabble as Brenda spoke with her father. Helen had never seen anything like that in her life, and was struck by the contrast to her own suburban milieu of manicured lawns and sailboats. She wondered how Brenda, with her rural roots, would fit into Joseph's world, or vice-versa. She pictured Joseph, with his long hair and leather book bag, showing up at the mobile home with the roosters.

Helen was certain that Joseph's father did not raise chickens.

Without a doubt, neither woman had ever met anyone quite like Joseph.

◆❖◆

Helen returned to the office at 1 p.m. on Sunday. These were full work days at the *Flambeau*. Jamie Wilson greeted her as she grabbed a typewriter off one of the desks in the sports department. She checked to see if it was missing any letters.

"How's that story coming along?"

"I haven't heard from my contact yet, but I somehow ended up at the carnival Friday night with the guy," she said. "My friend Brenda was with me, so don't get anxious, okay? I think she wants to date him."

"Don't get involved with the psycho," Jamie warned. "He's dangerous, and reporters getting involved with their subjects is always bad news." He tapped his foot on the scuffed wood floor.

"Hey, Jamie, come on," she said, growing aggravated. "Nothing happened. He's a nice guy who coaches little kids in football. Nothing is going to go wrong here."

"Just get the story and then stay away from the guy. I've been doing this long enough to spot trouble, and this guy is trouble."

"Look, I'm not getting involved with the guy. But I have to

interview him to get the story, don't I?"

Jamie shrugged and walked into his office. "Just do your job, Baxter," he said as he closed his door.

Later that afternoon, her stories filed, Helen called Joseph and asked him to tell her his story again. She needed his side of it in greater detail. He agreed.

They couldn't decide on a meeting place, so she gave him her address and directions. Her desire to get the story finished outweighed any fears she had about this "psychic." She called her friend Brenda and asked her to come by and hang out. She promised she would. She knew Helen didn't want to be alone in her apartment with Joseph. Besides, Brenda thought Joseph was "cute."

They worked late into the night. Brenda sat on the couch in the living room and listened intently to Joseph's tale. Helen crafted the newspaper story on her personal typewriter, an IBM Selectric, as they talked. He seemed to remember the details clearly. He recalled what happened and what his feelings were as he went through the ordeal of explaining his visions to investigators at the task force.

Near midnight, the rough draft was done. Joseph insisted the story be written a certain way because he feared that the sheriff's office would deny his involvement, and that would kill the possibility of getting the reward money to the girls and their families.

When he finally left, Helen was exhausted. She now had his full story, but she needed confirmation from Brand or someone from the task force in order to print it.

On Tuesday morning, before her first class, Helen drove to the news office and called Brand. He answered his office phone, but said he was busy and asked her to call back later that day.

She then called Dick Simpson, the sheriff's spokesman for the crime beat reports, to begin gathering the daily reports.

"You're early," he said. "I'll give you what I have, and I'll call you later this afternoon with the roundup."

When Dick finished relaying the last item on his list, Helen asked him if he knew about the psychic who had helped the task force catch Bundy. Simpson had been the spokesperson for the combined law enforcement task force during the pursuit of the Chi Omega killer, and then through Bundy's trial and conviction.

The phone line was quiet for several seconds.

"You there?" she asked.

"Yeah," Dick said, and fell quiet again.

She waited for him to speak again.

"Helen," he started, speaking quietly, "I've heard some new talk. I like you. I like working with you. But you don't want to touch that story. Don't ask anyone about it, either. Please."

She jumped on his words. "Come on, Dick, you know me. We've been working together for a while now. Off the record, then. Is it true or not?"

"I can't say anything," he whispered. "But you're playing with real trouble. Do you understand me? Off the record, you're playing with real, live ammunition if you touch that story. Drop it please." He fell quiet for a third time.

She thanked Dick for his help and hung up. She knew what his warning meant.

Earlier that morning, Joseph left a message with Laurie telling her that he had called Brand and asked for copies of his notes. He would have them later that day and would drop them by the newsroom.

When Helen picked up her messages and saw the note, she breathed and relaxed for the first time in days. It would be over soon.

Jamie Wilson came out of his office and asked Helen about the psychic story.

"Look, Baxter, write it or kill it. I don't pay you to waste time," he said. "And don't fool around with the psycho either, just get the story and get out." He waved her away.

The phone lines rang. Two of the calls were for Helen. She picked up the receiver.

"Stay away from the psychic story or you'll be screwed," a man said to her and hung up.

Helen nearly dropped the phone. Mike, the copyeditor, handed her a note telling her that Joseph was on hold. She punched the button that would connect them.

"Joseph, you there?"

"Yeah, have you heard from Brand?" he said with a friendly tone. He sounded nothing like the other voice that had just threatened her seconds before.

"Brand told me he'd get back to me, but I don't know when that will be."

"Great! Let me know how it goes. I'll be seeing him a little later today."

"Okay." Helen felt her optimism return. "Are you at home?"

"No, I'm calling from the Mecca. I'll be in class until almost one. You want to meet me for lunch?"

"No, I can't meet you today. Maybe tomorrow." Or maybe not. She wanted this all to go away.

"You know we're running out of time before the committee decides who to give the reward money to," he said.

Helen looked at her watch but did not say anything.

"Look, Helen, I'll be home all afternoon working on a project for my jazz arranging class, copying scores and stuff."

"Scores?"

"For music," he said. "Musical scores. Whatever. I'll talk with you later."

Helen finished the draft of her story on the lack of labor relations and job security in the sheriff's department and handed it over to Wilson for a read-through.

"It's good, Helen, really good," he said as he handed it back to her. "It's going to ruffle some feathers. But it needs a lot of editing, of course." He winked at her. "There's going to be blowback, you know."

Helen went to her classes but found she couldn't pay attention. The day dragged by. She cut her last class and returned to the office just before 2 p.m.

Wilson came out of his office just as she was about to sit down at her desk.

"Baxter, stay away from the psycho story for now. It's getting too weird. Is someone on the record?"

"No, not yet."

"Then can it. There's no story. We're getting threats now if we run the story. I'm going to call the cops on this psycho guy. What's his last name?"

"I don't know." She shook her head and shrugged. "Jamie, listen, I think it's the cops making the threats. There's something going on that makes everyone scared to talk about this guy."

"Stay away from the psycho and just write some other stories for now. Your PBA piece is coming together. You need to wrap that up. No psychic story. That's final." He glared at her until she nodded.

She sat down at her desk and called Dick Simpson for the updated crime stories. She thought he seemed a little cooler than usual, but she blamed that on their earlier conversation. She finished her calls with the Tallahassee and FSU police spokespersons. She wrote up her column with one eye on the clock. She was riding with the city police that evening, and had asked for a shift that would end at 11 p.m.

Near 6:30 p.m., Wilson approached her desk. She was gathering her cigarettes and getting ready to drive over to the Tallahassee Police Department to meet up with the patrolman she'd be riding with that evening.

"Your PBA story is done, and we're running it as the front-page story on Friday, unless the world ends or something," he said, smiling broadly. "We're doing some graphics, and a photo or two."

Helen felt a rush of excitement and happiness.

"Wow!" She was stunned. "The front page, with photos and everything? That's so cool!"

"Nice job, Baxter."

◆❖◆

Helen stepped into Laurie's office early in the morning before her classes began. Laurie was on the phone, but handed her a sealed envelope. She put her hand over the receiver.

"Your friend the psychic dropped these by for you this morning," she whispered. "He's actually almost cute." She winked at Helen. "I think he may be growing on me."

Helen took the envelope back to her car and got into the driver's seat. She opened the envelope. There were two pages of handwritten notes.

This is it? She was surprised. She thought there would be more. She scanned them. While she found them interesting, she noticed they were undated.

She put the envelope into the glove compartment and got out of her car. She locked the doors and walked across the campus to her morning classes.

◆❖◆

Joseph called Helen at work later that day. "Did you get the notes?" he asked.

"Yes, Laurie gave them to me this morning." She looked out the window. It was already getting dark, and she was not close to meeting her deadline. She'd have to buckle down and get her stories done.

"What'd you think? Are those what you need?" He sounded very eager.

Helen pulled the envelope out from under her notepad. "Well, actually, I was a bit... *underwhelmed*," she said. "I was under the impression there were more notes, more for me to work with. And while these seem to be pretty freaky, they're not dated. I'll need to get those dates verified."

"Brand could only find a couple of notes. He gave me copies of the ones he could find. He said he'd keep looking."

"Good, then, because I don't think these are even about Chi Omega, or the girl at the Dunwoody Street duplex, or what happened during the Tallahassee investigation. These notes seem to concern the abduction and murder of the little girl in Lake City."

"And Bundy did all of them," Joseph said. "Helen, as I told you, her death could have been prevented. Those are my notes about what he did to Kimberly Leach. I told you, I watched what he did to her."

She rolled her eyes.

"Okay," she said, "just let me know if more notes turn up."

It was Thursday evening and Helen felt like celebrating. The labor dispute story was a big one for her career, and she had spent many hours developing the sensitive piece. She called Brenda and they decided to go out that evening.

"Can you get Joseph to come out with us?" Brenda asked.

Helen told her she would try. She hung up with Brenda and called the number to Joseph's house. He answered right away.

"Brenda and I are going over to Poor Paul's Pourhouse," she told him. "For a couple of beers and to play some pinball."

Joseph said he'd join them. At the bar, he turned most of his attention to Helen, and they played backgammon until the bar closed. Disappointed, Brenda had gone home long before 2 a.m.

Helen and Joseph walked to Jerry's, a 24-hour restaurant, and ordered breakfast. They talked for hours and found they had quite a bit in common. Helen realized she was beginning to feel comfortable with him.

After they finished eating, they walked around downtown Tallahassee and the FSU campus until the sun came up over the tree line. Helen was excited about her story and wanted to see the newspaper when it was delivered.

◆❖◆

The cool November air was refreshing after being inside all

night. Helen and Joseph walked to the FSU Student Union where the daily *Flambeau* papers were dropped off for the distribution boys to take around the campus and the city.

Excitedly, she pulled out a copy of the newly-delivered edition. There was her story, on the front page.[2] She sat down on the edge of a concrete flower bed and studied the article and the graphics.

Joseph read the article and then looked at her oddly.

"I think you have trouble ahead," he said, shaking his head. "Real trouble."

"Yes, I know this is going to make some people unhappy. Particularly Sheriff Katsaris."

"No, Helen, you don't understand. This is going to be bad," he said. "Not just this story, but my story as well. Your sources are going to get worried. I think you may be in for some tough times. I'm sorry that both of these stories happened at the same time."

"Okay, I know that a few people are going to be upset by this," she said and pointed to the newspaper. "This is about the Sheriff of Leon County, and some of his people want job security. They want to know they'll have their jobs, no matter who the sheriff is, no matter where they are in the election cycle. I get that this is a sensitive story. We have unnamed sources here, but my bosses know who they are. We also have some people on the record. Why would this affect me? Why do you think I'm going to have some tough times?"

Joseph looked at Helen. He smiled. "You'll just have to watch and see. There's nothing I can do now but tell you not to trust anyone but Brand." He picked up his book bag.

"Thanks for the evening," Helen said. "I have to go home to shower and change."

She walked over to the *Flambeau* office, picked up her car, and drove home. It was going to be a long day for her, and there was no time for a nap. She showered and washed her hair. Then she returned to the FSU campus to begin her day.

---

[2] Waller, Susan. "Job security: Some cops have it, some never will?" *The Independent Florida Flambeau*, Nov. 7, 1979, p. 1A.

At 9:30 that morning, another threat came in. Laurie answered the phone and took the message: *Ms. Baxter and the news staff need to stop fooling around with police business, or you will all take falls. See what happens to the wiring on the newsroom if there is another story about the PBA trying to unionize the Leon County Sheriff's Department.*

When Helen arrived at work that afternoon after her classes, Jamie called her into his office.

"Baxter, your story is causing problems." He handed her the note and watched her read it.

"We've hit a nerve here, and we knew this was coming, or something like it," Jamie said. "But this is a clear threat against all of us. Warning about the wiring to the newsroom? Do you have any idea why someone would threaten us?"

"I don't know. Should we be worried? Are you afraid the building will be burned down?"

"I don't know," he said. "I think I'm more worried about something being planted in here, drugs or something. Or the phones being bugged. Repercussions from our stories are always a concern."

"We talked about the sensitivity of this for weeks as I was pulling it together." She sighed. She was tired. She had expected this story to make some people unhappy, but she had not anticipated threats. She wanted to feel good about the article.

"We knew it was going to cause a stir," Jamie said, "but I can't help but wonder if there's something else going on."

"It's a hotter story than we thought, that's all." She sat down behind the copy desk. "I've... *we've* put the sheriff in a bad spot. We knew he'd be angry about this story."

"Yeah, and he's called too." Jamie sat down on the edge of the desk. "Do you think these threats have anything to do with the psychic? Some people know you've been asking questions at the sheriff's department about him. Dick Simpson called me this morning. He asked me to pull you off that story. I went over to your desk and looked at your copy. It's a great story, Helen, but we're not going to run it. Not unless you can get someone on the record, and that's just not going to happen. Not now. Sheriff Katsaris is angry, first about the unionization story, and now about this psychic guy. I think he asked Simpson to call me."

"Simpson asked you to kill this psychic story?"

"Yes."

"And you agreed?"

"Yes." Jamie had tears in his eyes. "I think it's a great story, Helen, and it would blow everyone away if it's true. But I'm worried."

Helen put her head down on the desk. She was embarrassed that there were other guys in the newsroom who had heard their conversation. She was exhausted, and so ready for sleep, but she wasn't going to give up on the psychic story, not yet.

"What if I *can* the get corroboration, Jamie? Can we run it then?"

He reached out as if to touch her, then thought better of it.

"It depends on who corroborates it," he said. "I'm sorry, Helen, but the psychic story is done for now. Now go get tomorrow's news."

He turned away from her and walked toward his office. Once inside, he stuck his head into the hallway and looked at her. "If you don't like it, then go to charm school and write the advice column. Until then, do your job."

He paused for effect, as he knew the sports guys were listening, then said, "And Baxter, stay away from that psycho guy."

◆❖◆

Several days later, as Helen walked up the driveway to the newsroom from her classes later that day, Laurie stuck her head out of the door to the business office and greeted her.

"Hey, Bob wants to see you in his office. Now."

"Crap." Helen rolled her eyes.

Bob Martin was the general manager of the newspaper and was in charge of the day-to-day operations. It was his job to coordinate the advertising, newsroom, production, and distribution departments, and to ensure that the paper appeared each morning.

Department heads, including Jamie, as executive editor, reported to Bob throughout each day, and he in turn reported to the board of directors. Helen had little interaction with Bob, so she was nervous as she followed Laurie to his office. He rose slightly from behind his desk as she entered. She saw that Jamie was there. Laurie brought in a chair for Helen and then closed the door behind her. Helen sat down.

"Jamie told me about the threat he received last week," Bob said. "I was on the phone with our attorney about it today when another call came in. The caller asked for me. Some guy threatened me and our operations."

Bob looked sternly at Helen. "Now, I need to know the truth here." He stood. "I made some calls today to my own sources, and here is the story they've heard."

Jamie interrupted before Bob could finish. "Do you think we need to start with this, Bob?" he asked. "We haven't finished our discussion."

"Yes, I do." Bob lit a cigarette and Jamie opened the window next to him. "Helen, the story is that you and this psychic are sleeping together."

Helen was furious and struggled to keep her temper. *So, this is what it's come to?*

"No, sir," she said evenly. "I can assure you that nothing like that is going on with him." She looked at Bob, and then at Jamie. "I promise."

"Helen, some of my sources have told me that you've been having relations with some of the cops in exchange for information. Is that true?"

"No, no! That's not true at all." She was rattled by the accusation. "Nothing could have been further from the truth."

"Are you sure?" Bob asked.

She felt nauseated and betrayed. *Who would say that about me?*

"Oh my God, Bob," she said, fighting to keep the tears back. "I've never slept with anyone to get information."

The tears flowed down her face. Jamie handed her some tissues from a box on Bob's desk.

"I've only slept with one person in months, and he is a grad student. I don't think I've been out on a date since winter. No one asks me out. Not even the grad student. I don't really have any life outside of this place." Her voice cracked with emotion.

The men let her cry for a moment, but she quickly regained her composure. She was fatigued from a chronic lack of sleep, and now she had humiliated herself in front of both of her bosses.

"Do you want me to quit?" she asked.

Bob shifted in his chair and looked out the window.

"Just settle down, Baxter, and stick to the crime beat," Jamie told her. "No other stories for a few days, okay? Just do your usual report, but we're not going to run your byline on it for a week or so. Our attorney doesn't think you should do any shift rides with law enforcement. Not with the city cops, and especially not with the sheriff's office, for the time being, and Bob and I agree. Something's going on and we need to just let things calm down."

"Have you received any threats, Helen?" Bob asked.

Helen looked directly at him. "No, sir. I have not."

She had not mentioned the call she'd received the week before in the newsroom. And she had not told anyone about the calls she'd been getting at home. Most of them had been hang-ups, but the last caller had been a man breathing heavily into the phone when she answered. That call had come at 4 in the morning, and it terrified her. She was truly afraid, but she didn't want to tell anyone. And now she had lied to the two men who could help her.

Jamie cleared his throat. "Go ahead and make your calls."

Helen went back to the newsroom. The guys were uncharacteristically quiet. A Royal typewriter sat on her desk. No one said a word to her. She pulled out a notepad and began to make her calls. The spokesmen from the city and the campus police departments were courteous and professional.

When she reached Dick Simpson at the sheriff's office, he did not make any small talk with her. He gave her the crime stories for the day and quickly got off the phone.

Helen was saddened by this. Speaking daily with Dickie was a highlight of her life. They always made a little small talk and flirted a bit, but today the conversation was strained. She waited a few minutes and then called him back.

"Dick, I'm sorry," she said when he answered his phone. "But I can't ride with the deputies this week."

"I know," he said. "I was told you couldn't ride with them ever again."

Brokenhearted, she wrote the crime beat articles, and turned them over to the copyeditor.

"No byline," she told Mike.

"I know," he said.

◆❖◆

The phone was ringing when she walked into her apartment. She considered ignoring it, but answered it anyway. *Maybe they want me to come back in to work*, she thought hopefully.

"Hello?"

"Helen, it's Joseph. I called you at the office but they said you'd left for the day."

"Yes, I did."

She slipped off her shoes and looked around the apartment. Everything seemed okay, but things *felt* odd, like someone had been there. She pulled the long telephone cord through the apartment and pushed aside the blinds to make sure the windows were locked. She lived on the ground floor and was accustomed to checking the windows daily. She wanted to move to an upstairs apartment, but thought she'd wait until her lease was up, and then move to a different place, a house perhaps.

"Is everything okay?" he asked.

"No, not really." Helen wanted to take a shower, put on her

pajamas, and hide. Tears ran down her face. She wanted to be left alone to grieve.

"Do you want to have dinner with me?"

"No," she whispered. "Not tonight."

"Okay then, I won't keep you." He paused. "But I wanted to say, please be careful."

Helen couldn't think clearly and she didn't want to talk anymore that evening. She thanked him for calling and hung up.

This guy was the problem, wasn't he? So why does he feel like my only friend on earth?

Helen poured herself a glass of Chardonnay and put Tom Waits' *Closing Time* on the turntable. She cried her way through a shower and then drank another glass of wine.

She could not remember when she had last eaten; certainly, she had not eaten that day. There was no food in her apartment, but she didn't want to eat anyway. She flipped the album over to play the other side. And when that finished playing, she turned it over to the first side and played it again. She pulled out the envelopes with the two notes from the psychic and reread them.

Chapter 3: The Schoolhouse on the Hill

Helen pulled into her usual parking space and grabbed her backpack. She had classes and was actually caught up on her assignments for once. As she reached into the back seat of her Toyota Corolla for her umbrella, she noticed a tall woman walking toward her.

"Helen! I haven't seen you for a while," the woman said, and gave her a hug.

Joanie Harris was one of the *Flambeau* staff photographers and had sometimes provided photos for Helen's articles. The women caught up for a few minutes. Joanie was at least half a foot taller than Helen. She was model thin, and had a dazzling smile that showed off a wide gap between her two front teeth. Talented with a camera, Helen liked to work with her, but Joanie mostly preferred shooting sports events for the newspaper.

"I don't know what you've got going on this afternoon," Helen said, "but I have an idea." She asked Joanie if she'd like to ride over to Lake City with her that day.

"I've got a shoot tonight, but I could go this afternoon. Why? What do you have going on?"

"I've got a lead on what could be an angle to something I'm working on: a Bundy story. I'd like to check it out, and you could take some photos."

Helen briefly explained the situation with Joseph, and Joanie was game for an adventure. They agreed to meet back in the parking lot in an hour. Helen had some papers to turn in to her professors. The two women, each holding large umbrellas, walked off in separate directions.

The sky was dark with low-hanging storm clouds and rain poured down as they drove east on I-10 from Tallahassee to Lake City. The drive took two hours and their conversation was lively.

Helen showed Joanie one of the two notes Joseph had given her. In the note, he had described what could be interpreted as the abduction and murder of 12-year-old Kimberly Leach in Lake City.

"He said he turned in this note to the task force about one week prior to the little girl's disappearance," Helen explained. "But this copy of the note is not dated, so I don't know yet what to think."

"I had a dream," Joanie read from the note, "and in my dream, I saw myself standing on the hill next to the junior high school above the JM Fields shopping center near Lake Ella... you know, where the fence is tall. Below me, there was a van in the parking lot. I could see the distance from the van to Lake Ella. It was the same distance from the Chi Omega house to the Dunwoody duplex."

She turned to Helen. "So, what is he saying here? Is he predicting the little girl's death?"

"He said he was. There's another part of the note, he said, in which he 'dreamed' that he saw the killer grab her and throw her into the van. Joseph said he 'saw' the killer rape and murder her in the van. He told the investigator this dream was about the killer."

Helen pulled up in front of Lake City Junior High. She parked the car and the women got out. The school had been built on top of a hill, and there was a parking lot below the school. From where she stood, they could see a lake, just as Joseph had described in the note.

Joanie walked around and took photographs of the school building, the parking lot, and the view to the lake. The rain had diminished to a fine mist, but the skies were heavily clouded and blocked the sun.

"This area seems to fit the description in the note," Joanie said as they got back into the car.

"Yes, it does. But this brings up more questions than it answers, at least until I can get an official corroboration that it's true."

"Do you think this Joseph is real? Do you really believe what he's saying?"

"I don't know." Helen started the car. "I met with the investigator, and he assured me that Joseph was real and had helped them catch Bundy, but I can't get him to go on the record. Not yet, at least."

"I heard you'd been pulled off crime stories for a while, after the PBA story came out," Joanie said. "Is that true?"

Helen cracked the window and lit a cigarette. "I don't know what's happening right now. I'm still writing the crime beat, but I can't ride with the patrol units for a while." She exhaled and turned the windshield wipers back on.

"I heard it was more serious than that," Joanie said. "I heard that the sheriff has forbidden you from riding with his deputies."

"Well, that may be true," Helen said. She felt herself becoming sad again, and she fought the tears. "Look, if I can corroborate this story, and get it into the paper, and show how a psychic worked with the police, particularly with one of the sheriff's top investigators, I won't have to worry about keeping my job."

She rolled the window down and tossed out the cigarette butt.

"Oh, Helen, I don't know about that. If you run this story, keeping your job may be the least of your worries."

Joanie changed a lens on her camera and continued shooting photos of the town every time Helen stopped at a red light.

"Sheriff Katsaris is the most powerful man in Leon County" Joanie said. "And he's up for reelection. Aside from the university, this is a very conservative town, and Southern Baptist, and the sheriff won't ever want people to know they used psychics to solve the biggest series of crimes this town has ever seen."

"I have to admit that I'm skeptical, but I feel like I should try to see this through." Helen grabbed a sweatshirt from the back seat and wiped the fog from inside the windshield. She handed it to Joanie and asked her to wipe her side of the glass. "Do you want to get something to eat, or at least a cup of coffee before we head back?"

Helen pulled into a diner and stuffed the envelope with the notes into her bag. They sat in a booth and each ordered a late breakfast of eggs, toast, and coffee. While they sipped their coffees, Helen pulled the first note out of her bag and read it again.

"You have to admit, these notes describing the area around Lake Ella in Tallahassee sure do seem to match the description of the Lake City school where Kimberly Leach was abducted," Helen said. "What do you think?"

"Anyone can copy a typed paper and claim something with it. If this sheriff's captain guy didn't give you the note himself, I wouldn't trust it. Do you know who this Joseph really is?"

"No, not really, I don't." Helen put the note back into her bag. The waitress brought their food. "All I know is that things have become complicated the past couple of weeks."

"This is some pretty weird stuff, and I can understand why you would want to work on the story." Joanie paused and took a bite of her toast. "If it's really true that the task force used this psychic guy and you can prove it, that's great. But I don't want to meet him. Get Bob O to take the photos. This stuff scares the crap out of me."

"Me too," Helen laughed. "But I find psychic phenomenon absolutely fascinating. I really want to see if they did use a psychic here, and what the results were."

They finished their food and drank more coffee. As they left, Helen asked Joanie if she'd like to go over the Suwannee River State Park to see if they could find where the little girl's body had been found. "It's on the way back to Tallahassee," Helen said.

"As in, 'Way down upon the Suwannee River'?" Joanie sang. "That one?"

"That's the one." Helen smiled.

◆❖◆

Helen drove west on U.S. Highway 90 and they soon saw the sign for Suwannee River State Park. As they pulled in, they saw a small, brown cabin with a sign in the distance. It was the park ranger's visitor station.

Helen parked in the lot next to a small truck with a State Forest Service logo on the side. The women went inside the building. A tall, thin man sat behind a desk. He wore a traditional green forest ranger uniform and a pair of black-rimmed eyeglasses. He was in his early forties and had very little hair left on his head. He smiled and welcomed them to the park. He exuded contentment, and to Helen, he seemed like the most relaxed person she had seen in a long time.

Helen introduced herself as a reporter for the *Flambeau* and then introduced Joanie.

"You're a photographer, right?" the ranger said, and chuckled at his observation. Joanie was wearing her camera on a strap around her neck.

He winked at Helen. "Sorry, but that just seemed too obvious."

Helen and Joanie laughed. He looked them up and down.

"So, ladies, you're not dressed for a hike, so what can I help you with today?"

"Well, sir, we're thinking of doing a small article on Kimberly Leach," Helen said. "There's an angle I'd like to pursue."

The ranger frowned and pulled a bandana from his pants pocket. He blew his nose.

"Excuse me," he said. "Now, that's some bad business, what happened to that little girl. That was surely the worst thing I've ever seen in my life."

"What can you tell us about it?"

"Everything, but I'd rather talk about anything else."

He explained that searchers had combed the park immediately after the young girl disappeared from the middle school on February 9th, 1978.

"They came through and did several searches, and they even brought in a team of dogs to assist, but they didn't find her body, not for a while."

"Why was that, do you think?"

"It was February when she disappeared, and we'd had a cold winter. The ground was frozen, and we had a storm come through that day, and the temperature plunged and stayed cold for weeks. Her body froze."

The ranger's voice broke and he stared out of the window for a moment. His hands clenched into fists on the counter. Helen wrote some notes.

"Everyone was desperate to find her, and we hoped she'd be alive those first few days, but those hopes quickly faded, especially after we found the bloody rags. This is a small community. She could have been anyone's daughter. We all know her family."

"As I understand it," Helen said, "her body was not found until April, nearly eight weeks after she disappeared. Is that correct? Were you there when she was found?"

"Yes, that's right, and yes I was."

"Was it found in an area where you'd already searched?"

"Yes, she was under an abandoned hog shed. It was a horrible place for that little girl. Excuse me." He turned and went into a back room. When he came out, Helen noticed his eyes were red-rimmed. He'd been crying and didn't want the women to see. Helen felt guilty about upsetting the ranger.

"Sir, I'm certain it was an awful place for that little girl. I can't even imagine," Helen said softly. "How come she wasn't discovered before April?"

"Well, the area was searched multiple times. There were tire tracks, partial tracks, found in the area right after she went missing, so we searched there. People come into the park at night all the time, though not usually in February, so we thought those tracks were suspicious."

"I understand," Helen said as she continued writing notes. "Now, I came across something a couple of days ago, and I want to ask you about it, but I don't want you to laugh at me, okay?" She watched his expression.

"Go right ahead, miss."

"I read somewhere that a psychic, maybe from somewhere in South Florida, pointed to a spot on a map of the park and said that was where Kim's body was. Had you heard that?"

He nodded. "That's my understanding of it, yes."

"And that's the area where her body was found, right?"

"Yes. That was the place. I just had a feeling all along that was where that little girl would be," he said.

"And it didn't surprise you that the information came from a psychic, did it, and that it was correct?"

"Well, no. Like I said, I saw some tire tracks leading to the area, but we just couldn't find her."

"Can you show us where she was found?"

"I'll be happy to. I'm the only one here today, so I'll lock up this office and we'll walk out there as it's not raining." He grabbed his hat from the counter and his slicker from a coat rack. He looked at Helen's high-heeled black leather boots.

"Do you want to change your shoes into something better suited for the trail?" he suggested.

"Oh," Helen said and looked at her boots. She looked at Joanie's feet. She was wearing tennis shoes. "Well, these are my walking shoes."

"You can't tell she's from Miami, can you?" Joanie said to the ranger.

He laughed. "No, not at all. She looks right at home in the wilderness."

The women stepped outside and the ranger locked the building.

"I thought Tallahassee *was* the wilderness," Helen said. "Until I came here." She could already feel the dampness in her boots.

"We'll take my truck," the ranger said. "It's quite a hike back there."

Helen walked slowly and carefully on the muddy pathway to the ranger's truck, and quietly wished she had worn different shoes. But she hadn't planned on driving to Lake City and the state park when she left her apartment that morning. She was cold and damp and she knew she was going to ruin a beautiful pair of boots when she got out of the truck and checked out the sites. She made a mental note to keep a pair of jeans, a clean sweatshirt, and a pair of tennis shoes in the trunk of her car from now on.

"I can show you where the shed was, but it isn't there anymore," he told the women.

Helen shifted her focus from her footwear to the ranger. "No?" she asked.

"No. The police took it down when we found her body. Later,

we destroyed what was left and burned the wood. It's gone. We didn't want folks to look at it and be reminded of what happened."

"You'll take us over there though?" Helen asked. "Please?"

"Of course. It would be my privilege."

As he drove on a muddy pathway through the forest and toward the river, he pointed out the areas where he had seen the fresh tire tracks.

"You called them truck tracks before," Helen said, "but could they have been the tracks of a van?"

"Yes. They could have belonged to a van. They found a van, stolen from FSU, I believe."

"Yes," Helen said.

"See that area over there? Here. Let's get out here." He parked the truck and led the women to a rusted hand pump that brought up water from the river.

"We found a large tennis shoe and some bloody rags here," he said. "He must have used the pump to draw water to wash himself up."

Joanie snapped photos of the antique pump and the rocks surrounding it.

They walked a bit farther. "Over there," the ranger said, pointing to a clearing. "That's where the shed was."

Joanie moved closer to take more photos.

"Tell me," the ranger said, "what's your story about? The psychic who told them where to find the body?"

"No, that's not quite what I want to write." She chose her words carefully. "I met a man in Tallahassee who said he helped the task force catch Mr. Bundy." She paused for a moment. "He told me that he is a psychic, although he's not the psychic who told people where to find Kimberly's body. He gave me a note that described the school in relation to the lake, and then a second note that described how a young girl was abducted, put into a van, raped, and murdered."

The ranger stood still and waited for Helen to continue.

"Joanie and I drove over today to check that out, and yes, that description could easily have fit the Lake City Middle School in relation to the lake, and the parking lot he had described—or claims to have described. Now," Helen continued, "the psychic said he gave that information to someone on the task force a week to 10 days prior to the girl going missing. I won't know the exact date until I get verification from the investigator he worked with. The copy I have is not dated."

Helen knew she had the ranger's complete attention, so she decided to continue. Joanie had returned to them.

"This psychic, whose name is Joseph, told me he witnessed this murder as it happened."

This startled both Joanie and the ranger. Joanie moved closer to Helen, and the group began slowly walking back to the truck.

"How?" the ranger asked. "Was the psychic with Bundy when he killed Kimberly?"

"Well, here's where it gets kind of crazy, so stick with me. Joseph said he watched the murder happen in a dream. He said that after the Chi Omega murders, he first saw the killer's eyes in a dream, and the eyes blinked and looked back at him."

"You're kidding, right?" Joanie asked, and placed her hand on Helen's elbow.

"No, I'm not. This is pretty creepy, right?"

"Joseph the psychic said that he saw the killer, and the killer saw him? Is that what you're saying?" the ranger asked.

"Yes, that's exactly what I'm saying. Joseph said that when he had his visions, or dreams, or whatever they were, he could see the killer, and he knew the killer was looking for him. Joseph explained that the killer, Bundy, knew someone was watching him and was looking for that person. Pretty far out, wouldn't you say?"

"But Joseph wasn't here, right? He didn't do the murder, but he said he saw it *before* it happened?" the ranger asked.

"Yes. That's what he says, and I'm trying to get this confirmed."

Joanie paled, and looked like she would faint. "Joseph told you this? How do you know he didn't kill this girl?"

"I don't," Helen said. "But I don't think he did."

"Helen," the ranger said. "May I call you Helen?"

She nodded.

"If I'm understanding you correctly, Joseph thinks that the killer, Bundy, must have been psychic too, to be looking for Joseph." The ranger watched her.

"Yes."

"Well, that's what I thought all along, from the very beginning. I thought the killer must have been psychic, or sent by the Devil himself, because how in God's green earth did that man go into a school in the middle of the day and get that little girl to leave with him? Her folks said she'd never break the rules and wouldn't go anywhere with a man she didn't know. And then how did he know he could hide her body over there and it wouldn't be found until long after he left? We searched and searched that place. That man had some powers, alright, and none of them were used for good."

Helen shook his hand when they got out of the truck at the visitor's center. "You know things too, don't you?" she asked.

The ranger smiled. "I spend a lot of time alone, and sometimes I think about the different types of people among us. I knew that little girl was here, but I just couldn't find her. I wanted to help her family find some peace, and I asked God to tell me where she was." He picked up a branch that had fallen and put it along the side of the trail.

"Most of us are pretty good people," he said. "Me and you ladies, and most of the people we see around us, but there are some truly evil ones walking the earth. Bundy was one, and maybe your friend was given his visions to try to stop him. I believe that happens. I believe God chooses good people to fight against the evil in this world."

Helen and Joanie got into their car. The ranger stood by Helen's window. He thanked them for coming to the park.

"Always lock your doors, and drive safely," he said. "Good luck with your story."

◆❖◆

After Helen parked her car in the FSU lot, both women went into the newsroom. Joanie needed to speak with the sports editor about the event she was to cover that evening.

Helen greeted Mike, the copyeditor, and then went to her desk. Again, there was a working typewriter sitting there. She didn't know if that was a good omen or not. It was getting close to 5 p.m. and her deadline was at 7:00. She hadn't even spoken with anyone yet, and needed to make some calls quickly before her contacts went home for the day. She knew she had cut the time a little too closely, but she had enjoyed the day immensely.

As she sat down, she noticed there was a message in Laurie's handwriting next to the telephone. Captain Brand had called and wanted to meet in the morning, at Howard Johnson's on the Appalachia Parkway. 11:00 a.m.

Helen tried to call him immediately to confirm. The receptionist at the sheriff's office put her on hold, then someone else other than Brand answered the line.

"Who are you holding for?" the gruff voice demanded.

"Captain Brand, please."

"He's gone for the day. Do you want to leave a message?"

Something felt wrong about the guy on the other end. Helen suspected he may have been Sheriff Katsaris.

"No, thank you," she said politely, and hung up.

Helen knew she could call Brand at home. Most people had listed numbers in the telephone directory, but something told her to wait. She made her usual calls to gather the daily crime stories. She typed them quickly and handed them to Mike.

"No byline," she reminded him.

"I know. I'm sorry."

Helen drove home and spent the evening alone.

The next morning, Helen parked her car in the lot behind the

Howard Johnson's restaurant. She walked inside and looked around for Captain Brand. She didn't see him, so she chose a corner booth and sat down. The waitress brought her a menu. Helen ordered coffee.

Helen was the sole patron in the restaurant. The waitress, an older white woman, kept refreshing Helen's cup with coffee. Helen chain-smoked and wondered what was keeping Brand.

She knew that cops were never late for meetings, unless something was wrong.

30 minutes passed. The waitress asked if everything was alright and topped off Helen's cup for a fifth time. Helen placed her hand over the cup to indicate she didn't want any more. She was pretty jittery. The thought occurred to her that Brand had gotten caught with the psychic file.

Lunch patrons began to fill the restaurant. She'd either have to order some food or get ready to leave if Brand didn't show up. She looked at her watch. 45 minutes had passed. Where was Captain Brand?

A man from the motel's front desk walked in and looked around the restaurant. Helen watched as he said something to the waitress. She pointed at Helen. He walked over to the booth.

"Are you Ms. Baxter?"

"Yes."

"Your friend said he ran into some trouble and can't make it today."

She got up and put a five-dollar bill on the table. She left the restaurant, drove to the *Flambeau* office, and called the sheriff's department. She asked for Brand. She was told the captain would not be available for a while.

Helen then called Dick Simpson. He told her it was too early for the crime reports and that he would call her later.

Jamie came out of his office. He seemed surprised to see Helen already at her desk.

"I guess you missed out on the psychic story," he said.

"What? Why?"

"There was an article about the reward money in the *Democrat*," Jamie said. "The money was disbursed, with $5,000 going to the officer who arrested Bundy in Pensacola. The remainder was returned to the donors."[3]

"Nothing about Joseph, I guess," Helen said.

"No, nothing about the psychic. How did you miss the disbursement? Didn't Simpson tell you about it, or any of your other sources?"

"No. No one said a word."

"Well, you wasted enough energy chasing that story. I heard about your venture to Lake City the other day."

"Actually, I don't know if we're finished with the story yet."

"What do you mean?"

"I mean Captain Brand called yesterday and wanted to meet this morning at the Howard Johnson's. At 11:00. I waited, but he didn't show. Finally, the desk manager told me that Brand called and said that something came up."

"And you still think he'll come through for you? I think you're crazy. I think you're chasing the wind. Lay off this Joseph guy and his story. Brand is not going to back it. He'll lose his job if he goes on record, and I'm not running it without someone to verify it. Okay?"

Jamie stood close to Helen. The newsroom was quiet; it seemed as if everyone was holding their breath.

"Okay?" Jamie repeated sternly.

"Fine."

Helen did not want to talk about this story anymore, but she realized Jamie was still speaking.

"He's been playing a game and he will only hurt you. His ridiculous lies about being a psychic will land you in some hot water. Our building may be burned down. We're getting

---

3 Wireback, Howard. "Man wins $5,000 in Bundy arrest." *The Tallahassee Democrat*, Nov. 8, 1979, p. 1A.

threatening phone calls. You cannot continue with this story."

"What am I supposed to do then, Jamie?" She was frustrated and angry. "Am I supposed to answer phones, make coffee, and be your secretary, or do you want me to write? Tell me what I can do."

"Go ahead and ride with the city cops Saturday night. If they'll let you. But no talking about psychics, okay?"

"Of course," she exhaled. *Oh, thank God.*

He patted her on the back. "This will sort itself out."

Shortly after 1 p.m. on Thursday Helen went into work although she didn't have any idea what she would write about. She had ridden with a patrol unit from the Tallahassee PD the night before, but it was a quiet night. So quiet that she wondered if the cop she rode with deliberately did not take her to any interesting calls that shift. They'd been to a few car accident scenes, and all of those had been fender-benders.

"Have you mended fences with your sources yet?" Jamie asked her as she walked to her desk. The Royal was still there.

"No. I'm still in the penalty box," she said. "Which is pretty strange because these are the guys that gave me the PBA story to begin with."

"Did you see the article about George Brand in the *Democrat*?"

"What article?"

"It's a little one, but it's interesting. Let me get it."

He came back with the local section from that day's edition of the *Democrat*.[4] Brand had been suspended for three days without pay from the sheriff's office. Dick Simpson said that Brand had "discharged his firearm into the ceiling of an office in the Leon County Courthouse" on Thursday morning.

The morning he was to meet Helen.

---

[4] Grant, Dean. "Sheriff's captain suspended 3 days for accidental shot." *The Tallahassee Democrat*, Nov. 11, 1979, p. 1A.

"At the risk of upsetting you, I'd like to know why we don't have this story?" Jamie asked her. "Why didn't Dick Simpson give this to you?"

"How the fuck should I know?" Helen was very upset. She clapped her hand over her mouth. She didn't know why Simpson hadn't given her the story, but she suspected someone was punishing Brand. And her. And she didn't know who to believe anymore.

"Okay, let's just put this behind us and start over again." Jamie pulled a chair from the arts and features desk and sat down next to her. "Did you ride with the city last night?"

"I did." She was trying hard to keep from crying, or from screaming.

"Do you have some good stories to tell? What did the guys say when you went to Jerry's?"

Jamie knew that she always went to Jerry's with the city cops when they had down time, usually around 4 in the morning. They would eat breakfast, drink coffee, and work on their reports. Helen often proofread the officers' paperwork and corrected their misspelled words.

Helen looked at Jamie. "No. I don't have any stories. I went to car accidents. We responded to calls about cars parked illegally behind the Tennessee Street bars. We had those cars towed. I didn't ride with either George or David or Phil. I had to ride with a cop I didn't know. He wasn't very friendly. I think he'd been told not to talk to me. We didn't go to Jerry's."

She felt like she'd been kicked in the gut.

"I don't have a story," she said. "I'm shut out, Jamie. I'm finished here."

She was in tears. She lost her last shred of confidence when she learned the story about Brand had been given to the *Democrat*, and not to her.

"Hey, come on Baxter, you're a good reporter. You've just been caught up in a game, that's all." Jamie smiled, but he seemed very concerned. "Just overworked."

Helen said nothing. She lit a cigarette and exhaled. She felt numb. Joseph's warning came back to her. Her pursuit of the PBA story and her attempt to verify Joseph's involvement with the Chi Omega Task Force had torpedoed her career. *Some trouble indeed.*

"Thanksgiving is coming up," Jamie said. "Why don't you take some time off and come back at the beginning of January when the new quarter begins? Finish your classes. I've heard you're behind in all of them. Go home, see your family, and come back ready to do something else. We'll find a different beat for you."

It was true. She was tired, and confused about every aspect of her life. Her grades were a mess, and she had gotten herself into trouble with her sources trying to prove a story about a psychic who said he'd helped catch Ted Bundy.

The PBA story hadn't helped, either. She had underestimated Sheriff Katsaris' power in Leon County and realized she'd been used by a handful of officers to further the agenda of the man's political opponent, Eddie Boone. She'd jeopardized her job. Newspaper work was the only thing that gave her life meaning. She loved it and she had loved working the crime beat. But everything was out of kilter. She was too angry and stubborn to admit to anyone that she may have made a dreadful mistake in chasing the psychic story, on top of publishing the heavily-sourced PBA article.

Was the psychic story the reason Brand had been suspended? To keep him quiet? The story that he'd discharged his firearm into the ceiling at the courthouse seemed wrong.

"Damn it, this is such fucking bullshit. You know very well that I did not do this PBA story alone. You, Bob Martin, and the lawyers—everyone knew about this story as I was writing it. It was completely vetted. You knew who my sources were and no one thought I was being used by Eddie Boone."

"Helen, you're right. Just calm down," Jamie said. "Let's work this..."

"No, Jamie, I'll leave now," she interrupted. "I don't know if I'll be back. If I can't work the crime beat, then I guess I'm finished here."

She cleaned out her desk and walked out the door. No one said a word. No one tried to stop her. Her 21-year-old heart was broken.

◆❖◆

The phone rang in Helen's apartment. She was trying to finish a term paper before it was due, for once. The next day was Thanksgiving. Despite her mother's offer of a last-minute plane ticket home to Miami, she was going to spend the holiday alone. She had quite a few assignments to catch up on before the quarter ended.

"Helen?"

She recognized Brand's voice.

"Your friend Laurie gave me your home number. She said you walked out and hadn't come back to work yet."

"I'm not going back. I need to concentrate on my school work. I'm pretty far behind."

"I wanted to apologize for standing you up that morning at the Howard Johnson's." She heard him light a cigarette and waited for the exhale. "I guess you heard I was suspended."

"I did. I read about it in the *Democrat*. I knew I was in trouble when Dickie didn't even give me that story."

"Ah, Dickie didn't want to hurt you. But someone wanted to teach you and me a lesson. That reporter at the *Democrat* couldn't write a story correctly if his life depended on it. Come on down and see me at the courthouse on Monday."

"You know I'm not a reporter anymore, right?"

"Don't worry about that. We can fix it."

Helen was ushered quickly into Brand's office. He held his finger over his lips and shushed her. He pointed at the ceiling. Helen looked, but she could not detect where the plaster had been damaged by Brand's discharged bullet.

She looked at him questioningly.

"Never happened," he whispered. "Someone wanted me to get the message."

"Really?" Helen didn't know what to make of this. "Did you get the psychic file?"

Brand was quiet for a moment.

"No, it's disappeared. I know where it is, but for now it is hidden and will stay that way. Some things are better left untold for now." He took a deep breath. "You see, Helen, if the defense were to get hold of that information in the file, it could open up a whole new set of problems. It could maybe get the bastard acquitted, and we don't want to have to retry that son of a bitch. It might get our mutual friend in trouble, too. Someone might read his notes and think he did it. I don't think we would want that to happen. Am I making myself clear?"

Brand gave her a stern look. "If you wait and are patient, I promise you you'll get the story of what really happened. It might take a while, but I've arranged that for you in exchange for your silence. Is that clear?"

Helen nodded. "Can the other people involved be trusted?" she asked.

"Hell yeah," Brand smiled, "I give you my word. When Bundy's executed, doors will open and you will have the story. The whole story."

"How will I know when to contact you again?"

"After the son of a bitch is dead. Good luck, Helen."

They shook hands once again and Helen left his office.

Chapter 4: Gallows Pole

It was January 19th, 1989. More than nine years had passed since Helen had met Joseph and George Brand. 11 years had passed since the Chi Omega murders in Tallahassee.

Helen heard a news broadcast on the radio that Governor Bob Martinez had signed a death warrant for Theodore Robert Bundy. He was to be executed in five days, on January 24th, for the abduction, rape, and murder of Kimberly Leach, who had been 12 years old when Bundy lured her from a Lake City, Florida, middle school. She was thought to have been his final victim before he was arrested on February 12th, 1978, in Pensacola, Florida, by patrolman David Lee.

News of the warrant caught her attention. Helen picked up the phone and called Joseph to see what he thought about it.

"It's good news, finally," he said. "You just watch, Bundy's going to start confessing."

"What do you mean?"

"Bundy's going to spill his guts."

"How do you know?"

"Because it's time," he said softly. "He's going to talk, a lot too, and offer to help investigators find bodies of some of the women who disappeared. He wants to buy himself more time. He also wants to get out, to help them look for the bodies."

"Why? So he could try to escape again?"

"Yes. Just watch."

◆❖◆

As Bundy's execution date approached, he began talking just as Joseph predicted. Confession after confession poured out of the convicted killer. The number of women he killed, then raped and mutilated, reached more than 32. Some members of the FBI and other law enforcement agencies estimated that perhaps more than

100 women may have been murdered by Bundy. He tried to strike a bargain to buy himself more time. He offered to show investigators where he had buried the remains of victims that were still missing.

Helen nervously waited for the last chapter to unfold in the secret story she had been living with for nearly a decade. Soon, the media became electrified over Bundy's execution. The evening and late-night news shows were filled with story after story of Bundy's confessions, and quotes from Governor Martinez that there would be no dealing with Bundy.

On the day before the execution, hundreds of people and reporters from all over the nation began to gather at the Florida State Prison in Starke. Cars, trucks and a dozen mobile satellite transmitting vans filled the parking lot. Someone made a comment urging the television stations not to transmit any live news feed when "Old Sparky," the electric chair, was fired up to electrocute Bundy. The joke quickly passed through the assembling crowd. They wanted to make certain there "was enough juice to fry the bastard." People grilled hamburger meat to a crisp and called them "Bundy Burgers." T-shirts were sold with anti-Bundy slogans screen-printed on them. "Burn, Bundy, burn!" indeed.

A small group of about three dozen people protested the execution. They stood quietly while the crowds heckled them. The media circus Ted Bundy created while on trial for the Chi Omega murders in Tallahassee 10 years earlier was nothing compared to the execution party he inadvertently created outside the prison walls that Tuesday morning.

On the evening before Bundy's electrocution, Helen spoke with friends who were into metaphysics. They speculated on the idea of Bundy's "evil spirit" astral projecting into someone else's body. There was a thought, among the spiritualists, that when a person knew he was going to die, such as Bundy did, he could will his spirit out of his body just prior to his death. His spirit, they thought, would then live on in another's body, a possession of sorts, and continue to wreak havoc and mayhem in the world.

Late that evening, Helen called Joseph again and asked him what he thought of the concerns her friends had about Bundy astral projecting.

"I have no idea about that stuff or what his spirit might do."

Helen did not sleep well that night.

The morning news was filled with the reports of Bundy's death at 7:16 a.m. Helen thought about George Brand, and Joseph, and the events in Tallahassee that had led to her losing her reporting job. She wondered if she should begin making some telephone calls again.

Later that day, Helen telephoned a friend, Alex Silverberg, who was the Gainesville Bureau reporter for the *Jacksonville Times-Union* newspaper. She briefly told Alex that a psychic had worked with an investigator in Tallahassee to help capture Ted Bundy.

"Helen, are you kidding?" Alex had asked. "Who's the psychic?"

"Nope. You call Captain George Brand and ask him. Tell George I told you a little about the story."

When Alex called the Leon County Sheriff's office, he discovered Brand no longer worked for the department. He had resigned years earlier. Alex called Helen back and asked for help to find Brand.

Helen made two phone calls and found Brand's contact information. She passed it over to Alex. By the end of that day, Alex had spoken with George Brand and confirmed the story that a psychic had worked to help catch Bundy.

"Helen, he asked about you. He wanted to know why you aren't writing the story. I told him that you had three small children and were in the process of getting a divorce. I gave him your phone number, because he asked and I thought it would be okay with you."

"That's fine. It would be nice to talk with him again," she said. "Are you going to do the story, Alex?" She heard computer keys clacking on his end.

"Can't. I ran it by my editor and he wants the *immediate gratification* stories that everyone else is running."

"Such as?"

"Oh, some reporters dressed in scrubs and tried to crash the morgue. The *Enquirer* allegedly got a photo of his head, shaved, with the electrode burn marks on it. He wants me to run it down, and get some comments from Tallahassee locals and Lake City PD."

"Did you ask Brand for a comment?"

"Officially, he declined. Off the record, he said, 'Good, I'd have pulled the switch myself to kill that SOB and then I'd pull it again just to make sure he was dead!'"

"Oh, that sounds like George Brand." She giggled.

"Hey, Helen, my editor wants me to find Bundy's wife, the one he married in the courtroom and then had a baby with. Any ideas?"

"The last I heard, she was living in northeast Gainesville. Rental house. She shouldn't be too hard to find."

"I heard she packed up and left in the middle of the night when he started confessing. She always insisted he was innocent."

"I guess she finally realized what the rest of us knew all along. Ted Bundy was a dangerous sociopath who murdered women just for the fun of it."

"Seriously, Helen, you should think about writing that story."

"How would I even start, Alex?"

"Get Joseph to keep the kids for a few days and go to Tallahassee. Interview George Brand and everyone else. You know all those people. Then get a divorce and I'll help you write the story in my free time. We could write a book."

She laughed. "Easier said than done."

"Hey, who is the psychic?"

She thought about this for a second.

"Alex, the psychic is Joseph."

"Get the fuck out of here!"

◆❖◆

Helen had arrived in Tallahassee the afternoon before and had spent the night with her old friend Laurie Jones. Laurie no longer worked at the *Flambeau* and now had a job with the support staff of the Florida Legislature. They went out to dinner, and then for dancing and drinks at Tommy's Deep South Music Hall, one of their old favorite hangouts.

The next morning, Helen drove over to the Doak Campbell Stadium and picked up a visitor's parking pass from the attendant. He sent her into the visitor's office, where she signed in and received a badge. The woman walked Helen to an office.

Helen knocked.

"C'mon in," Brand called.

She opened the door.

"Hey there, I know you," he said. He had a bad head cold. "I'd recognize you anywhere. Long time ago, you worked for the mullet wrapper."

"That's me." She smiled and they shook hands.

"It's been a long time, hasn't it?" Brand leaned back in his chair.

Helen pulled out a small pocket tape recorder and set it on the desk. Before Brand began to tell his story, she made sure the tape recorder was working.

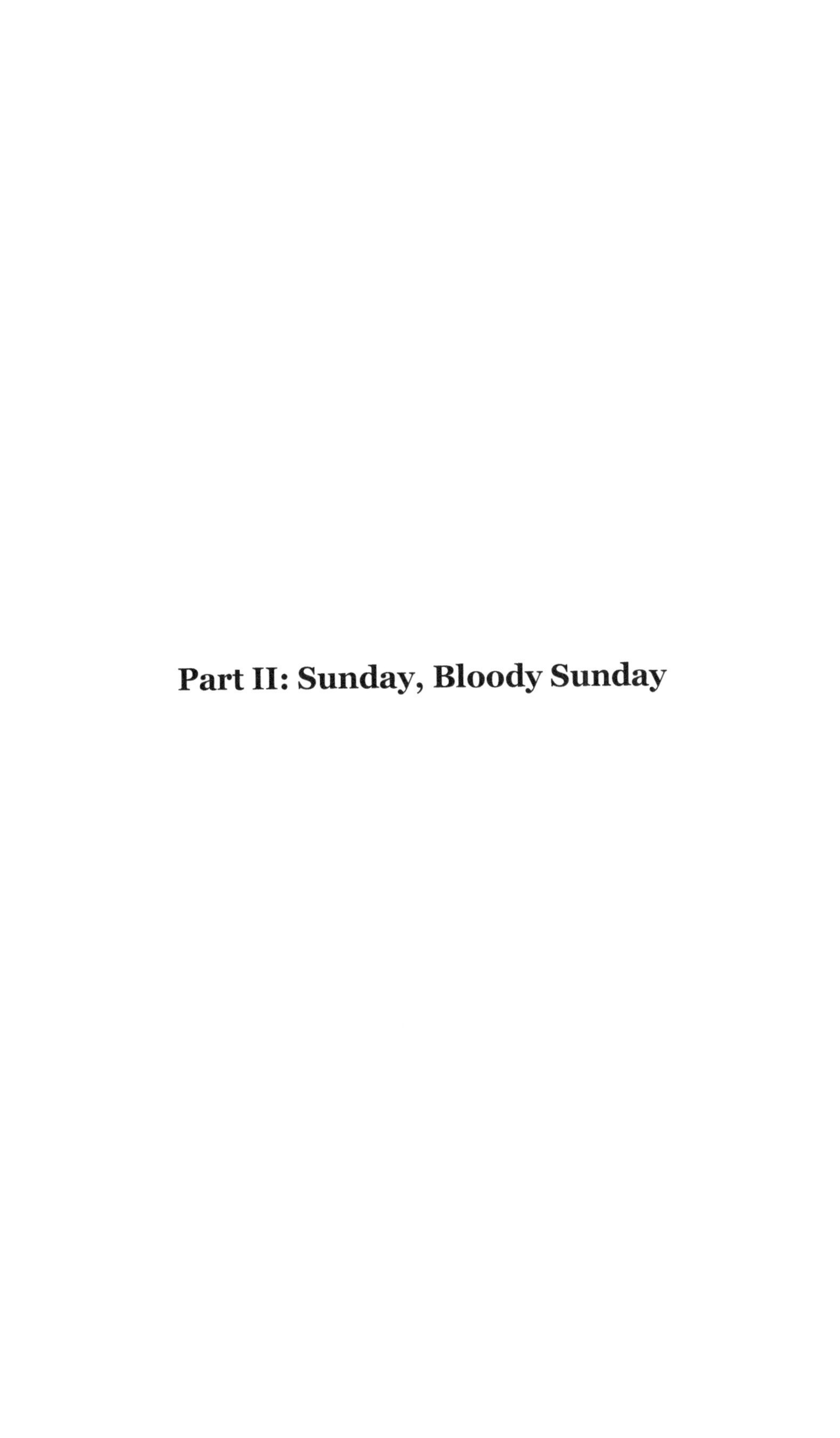

Part II: Sunday, Bloody Sunday

Chapter 5: Shattered

Brenda pulled into the parking lot of her small, one-bedroom apartment across from several sorority houses. She loved living just blocks from her classes, but found being in such close proximity to the noisy girls' clubs to be distracting. *Those girls partied.* She planned to move as soon as her lease was up.

It was just after midnight, and she was two hours late getting off work that night. *So much for a night out*, she thought as she gathered her book and notebooks from around the inside of her small Datsun sedan and jammed them into her backpack. She grabbed her cigarettes and lighter, got out of the car, and hefted the bag onto her shoulder. She pushed the lock and closed the door.

The night was below freezing and spits of rain were falling. She was cold and pulled her coat tightly around her as she headed toward the stairs. She pushed her long brown hair under the jacket hood.

Out of the corner of her eye, she became aware of a small movement near the large oak tree at the edge of the lot. She stopped for a second and looked at the tree, which was in shadows. The parking lot was only dimly lit, and she felt a little spooked, but blamed the movement on the wind. She began walking again, faster, but kept her eyes on the area of the tree.

"Come here," she heard someone whispering to her. "Come over here." Then she saw the source of the movement. Someone was leaning against the tree. "Help me," she heard. Or had she? She wondered if that person, if that's what it was, had actually called to her or if she was imagining it.

She shrugged her free arm into the other bag strap and began to walk toward the tree.

"Stop!" a voice shrieked. "Stop! Don't go over there! Run, run! Get out of there!"

It was her mother's voice. Her mother was screaming in her head. She turned and fled up the stairs. She unlocked the door and slammed it behind her. She made certain she was locked in, and then she pushed a table with the TV in front of the door. She was terrified.

Her mother had been dead for nearly eight years.

◆❖◆

The date was Sunday, January 15th, only hours before the start of the 1978 Super Bowl. Everyone living in or visiting Tallahassee at that time remembers it well. The events of that day changed the city forever. It was the weekend of the Chi Omega murders.

The weather was very cold and wet, typical for Tallahassee in the winter. The attacker struck his first victim around 3 a.m., just after most of the sorority girls had returned home from their Saturday night outings. It was only after one of the wounded girls was found staggering in a hallway, bleeding profusely from a head wound, that anyone realized something truly awful had just happened in the house. It was strange that no one had heard anything.

Chi Omega sorority sisters Margaret Bowman and Lisa Levy had been beaten and strangled to death while they slept. Their bodies were gruesomely mutilated.

After clubbing and strangling Bowman, the killer mutilated her body. The nipple of her right breast was nearly bitten off and dangled by a tiny piece of skin. A pair of pantyhose was found wrapped tightly around her neck. The police didn't notice the nylons at first because they were embedded so deeply into her flesh and neck. The makeshift garrote had nearly decapitated her.

The killer had smashed in the right side of her head with what seemed to be a long wooden club. It left a hole so large that crime scene technicians could see her brains clearly. The opening began above her right eye and ended at the back of her head. The hole in her skull behind her right ear was as large as a man's clenched fist.

Blood and pieces of head matter were splattered throughout the room. Shards and slivers of oak wood and bark were discovered amidst the carnage. Most of the shattered skull fragments were driven deeply into her crushed brain.

Her panties had been torn off with enough force to burn the skin. Oddly, no semen or any obvious traces of the killer were found on or around the victims, even though evidence suggested these had been sadistic and sexually motivated killings.

Down the hall, in Lisa Levy's room, technicians found a hair spray can had been used to rape Levy, both vaginally and anally. Deep bite marks and bruising were found on her breasts and buttocks, where the killer had attacked the woman and sucked blood from her wounds.

To those who responded to the calls for help, the scenes looked as if a cannibal or vampire had committed the crimes.

Karen Chandler and Kathy Kleiner, two other sorority sisters, had also been attacked in their rooms. They received severe injuries but survived the killer's rampage.

Chandler was the first victim to be discovered. She staggered down a hallway, dripping blood. She had sustained a concussion and her jaw was broken. Several of her teeth had been knocked out. Her arm was broken. She also suffered facial fractures and lacerations, and a crushed finger. Kleiner's jaw was fractured in three places and her teeth were loosened by the blows from her assailant. Her shoulder had suffered several deep cuts, and she had whiplash on her neck. A large pin had to be placed in her jaw.

Both girls were hospitalized for over a week, and their jaws were wired shut for weeks thereafter. They were lucky to be alive.

Within minutes of the emergency calls, police and paramedics arrived and began to work the murderous scene. The dead girls were found in their nightgowns with bedding pulled up over their shoulders. They appeared to be sleeping peacefully, until the bed covers were removed and the ghastly scenes were revealed.

As police officers went through the house waking up the other residents, the horror of the night began to expose itself. A head count was made of the women as they huddled, terrified, in the large downstairs dining room. Several girls were missing. Officers checked their bedrooms to make sure they were not victims. Confusion and hysteria set in among the residents. Several girls collapsed in the stairwell, causing problems for police officers and paramedics trying to reach the bedrooms.

Lieutenant George Brand of the Leon County Sheriff's Department was the first high-ranking officer to arrive on the scene. Captain Jack Poitinger, Brand's superior officer, walked in several minutes later. Both had been awakened from a sound sleep only minutes before.

Soon, more than 50 police officers from local and state law enforcement agencies were at the scene. It was a madhouse, with medics yelling orders to help the victims while others gave commands to secure the area. The ambulances left for Tallahassee Memorial Hospital with their sirens screaming.

Lieutenant Brand asked the officers if anyone had seen anything suspicious. He was informed that one woman, Nita Neary, had seen a man leaving the house as she arrived home from a date.

Nita Neary? Brand stopped in his tracks. He knew the woman from a similar but less devastating attack that happened several months earlier.

Without hesitation, he asked to have Nita taken to the sheriff's department to be hypnotized and held for questioning. This was a very unusual request, but Brand wanted to obtain as much information from the young woman as quickly as possible. He would interview her.

"Make sure the doc asks her one thing," Brand said to the deputy he tasked. "See if she's had any experience with Satanism."

Chapter 6: For What It's Worth

"I'm in charge now."

Those were the first words Leon County Sheriff Ken Katsaris said as he arrived at the Chi Omega house moments after the two surviving victims had been rushed to the hospital. Nearly 30 other girls were huddled together in the dining room. They all watched in horror as Margaret Bowman's body, covered with a blood-soaked sheet, was wheeled out of the house on an ambulance gurney.

Many of the law enforcement officers were not surprised by Katsaris' remark. It was common knowledge that few of those who came in contact with Katsaris cared for him. Many considered him self-centered and egotistical.

It was not necessary for Katsaris to exert control of the scene. As the Sheriff of Leon County, he was the highest-ranking law enforcement officer. Katsaris declined to go upstairs to examine the crime scenes firsthand.

Several officers, including Brand, briefed the sheriff on the situation.

"Lieutenant Brand will be in charge of this situation," Katsaris announced. "All reports will be made to him."

Brand was bemused. As soon as he was able, he pulled the sheriff aside to speak with him privately.

"With all due respect, sir, I'll be reporting to Captain Jack Poitinger, like I always do."

The sheriff was momentarily perplexed by Brand's comment. He had forgotten about Poitinger.

George Brand had proven himself to the sheriff a year earlier, when Katsaris took office. The crime wasn't a brutal murder, but an unusual event which demonstrated Brand's ability to remain level-headed under pressure.

It was during January of 1977, a few days after Katsaris was sworn into office. The department received a bomb threat. George

Brand was a sergeant then.

The new sheriff ran excitedly into Sergeant Brand's office and told him that a bomb threat had been called in. The main Tallahassee post office was the target. He ordered Brand to check it out.

At the time, Brand's parking spot was a long walk from his office. The sheriff and other high-ranking deputies had reserved parking spaces in a garage underneath the courthouse. Because of this, he was the last to arrive on the scene.

The first thing he noticed when he entered the post office was that the sheriff stood alongside Captain Poitinger, the postmaster, the district attorney, and several other deputies from the department.

"Well, George," Katsaris said when Brand entered. "What should we do now?"

"Well sir, I'm going across the street and I'm going to wait to become the next appointed Sheriff of Leon County," Brand replied with a straight face. "I'll have no competition."

The sheriff did not understand what Brand meant. The others in the post office began to leave the building.

"What? What did you say?" the sheriff asked. "What do you mean?"

Brand grinned and saluted his boss. "Sir, there's a bomb threat on this building. I just stopped in to make sure it was being cleared and secured for the bomb squad."

He paused.

"With all of you standing here, if this place blows up, I'm the new sheriff."

Brand walked out the door, chuckling to himself.

Katsaris never forgot that lesson. A short time later, he promoted Brand to the rank of lieutenant, a title that brought with it a reserved parking spot underneath the courthouse.

Now it was a year later and Katsaris faced the worst situation of his career. As self-absorbed as he was, Katsaris knew that an officer's gut reaction was his most important asset, and he trusted his officers' instincts to react appropriately when the pressure was on. He allowed the men to do their work.

The paramedics were instructed to stop while a deputy asked the sheriff if he wanted to see Margaret Bowman's body before it went to the morgue. Katsaris declined. He asked who was doing the crime scene analysis and learned that Howard Winkler, one of his top technicians, was in charge.

Most of the officers working upstairs, gathering evidence, tagging exhibits, photographing the room, and taking inventory of the victim's personal belongings had been Katsaris' students at the police academy before he had been elected sheriff. He was confident they were following procedure. He said he didn't want to further contaminate the crime scene by walking through it.

The sorority house was a mob scene of patrol officers, deputies, paramedics, and residents. Winkler, a meticulous crime scene specialist, came downstairs to find Katsaris. He worried that the medics had handled the bodies too much to get any reliable fingerprints.

"We can't wait for fingerprints while trying to save victims," Katsaris told him.

Winkler went back upstairs in a huff.

Eddie Boone, head of investigations at the Florida Department of Law Enforcement (FDLE), the statewide agency, entered the sorority house. He came to offer the services of his best investigators. Katsaris refused the help. There was no love lost between the two men. There were already rumors that Boone planned to run against Katsaris in the next election.

Boone had been Katsaris' original choice to be the number-two man at the sheriff's department. Boone initially accepted the position, but backed out days before he was to begin work at the department. That made for bad blood between the two men.

Lieutenant Brand and Captain Poitinger decided they needed to place a security net around the perimeter of the Chi Omega house. Katsaris agreed.

Brand and Poitinger requested that several officers be dispatched to go door to door in the neighborhood to learn if anyone had heard or seen anything unusual. The sheriff readily agreed. There was a large crowd of people gathered outside the sorority house. Katsaris instructed Brand and Poitinger to send officers to interview the individuals as well.

It was nearly 4 a.m. It was freezing cold and damp outside. One thermometer read 24 degrees as the officers began to question the onlookers and the nearby residents. His men were doing all they could, so Katsaris left the scene in his car and went home.

Some of the detectives left the sorority house too, to catch some fresh air and get some warm coffee. Brand was one of them.

He picked up a cup of coffee and was sitting in his car in a gas station parking lot on Woodward Avenue when he realized what he was wearing. He had on a hunting jacket but no shirt, pants but no underwear, and loafers without socks. He wasn't exactly complying with departmental dress code. He'd grabbed the first things he found, not planning to be out long, hardly imagining that he'd be involved in a bizarre murder case.

As Brand sat in his car sipping hot coffee, a new set of emergency calls crackled over his police radio. Another attack had taken place. Brand recognized the address. It was just two blocks from where he was parked. He hurriedly drove to a rundown Dunwoody Street duplex and joined several squad cars. Officer Wilton Dozier was already out of his car with his shotgun in hand.

Brand ordered the officers to gain access as quickly as possible. Dozier was about to break down the front door when Nancy Young, who lived in the duplex next door, remembered the location of a spare key.

Officers went in and found Cheryl Thomas, an FSU dance major, on her bed bleeding and semiconscious, but alive. Thomas had been beaten with a club and had suffered multiple skull fractures. Her shoulder was dislocated and her face was swelling with purple bruises. All of her clothes except her panties had been torn off. She would never walk normally again, and suffered permanent hearing and equilibrium loss. Her dreams of being a professional dancer were shattered forever. But she was alive.

Her attacker appeared to have escaped through the kitchen window, which seemed to have been the way he entered.

Brand instantly knew this new attack was related to the Chi Omega crimes. Paramedics arrived on the scene minutes after having delivered the surviving Chi Omega victims to Tallahassee Memorial Hospital.

After Cheryl Thomas was rushed to the hospital, the crime technicians discovered a mask in her bed sheets. It had been cut from pantyhose and yielded several brown, wavy hairs. The pantyhose were of the same brand and had been cut exactly like the one found in Margaret Bowman's room at the Chi Omega sorority house.

Standing outside in the freezing cold, Brand remembered an expensive platter of sandwich meats and cheeses wrapped up in the refrigerator at home in preparation for a Super Bowl party. He knew that wasn't going to happen. In fact, he knew it would be a long time before his life would be normal again. He took a deep breath, went out and bought another cup of coffee, then headed back to the Chi Omega house.

He prayed there would be no more attacks that day.

Chapter 7: One Piece at a Time

Crime technicians are a special breed of police officer. They conduct crime scene work such as dusting for fingerprints, photographing the area and victims, and logging evidence. They are also responsible for establishing and enforcing the chain-of-custody requirements for all evidence gathered from a crime scene to ensure its admissibility in court. Crime scene analysis for violent crimes and homicides is considered by the professionals to be the most crucial part of an investigation. Convictions hinge on the quality of their work.

The Chi Omega murder cases, which included the attack on Cheryl Thomas in her Dunwoody Street duplex, presented the most challenging set of obstacles Howard Winkler and his fellow Leon County crime technicians had faced up to that time. The scarcity of clues was compounded by the scores of officers and medical personnel who had trampled the crime scene. There were also hundreds of fingerprints in each room, some possibly older than 15 or 20 years.

Some types of surfaces and materials retain fingerprints longer than most people live. The sorority rooms held years of living history. Dozens of girls had lived in these rooms, and hundreds of their friends and family members had visited. Technicians applied chemicals to each room where an assault was committed. To their dismay, they found fingerprints on almost every square inch of the rooms.

The sheer number of potential matches to the fingerprints made the task of determining who had been in the rooms that night impossible. At any given time, the Chi Omega house had up to 40 girls living in it. The staff included house boys, housekeepers, kitchen and other service employees. There were outside maintenance personnel who had access to the building, as well as delivery people, plumbers, vending route men, and many others who walked right in or had their own keys to the service entrance door. And, oftentimes, as in every dormitory and many apartments throughout the city, doors were left unlocked.

Then there were the boyfriends. Men weren't allowed upstairs in the sorority house, but their fingerprints turned up there, anyway. The stories the girls told while they tried to help the police piece together the timeline of the night revealed that many routinely broke the house rules.

Eventually, the technicians would match over 250 sets of fingerprints from the crime scene.

In several of the victims' rooms, Winkler's men found small bags of marijuana, pornographic magazines, vibrators, rubber penises, and other sex toys. This intensified the situation for the police. Now they were forced to deal with complicated and sensitive issues regarding the moral reputations of the victims. They didn't want the parents—or worse, the press—to find out.

The technicians threw the marijuana away and gave the sex toys and magazines to Lieutenant Brand.

During the autopsy, when the photographer took pictures of Lisa Levy's buttocks, investigator Steve Bodiford impulsively laid his plastic ruler next to the bite marks. Later, this was to be the only evidence that would conclusively tie the killer to the crimes, for the photograph gave the prosecutors the exact dimensions of the killer's teeth. This piece of evidence would not be discredited.

The medical examiner, Dr. Thomas Wood, surgically removed the entire bitten area from Lisa Levy's body and attempted to preserve it. The killer sometimes bit more than once in the same area, so the teeth marks overlapped. Based on the amount of blood found in and around the bite marks, Dr. Wood determined that Lisa was already dead when the killer mutilated her body.

A piece of chewing gum with a perfect set of teeth prints was removed from the hair of one of the victims. This gum was considered extremely important. It was placed in an envelope and immediately mailed to an FBI laboratory in Atlanta, Georgia, for processing.

Laboratory technicians found blood, pubic hair, and fecal matter on the hair spray can, but as far as they could discern, they had no fingerprints from the killer. The lack of evidence was alarming. And disheartening.

Chapter 8: So Begins the Task

Sheriff Katsaris appointed Captain Jack Poitinger, a stocky man with short, dark hair and a stern face, as the coordinator of the investigation. Poitinger would report directly to Katsaris. A lawyer by training, he was a strong leader who chose his words cautiously. His first directive was to assemble a large search team and set up a mini-command post inside the sorority house.

Before dawn, a meeting was held with representatives from several local law enforcement agencies. The Tallahassee Police Department was represented by Captain Burl Peacock. Captain Steve Hooker came from the FSU Police Department. Several members of the FDLE, including Eddie Boone, were present.

Poitinger knew that a piece of oak had been used to break the skull of one of the women. It was estimated to be the size of a small club. It had to be somewhere, and it was likely covered with blood.

But with daylight coming on, Poitinger knew that potentially thousands of students would soon be walking and driving through the two crime scenes, oblivious to what had occurred. He knew that people would be using their fireplaces and wood-burning stoves, and would go outside to gather suitable firewood to heat their homes.

The group decided to begin with a "hot search." They immediately assembled a large group of officers to conduct a systematic search of several blocks surrounding the Chi Omega and Dunwoody residences.

The men were divided into squadrons. For his search team leaders, Poitinger selected men with professional homicide law enforcement backgrounds. These men would lead the searches with current officers or officers-in-training from several different law enforcement agencies, including a group of new cadets from the Florida Highway Patrol Academy, located in Tallahassee.

Hundreds of people during the course of the day would become involved in the search sweeps. Nearly every law enforcement officer not assigned to an immediate crime in progress was included in the searches. Men walked at arm's distance from each other, sweeping through the area, looking everywhere for clues and potential suspects.

They looked under houses, on roofs, and in trash bins, gutters, and toolboxes. They searched under bushes, in firewood piles, in and under cars and trucks, along wall cracks, in trees, and under porches... wherever they could see at least a one-inch opening into which someone could have shoved a weapon or bloody clothing. They went over and over the areas, each time changing the sweep angle and rotating the men so they didn't walk the same area twice.

After several hours of scrambling, climbing, crawling, and lifting, the search was completed. A sizable stack of oak wood had been collected. Each piece had to be examined carefully to see whether or not it could have possibly been used as the murder weapon.

Mountains of discarded clothing were also gathered during the neighborhood sweep. Each piece was examined and checked for blood. Eyewitness Nita Neary had described the killer's clothing, but nothing similar had been picked up. They looked for a sock that may have been wrapped around the club, as Neary had seen. Nothing was found to indicate who or where the killer might be. The officers swept the areas again.

Roadblocks and special surveillance teams were established in the perimeters of the neighborhood. Identification was checked and residents were asked if they had seen or heard anything unusual.

Teams of officers knocked on each and every residential door. The officers insisted upon interviewing everyone they could find. They wanted to know who was home, and who *wasn't* home, during the timeline they were trying to establish for the attacks. They scrambled for any clue that could identify the killer.

Time was of the essence, and Captain Poitinger and the other agency delegates attempted to coordinate through their different agency locations. He realized they needed a place for all of the investigators to work under one roof. It was decided that a central command post would be necessary to work effectively and efficiently.

Sheriff Katsaris called several people familiar with local commercial real estate. He was looking for enough office space to establish a task force command center that would allow the investigators to work separately from the other agencies.

A two-story office building, located at 307 E. 7th Avenue, was secured within hours. It was conveniently located across the street from the Tallahassee Police Department. Syde Deeb, a local real estate developer, donated the empty space.

The building seemed to meet all of the anticipated needs of the task force members. There were plenty of rooms on both floors. Katsaris requested there be a coffee maker placed into each office, except the interrogation rooms. He requested someone be brought in to keep the coffee brewing.

Brand designated the lines of communication for the command post. He used standard military procedures learned through his 20-plus years with the National Guard, the last eight of them as a regional commander.

Throughout the afternoon and night, crews from the telephone company set up the phone lines in the 7th Avenue building. Truckloads of desks, chairs, and file cabinets donated by local business supply companies filled the rooms within the building.

The owner of the local McDonald's restaurants volunteered an ongoing supply of hamburgers, fries, and drinks for the task force personnel.

As the command post and other operations started to fall into place, Brand became more confident of finding the killer.

Throughout the day, a crowd of people estimated at over 150 gathered near the roped-off crime scene areas. They wanted to know what had happened. Stories began to circulate that several sorority girls had been murdered. By the afternoon, the gossip was that most of the girls in the Chi Omega house had been injured or killed by a roving gang of angry Iranians, or more likely, a fraternity prank gone bad. It was clear that hysteria was growing, and a witch hunt could result unless a suspect was caught soon.

News reporters arrived on the scene very early in the day. One began to make comments about other killings that might be related. His comments were intended to rile the bystanders and to get someone to go on record, worried that the killer would strike again.

One reporter overheard that Nita Neary, an eyewitness in an earlier case, had seen the killer leaving the house.

These reporters quickly discovered the police were in the process of contacting every person in the area. A massive door-to-door search by the police had never taken place before in Tallahassee. While the media had few details at this time, it was obvious that a massive news story had occurred.

Several reporters monitoring police radio transmissions went to the Dunwoody Street duplex. The officer stationed at the house was excited by the attention of the press. He eagerly showed Ms. Thomas' apartment with the broken window to the reporters. He then introduced them to Nancy Young and Debbie Cicerelli, Thomas' neighbors, who had heard her struggling with her assailant and called the police.

Nancy and Debbie naively identified themselves to the reporters. They told them where they worked. They gave their telephone numbers to the reporters so they could be easily reached.

Later that afternoon, Lieutenant Brand arrived at their duplex with an advance copy of the Monday Regional Edition of the *Democrat.* He explained to the women how they just let the assailant know that they had heard the attack on Thomas. They were in a dangerous situation. The killer would not only learn he had left witnesses, but he would know exactly where to find them.

Brand was furious with himself for not removing the two young women from their duplex apartment immediately after Cheryl Thomas was attacked. When he learned of this information leak, Brand called the editorial staff at the *Democrat* to attempt to stop the publication of the women's identities. Unfortunately, the early edition had already gone to press. Nancy Young's full name was printed, as well as the name of the only eyewitness, Nita Neary. The killer now knew who they were.

At least one of the witnesses was safe, Brand thought. Nita Neary had already been put on a plane to her family home in Muncie, Indiana.

In 1978, the *Democrat* printed three editions a day. The Regional Edition was published the evening before, the Sunrise

Edition was printed during the night, and the daily Home Final Edition was printed in the morning for afternoon delivery.

As the damaging articles hit the streets, Lieutenant Brand urgently made phone calls and called in favors owed him. He knew the Dunwoody girls might have to stay in safe hiding for a long time. Different jobs and a place to live were quickly found for them and by Monday night, Brand had helped Debbie and Nancy relocate to a new apartment. When reporters tried to contact the girls again, they discovered that the apartment phone number had been disconnected and their work information was no longer correct. The duplex doors were locked and the apartments were empty. Debbie and Nancy had vanished. Cheryl Thomas' apartment had also been cleaned out.

One of the people Brand called for help was his good friend, State Senator Don Tucker. The senator helped Debbie Cicerelli get a new job with the Sergeant of Arms in the legislature.

Nancy Young's new job was as a waitress with the Round Holiday Inn Restaurant on Tennessee Street. Only Brand knew where the two girls lived and worked. Poitinger and Katsaris never knew what happened to the girls, except that Brand took care of them and that they were safe.

Brand called Sheriff Katsaris to tell him about the newspaper articles. Upon learning what had already happened with the press, Katsaris decided to withhold information, and even gave the media false details about the crime to weed out compulsive confessors and copycat killers. He feared that a copycat might use these murders as an opportunity to kill other women, such as a wife or girlfriend, to add to the body count of the Chi Omega killer. Several confessors still came forward using the false facts planted in the articles by Katsaris. These imitators were quickly discredited.

Chapter 9: Jigsaw Puzzle

Early Sunday afternoon, Sheriff Katsaris appointed Captain Poitinger as chief of the newly formed multi-agency investigation task force. The men assigned under Poitinger were divided into several investigative teams.

The first divisional assignments were to research the backgrounds of all victims to see if there were common denominators connecting them. This was standard procedure for multiple homicide investigations. Within this unit, a smaller division was assigned to compare the Chi Omega case with another attack that occurred several months before at a park on Spring Hill Road. The two cases were similar in many respects.

The previous attack involved a young FSU coed, Linda Sue Thompson, who was also a Chi Omega pledge. The previous May, she was clubbed and kidnapped from Dorman Hall, only a few blocks from the Chi Omega house, at around 3 a.m. Then she was taken to a lake area in southwest Tallahassee. Police knew the assailant was a black man because of pubic hair found on the woman. She was left in the park unconscious, naked from the waist down, and covered with pine needles.

Thompson's roommate, and fellow Chi Omega pledge, was Nita Neary. Poitinger found it strangely coincidental that Neary was tangentially related to both brutal attacks involving the Chi Omega house. Investigators studied the possibility there were two attackers at the Chi Omega house: the black assailant of Thompson, and the white man Neary saw leaving the house.

A different investigative team was assigned to discover how each victim could be linked to Cheryl Thomas and the Dunwoody Street duplex, and what might have linked her to the Chi Omega house.

Captain Poitinger appointed Lieutenant Brand as chief of the command post. The officers directly under Brand were Larry Clark, Steve Bodiford, W.D. (Dee) Phillips, Stephanie Wright, and Bill Gunter. These detectives became group leaders responsible for tracking down suspects and questioning them.

Under Brand were in-county and out-of-county investigation teams. Phillips was designated commanding officer of the extra-county unit. Phillips' men were assigned the task of tracking down all of the leads that originated outside Leon County, and finding suspects currently living outside the county but who may have been in Tallahassee at the time of the murders. The investigators in Phillips' unit would spend long hours driving hundreds of miles each day, following up every possible tip that came into the task force.

As news of the murders spread throughout the country, dozens of law enforcement agencies called in with information about fugitive men from their jurisdictions. Phillips quickly amassed files on serial killers, escaped murderers, and other unusual criminal types who could possibly be the Chi Omega killer.

The in-county team began working the flood of incoming telephone leads. These calls were mostly from women calling to report that their husbands and boyfriends were not home that night.

Within minutes after the assignments were given out, the investigators began asking the sorority girls some tough questions about the personal lives of the victims. Confessions poured in from the girls, and this helped the officers uncover the personal affairs and acquaintances of the victims.

The detectives were surprised about the number of different boyfriends several of the victims were sexually involved with at the same time. One victim had five sexual partners she saw regularly. She had kept an appointment book. The investigators tracked down each of the men who were named and interviewed them. The officers tried to keep this information quiet, as several of the men were married.

While under hypnosis, sorority sister and eyewitness Neary was able to describe with great detail the man she saw leaving the sorority house. She said he was clean-shaven and looked like Ron Eng, one of the Chi Omega house boys. Eng was a music major at FSU and studied classical guitar performance. He was short, thin, and had a long, sharply pointed nose. He had a light-tan complexion. His signature trademark was the pencil-thin mustache he cultivated.

Eng was adored by the Chi Omega sorority sisters. After the attacks, the girls asked him to spend nights at the house to protect them. The *Democrat* ran a story about him spending nights downstairs on the couch. The story didn't mention that Nita Neary had described the killer as resembling Ron.

Since four of the five victims lived in the Chi Omega house, it was easy to find common elements in their lifestyles. Many of the sorority sisters went to the same bars and attended events together sponsored by the sorority house or the Greek Council. Even so, detailing the lives of the victims would be a long and time-consuming process.

Eventually, the only common denominators linking all five of the victims together was their attendance at FSU and the killer's methodology of attack. One of the investigators noted that all of the girls had brown hair.

The angle that Poitinger favored was that Cheryl Thomas was the killer's intended victim. She was the outlier, and had little in common with the Chi Omega victims. There were no known links between Thomas and the four Chi Omega victims. Poitinger guessed the killer had seen Thomas at the Montgomery Gym on the FSU campus. Poitinger surmised the killer may have watched Thomas practice dance routines at this gymnasium.

He speculated the killer could have followed her home one day, and thus known where she lived.

Poitinger reasoned that the killer had stalked Cheryl Thomas and had decided to attack her on Saturday night. But Thomas unexpectedly had plans that evening. Had the killer spent the evening waiting for Thomas to come home?

He also suspected that because of the close proximity—mere blocks—between the Dunwoody apartment and the Chi Omega sorority house, the killer would have been familiar with the area as he prowled, searching for his next victim. Someone who watched closely would have observed that the back door on the Chi Omega house had a broken lock. The door was not secured, even late at night.

A hunter intent on selecting his prey would have been quite excited at such a fortuitous invitation, and would have been hard pressed to not enter the sorority house with so many girls to choose from.

Poitinger believed that as the night passed by, the killer worked himself into a frenzy.

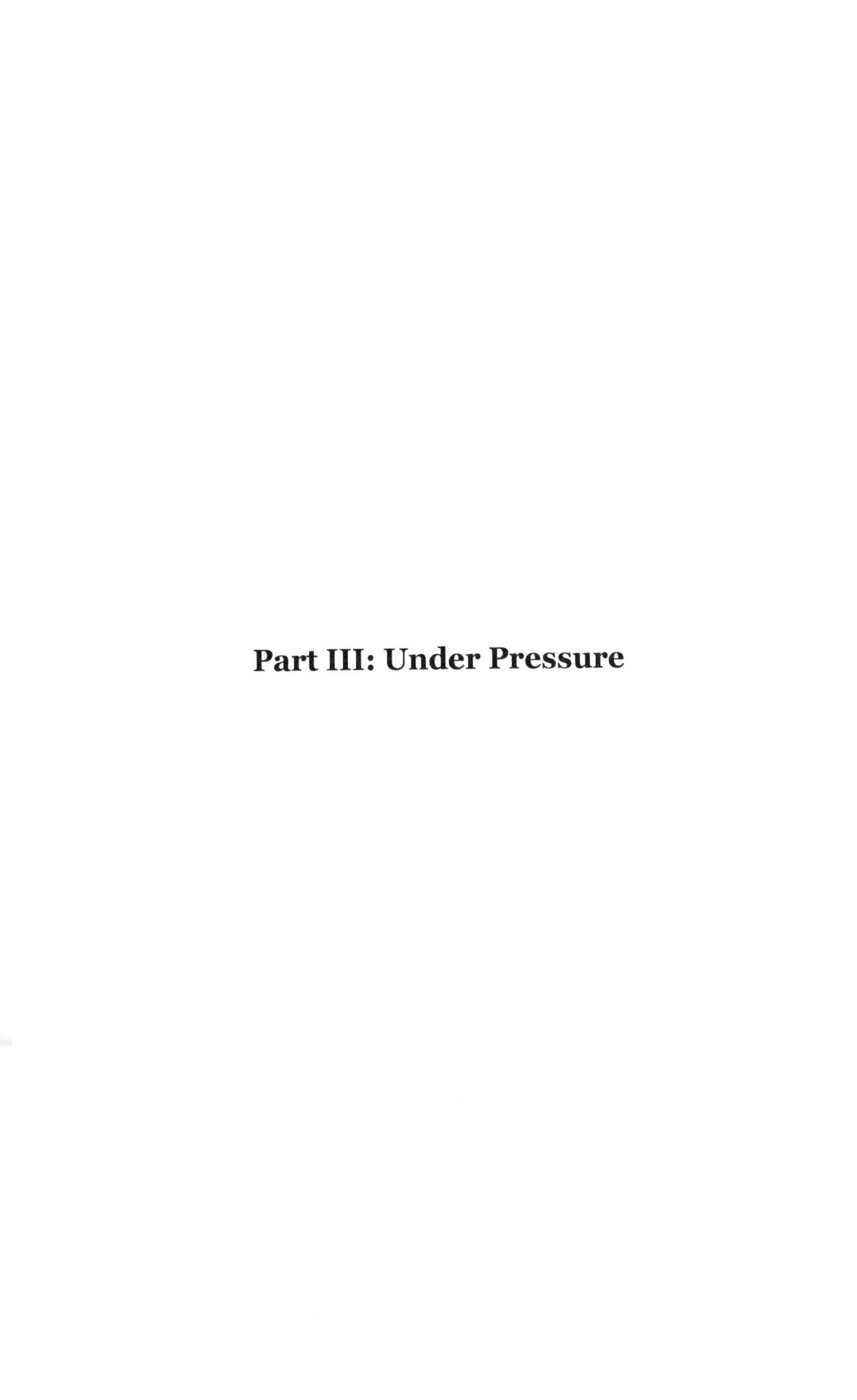

Part III: Under Pressure

Chapter 10: Into the Mystic

Among the residents of Tallahassee who awoke to a cold and rainy Super Bowl Sunday was a 22-year-old FSU music student named Joseph. He had made plans to watch the game that day with a handful of friends from the music school at the Past Time Tavern on Tennessee Street.

When he arrived at the bar just before the game started, he was surprised his friends weren't there yet. He figured something must have happened and they'd be along soon.

The Past Time was a large bar, conveniently located across the street from the FSU campus. The front door faced Tennessee Street, also known as U.S. Highway 90, and the bar was a popular hangout for students.

Joseph sat on one of the tall, wooden barstools behind the party tables in front of the big-screen TV. The barstool gave him an excellent view of the TV. He kept two other barstools on either side of him for his expected friends. One of the empty stools served as his personal table for his beer, popcorn, and sandwiches.

Finally, the Super Bowl teams and players were announced. The people in the bar grew excited. They cheered, whistled, and danced around the bar.

Tony Dorsett, the Heisman Trophy-winning rookie running back for Dallas, scored the first touchdown. All the Dallas fans went absolutely wild. Then words began to crawl across the bottom of the screen:

...TALLAHASSEE POLICE HAVE NO LEADS IN BRUTAL KILLING OF TWO FLORIDA STATE UNIVERSITY SORORITY WOMEN IN THEIR DORM ROOMS... SEVERAL OTHER WOMEN WHO WERE BEATEN WHILE THEY SLEPT REMAIN IN CRITICAL CONDITION... MORE ON THE EVENING NEWS FOLLOWING THE GAME...

The crowd in the bar fell silent. The headlines ran slowly across the big-screen in a continuous loop. People were stunned by the news and began to whisper as the game continued, eventually unnoticed by all.

Joseph's immediate reaction was shock. He sat there with his hands on his knees as he read the words. He slipped into a trancelike state. He began to see images, but he could not quite make out what they were. The energy that flowed through him stripped away the excitement about the game he had felt only moments before. His thoughts flashed back to his visit with his family in Miami the past Christmas season.

Joseph's mother, Ellen, wondered about her son's psychic capabilities. She took him one evening during the holiday vacation to see Ruth, a renowned Miami psychic who was teaching a small group of people how to work with their extrasensory perceptions or clairvoyant talents.

Joseph recalled that Ruth was very overweight and her face was disfigured from a bad automobile accident. Her skin was deeply wrinkled. Heavy face makeup turned her face orange and disguised the true color of her skin.

Each of her students took a turn discussing his or her particular talent. Joseph declined to participate in the activity. While *he* was not comfortable, he noticed that belonging to the group made his mother happy. She had fought cancer several years before and remission had given her the opportunity to discover new interests and to enjoy life with an abundance of optimism. He was glad she had found these people.

After they had finished sharing, it was time for personal readings. Ruth asked Joseph to come to the front of the room and sit with her. The others cheered him on. Reluctantly, he sat down in a chair directly across from Ruth. Their eyes locked.

At first, the conversation was friendly and they asked each other questions. Then Ruth became serious.

"You have great talent, young man. I would say your IQ is over 160, maybe 170. You have something very special. You have a great path filled with wisdom. I don't mean book wisdom, but true wisdom. It is the rarest of gifts." She paused. "You understand me, don't you?"

"I do," Joseph said.

"Alright," she continued. "You have a great destiny. I see it all around you like a great light. You will make national headlines with your destiny. I sense you already feel something about what it is I say to you."

Joseph nodded. "Maybe my music and writings. It's a destiny I've always felt... to become famous for my music."

Ruth laughed, clearly pleased with her observations, and continued with great excitement. She waved her arms as she spoke.

"I feel power coming from your center. That is the most powerful place of all. It is the strongest part of the psychic's body, only the heart is more powerful." She looked around at the faces of her students, and lingered on Joseph's mother for a moment.

She turned her attention back to Joseph.

"Your great deed will be shown to all, in national newspaper headlines and on television. Joseph, you will be in the center of power."

She paused to catch her breath and then continued in a much quieter, less exuberant voice. "Regretfully, no one will truly understand you."

Ruth continued to praise Joseph's intelligence and his psychic awareness. Joseph listened with one ear. He'd heard about psychics who heaped on the "visions" just before they asked for a donation. To his surprise, Ruth didn't ask Joseph for money.

"I don't accept money from authentic psychics, young man. This is my pleasure. For you, this is a professional courtesy," she said as she accepted cash from everyone else in the room, including Joseph's mother.

The news banner with the announcement of the murders was still running on the television station when the Super Bowl concluded that Sunday night. People had been leaving the bar throughout the game. No one felt much like partying with the constant reminder of the murders snaking its way across the bottom of the screen. The few remaining patrons left quietly. The initial confusion over the news had turned to fear. Where was the murderer and who would be next?

The murky images Joseph had seen earlier began to form

distinct pictures in his mind. One was of two square oak sticks, and the other was of an old colonial-style house.

That night, as Joseph lay in bed with his eyes closed, chasing sleep, a set of eyes appeared. The eyes seemed to be looking for him. Terrified, he forced himself to open his eyes. He thought he'd been dreaming, but when he closed his eyes again, the eyes reappeared, startling him.

The Bible story about Cain and Abel flashed through his mind, from Genesis 4:9-10:

"And the LORD said unto Cain, Where is Abel thy brother? And he said, I know not: Am I my brother's keeper?

And he said, What hast thou done? the voice of thy brother's blood crieth unto me from the ground."

Joseph now understood what this passage meant. He knew he would have to try to help the police catch the killer.

Chapter 11: Sorrow

Later that afternoon, the parents and families of the five young women who had been brutalized earlier that morning were gathered in a banquet room of a local motel in Tallahassee. George Brand faced the tears of two mothers who had just lost their daughters. This meeting was the most solemn of Lieutenant Brand's career.

The management of the Holiday Inn on Appalachia Parkway had agreed to let Brand meet secretly with the families. The anger, fear, and shock of the vicious crimes weighed heavily on the families of the victims.

Brand had asked for the meeting, with the knowledge it would be a painful and difficult session but it was a necessary protocol. He walked to the front of the room and looked, in turn, at each person seated before him. He took a deep breath and expressed, in a gentle way, his feelings about the grotesque killings and assaults.

"It is never easy to say what will happen or if the results in finding this killer will be positive, but I pray to God to help us do the right things to bring about some kind of justice for your loved ones." Brand then made a vow. "I promise to do anything, work with anyone, try everything, whatever it takes... to find the person, or persons, responsible for these tragic, violent crimes. You have my word that every angle will be explored, every rock will be turned over."

One of the mothers questioned how someone could commit such horrible crimes.

"Ma'am, I don't know," Brand replied. "I cannot explain this behavior, but, as we've just seen... well," he shrugged. "I don't know." He answered several more questions from the bereaved parents.

"I beg you to put your trust in me and stay calm," he said. "Please, don't speak with any members of the press, under any circumstances. Your comments, however innocent and well intentioned they may seem, could aid the killer and neither you nor

I want that to happen."

As the meeting drew to a close, the families joined hands and asked God to help the police find the killer and bring about justice in their daughters' names. Everyone in the room cried unashamedly. It was a terrible day for all of them.

Brand vowed never to forget his promise to find the killer, no matter what.

◆❖◆

The weather was cold and the sky was clear and bright as Monday morning dawned. The air was crisp and fresh. It was a beautiful day, but few took note of the weather. Everywhere, people were reading the newspapers, carefully examining every word printed in the *Democrat* or the *Flambeau*. Some people purchased both newspapers, and cross examined them to compare details of the news stories.

Silence filled the halls of every building and office. Overnight, Tallahassee had become a city of suspicious strangers. People were frightened, and hurried to classes or to work without stopping for the usual high spirited conversations normally found on college campuses. Optimism had been replaced by fear. They stopped talking with one another. The usual din of the campus cafeterias and local diners was missing that day.

The papers carried a vague description of the killer. The assailant was described as a white male, approximately 5'10" and weighing 160 lbs., with short brown hair. Most found this description so unexceptional that it only added to everyone's unease. Women looked at the men around them and wondered, *Could he be the killer? How old is the killer? Is he a student? Is he in this classroom?* Women no longer made eye contact with any man on the campus that fit the ambiguous description. Girls walked quietly together in groups, their eyes downcast. The question on everyone's mind was, *Is the killer going to strike again?*

◆❖◆

Scattered around the FSU campus were several diners that

served fairly cheap meals to students and faculty. One of the student favorites was the Mecca on Copeland Street, a small luncheonette and convenience-type store across from the front gates of FSU. It was right by the older part of the campus, where the administration offices, music and English departments, and most of the other liberal arts buildings were. The area held some of the older dormitories and was surrounded by sorority houses. The Chi Omega house was nearby.

The Mecca was divided into two sections. The south side was the dining area where everyone's friend, Clyde, stood in his white apron. He could be counted on for the jokes he told the guys, and the way he flirted with the girls. He sought to draw smiles from the students he fed. Wiry thin, he continuously ran behind the counter, serving food and then ringing up purchases at the register. That day, Clyde stood silently behind the cash register. He carefully examined every person who came through his door. He glanced down only to make certain he gave the correct change.

Someone dropped a fork and many students jumped at the sudden noise. The sound reverberated. It was eerily quiet.

The Mecca was always crowded, especially with students and faculty of the music and English schools. Normally, it was hard to get one of the few booths, so students often shared tables with strangers. They typically parted friends.

After Joseph finished his first few classes at the music school, he walked over to the Mecca. He spotted his friend, Tracy, a music major who studied pipe organ performance. Typically, they would shriek each other's names in greeting, but today Tracy looked at Joseph as he quietly slipped into the booth beside her. Three other music students were squeezed in close together on the other side of the booth. Joseph greeted them.

Tracy pushed her newspaper midway between them so they could read it together. "I'm really afraid," she said quietly.

"I don't think you have anything to worry about," Joseph said to calm her.

"Really? How could you know?"

He wrapped his arm around her shoulders and moved closer to her. They continued reading the paper. He noticed a small sidebar article announcing a reward of $2,500 for information leading to the arrest and conviction of the Chi Omega killer. There were details on how to respond, with a secret code number. A cartoon illustration showed the proper way to tear a letter so pieces could be matched later if the information proved correct. The contest deadline was six months away and would continue at the discretion of the editor.

"Shoot the bastard..." he heard someone whisper at a nearby table.

"That's too good for him," another person said. "Beat him to death."

"So, you're going to do something about it, right?" he heard someone say.

"Do something about what?" Joseph turned his attention back to Tracy.

"About what? What, about what? What are you talking about? You all here, Joseph?" Tracy spoke in her exaggerated Brooklyn accent. "You are the biggest space-case I know." She rubbed his head and wrapped her fingers in his long hair.

"I thought you asked me a question."

"Nope."

"You know, Tracy, the person they're looking for is not from Tallahassee," Joseph stated.

"How do you know? You psychic or something?" Her accent was even thicker now.

"Maybe." He moved away from Tracy and shrugged. "I have things I have to do, you know, to help."

"Like what, Sherlock? Go down to the police and tell them you're psychic and you know how to find the killer? You are so weird sometimes. You know that?" Tracy gave Joseph's shoulder a push with the palm of her hand.

"No, I don't. Something is..." Joseph hesitated, then realized he needed to be quiet. He stood up and said goodbye to Tracy and the other people seated in the booth. As he left the booth, Joseph smiled strangely at his friends.

◆❖◆

Joseph received a telephone call from his father that evening. He was quite concerned about the safety of his sons. Joseph's younger brother also attended FSU.

"Keep an eye on your brother, okay?" he asked. "Just in case the killer decides to attack some of the male students next time."

"I'm sure we'll be alright," Joseph assured him. "But I'll check in on Bobby."

"There are all kinds of nuts out there," his father said.

Joseph sat with two of his three roommates to watch the 11 p.m. news. Almost the entire show was about the murders and how the police had little evidence. The TV news team talked about the condition of the girls who had survived, and eulogized the two who had died.

Film footage was shown of a special memorial service held that evening in the Ruby Diamond Auditorium on the campus. Thousands of students and faculty packed the hall for the service. Every young woman seen on camera was crying. The impact of how horrible and devastating the attacks were replayed over and over again for the people of Tallahassee that night.

Every politician and business leader who was interviewed asked for help from the citizens in Tallahassee. Sheriff Ken Katsaris promised to catch the killer as quickly as possible and the news people talked about how gun sales were not up, but security precautions were being taken. One person commented on how it always seemed to require a tragedy before people became aware of the need to protect themselves and each other.

After the news, everyone headed off to bed. Joseph went to his room to play his guitar, but practicing didn't feel right, like it usually did. His attempts to quiet his mind were interrupted by the sounds of someone rummaging around in the kitchen. He put his guitar aside and walked out to investigate.

Marty was fixing a late-night snack.

"You heard anything yet from your friends at the hospital?" Joseph asked.

"I haven't heard a thing except that Don Allen called me and said he got the call to the Chi Omega house. Everyone's really being quiet about the whole thing." Marty took a bite of his sandwich and chewed deliberately.

"I tell you what, the girls who lived were lucky that Don was on the ambulance that night. He's good, I mean he's really good. It's probably the only reason they're alive right now. That was one screwed-up situation."

He took another bite and chased it with a swig of beer. "It was really bloody, as bad as it gets. People don't realize it takes a lot of deliberate brute force to crush skulls and fracture faces. Whoever did it was either very, very sick or really pissed off at those girls."

Joseph reached into the fridge and pulled out a beer. He popped the tab and took a long swallow. "Was it one killer, or two, do you think?"

"*No one* knows." Marty finished his sandwich. "I mean, they don't know who they are looking for. They have no idea if there's more than one killer, who the killer is, or if he's going to strike again." He washed his plate and wiped off the counter. "I wouldn't want to screw with the cops, for any reason, for the next few weeks or until they make an arrest. They're going to be mad as pissed-on hornets and looking for anyone to pin the shit on. It's going to be hell around town for a while, so watch out how you drive. Don't carry any weed." He turned around for a second, then added, "Keep it cool for a while, Joseph, I mean real cool."

"Yeah, I see what you mean," Joseph agreed. He went back to his room to play his guitar for a while, then crawled into bed.

As he lay there, the skin on the back of his neck seemed to be pulling at his ears, moving in waves. It felt like someone was tugging on him. The familiar sensation unnerved him. Joseph loathed that feeling.

In the silence of the house, he heard the front door close. He got up to check it out. It was their roommate, Melanie. She was home from visiting her friends. Marty came out to the living room, and he and Joseph told her they were more than a little worried.

She apologized for not calling to let them know she was running late.

Joseph went back to the darkness of his room. His visions returned as soon as he closed his eyes. He tried desperately to relax, but his thoughts were robbing him of sleep. A feeling of terror came over him. He abruptly sat up in bed and frantically scanned the darkness for an unseen intruder. He felt for his nunchacku. He had dreamed the killer watched him from the foot of his bed.

His heart pounding wildly, he breathed deeply and asked the darkness to let him sleep.

As though there had been an answer to his request, he laid back down, and in what seemed like mere moments, he opened his eyes to see the bright morning sunlight pouring into his room.

He knew he'd slept, but he felt far from rested.

Chapter 12: Lost in the Flood

The special hotline number that was set up early Monday to encourage people to provide any information about the attacks, or the suspect, was broadcasted by television and radio stations hourly, and both the *Democrat* and the *Flambeau* had agreed to run the plea for information in their daily editions until someone was charged. Calls flooded the hotline and the phones at the command post rang 24 hours a day for days.

By the end of the first week of the investigation, more than 4,600 calls had been logged in. No one knew quite how to tackle the staggering number of leads.

Two uniformed police officers who specialized in hotline communications were in charge of the incoming calls. They were assisted by two male student interns from the FSU Department of Criminology.

"This will be the toughest internship ever," Brand warned them. "You two are in the middle of an intensely bizarre murder investigation. This is the equivalent of going to war. You are on the front lines in the communication unit, so expect the roughest ride of your lives."

Members of the team answered the phones in shifts lasting up to 18 hours a day.

The four heard just about every variation of the English language there was, and the messages were often cryptic and vague, misleading and misogynistic. Sometimes the callers spoke rapidly, or they spoke in whispers, making it hard for the interns to understand the words. Many of the callers were women who were afraid of their husbands, boyfriends, fathers, or brothers. Most could not verify where their men were during the approximate times of the attacks. Some callers wanted to talk, and others sincerely wanted to help the investigators catch the assailant.

During the first day, the investigators received a tip that a local psychic, Brandon Hill, had predicted "horrible deaths" in Tallahassee for 1978. This statement had been part of a New Year's prediction that the psychic made in December 1977, just weeks before the Chi Omega attacks. Hill had told his followers that he felt the presence of evil coming to Tallahassee, and that this evil would bring the town great sorrow.

This prediction made some people suspicious, especially during the aftermath of the Chi Omega murders. Sheriff Katsaris knew of the flamboyant Brandon Hill and wanted to talk with the self-proclaimed psychic as soon as possible. He reasoned that Hill quite possibly wanted to market himself as a gifted psychic and, consequently, committed the crimes to gain notoriety.

Brand wrote Hill's name on the suspect blackboard. Several people recognized his name and joked that they could use a good psychic to help them solve the case.

Hill suggested to the investigators that he "might" be able to help them, but he would never provide them with information. Brand speculated that the psychic wanted to charge a fee for his services.

Ken Katsaris was a political pragmatist. He didn't care where the information came from. He wanted the killer caught before he struck again, and he was willing to entertain any leads the investigators brought to his attention. He was determined to resolve the case as quickly as possible. He knew his electorate. The voters of Leon County didn't care how he got the job done. They just wanted the killer caught.

Captain Poitinger, however, was not as open-minded as his boss. He didn't care for psychics or people who claimed to know the future. Poitinger wasn't keen on very many people, and he didn't want to be bothered by Brandon Hill or anyone else who claimed to have "seen" things. He thought such *leads* were a waste of valuable resources. He was a no-nonsense law enforcement officer *and* an attorney. He loved his work and the authority that came with the job, and he approached law enforcement and the law with logic and practicality. Poitinger wanted concrete evidence to build the case upon. He did not want to deal with nebulous notions or "evidence" that would require additional effort to defend in court. He did not want to waste valuable manpower chasing phantoms on the advice of someone with *a feeling*. Using psychics to solve cases was, according to Poitinger, a monumental waste of time. He imagined the cross-examination by defense attorneys.

"So, Mr. Poitinger, where exactly did this 'damning' information come from?" the defense attorney would ask him when he testified. "A crystal ball? A gut feeling? Tea leaves? A psychic, huh?"

He was not going to be the butt of a defense attorney's joke.

◆❖◆

The phone rang at the task force.

"Good afternoon," a male caller said to one of the interns. "I'd like to speak with the chief investigator, please."

"Sir, may I have your name, please?"

"I would rather not give my name," the man said. "I would like to speak directly with the head of the task force, please."

"Lieutenant George Brand is the chief investigator," the intern said.

"Then I would like to speak with Lieutenant George Brand, please," the caller said.

The intern took the message and passed it to the sergeant in charge, who delivered the note to Lieutenant Brand. Brand reached out for the note. He read the message.

"Damn it all to hell, I'm in the middle of trying to solve the worst crimes this town has ever seen," he groused, "and someone calls and doesn't trust telling what he knows to anyone else! He's got to talk to the boss," he said in a sing-song voice, nodding his head with the cadence. He tossed the note onto his desk.

Brand pulled a cigarette out of his shirt pocket and lit it. He picked up the note and grabbed the receiver of the phone.

"But you never know, do you?" Brand said, and waved the officer away. "Close my door." He punched one of the blinking buttons on the phone. "This is Brand."

"Are you Lieutenant Brand, head of the task force?" the caller asked.

"Yes," Brand replied. "Who is this?"

"We need to meet. I am the only person who can help you. Is there someplace private we can talk?"

"You're the only one who can help, huh?" Brand barked at the caller. "Okay, well I'm a little too busy to meet you unless you come down to the command post. I've got an investigation to run, and it's impossible for me to get away to meet with some secretive person."

The phone line was quiet for a few seconds. Brand tried a different approach. He had no idea who he was speaking to.

"What's your name?" he asked gently.

"I'd rather not give you that at this time."

"Well, fine, when you're ready to give me your name, come on down to the command center. I'll know when you're here and then we can talk."

Brand instinctively felt it might be wrong to blow this guy off. *Could this be the killer?* he wondered.

"My name is Joseph, sir," the caller said. "I only work in secret. I do not want anyone to know that I'm working with the task force. I don't like people to know what I can do."

"Well, whatever it is you do, if you want to see me, you'll have to come down to the command post."

Brand was curious. He wrote the man's name, *Joseph*, on the edge of a sheet of yellow legal paper. He tore the edge of the page and put it into his shirt pocket, next to his cigarettes.

"Joseph?" Brand asked.

"Yes, sir?"

"I'm sorry, but there just ain't no other way. I can't put everything down and come running just because you've called. Please understand me, son, I don't even know what this is about."

"I live just north of Lake Ella," Joseph said. "I'll walk over in a few minutes."

Brand smiled. "Good, I'll see you when you get here."

He turned his attention back to the names on the blackboard. At that moment, he received a call from Mike Fisher, an investigator in Colorado Springs.

Fisher had called the task force bright and early Monday morning, as soon as he had learned of the Chi Omega attacks. He had suggested that Ted Bundy may be who they should look for as their killer. Fisher said that Bundy had been convicted of kidnapping in Utah and faced multiple charges in Colorado. Charges of kidnapping and murder were also being considered by Washington state.

On December 30th, Bundy had escaped from the Glenwood Springs, Colorado, jail.

Members of the task force thought Bundy was a longshot. Chi Omega happened just 16 days after Bundy broke out of the Colorado jail. One of the interns looked up the distance between the two cities. They were nearly 1,800 miles apart.

How could someone with no money or car, wearing only the clothes on his back, travel that distance in 15 days and show up to brutally attack five women in Tallahassee?

Task force investigators thought it was improbable, but they put his name on the suspect board anyway.

Fisher had overnighted an extensive file of Bundy's crime to Brand. Fisher was convinced Bundy was the man they sought.

"The types of crimes and mutilations you've got in Tallahassee are mighty similar to Bundy's style," Fisher said. "I'm certain Bundy is your killer."

Brand thanked Fisher and said he welcomed the information. He dropped the phone into its cradle and went out of his office to the hallway. He asked one of the younger detectives to find the package of information and bring it to him.

Once he had the Federal Express package in hand, Brand requested that Dee Phillips be sent into his office. Phillips, tasked with handling all leads generated outside of Leon County, should have been given this packet of material on Bundy.

"You need me, George?" Phillips asked.

"Dee, keep this file on this Bundy guy. Make it a low priority for now. That boy would be a long way from home."

Phillips took the file. "Yes, sir." He left the room.

Brand went into the conference room and stood in front of the blackboard. Bundy's name was already on the list of suspects. It was one of the first names Brand had written.

He pulled the piece of torn yellow legal paper from his pocket and unfolded it. He looked at the name: *Joseph.* As he reached for the chalk, he heard someone call his name. "Brand, George Brand, are you here?"

"I'll be right there." He tucked the paper back into his pocket and left the room without writing Joseph's name on the blackboard.

Chapter 13: Masquerade

Joseph slowly hung up the phone. He tried to envision meeting Lieutenant Brand, but he only saw images of people without faces.

He lived on the back porch of the house, which had been converted by the landlord into a bedroom. He loved the room because he could look out past the overgrown rosebushes under the canopy of giant oak and magnolia trees, to a picturesque view of Lake Ella.

His room measured 8' by 9' and had no storage space of any kind. He kept his clothes in a hallway closet on the other side of the house. The room held a small, wobbly wooden desk that doubled as a dresser, a single bed, and a barstool. He sat on the barstool when he practiced guitar or sang songs for visiting friends.

A small Bible was on the desk. He picked it up and looked into a full-length mirror. He quickly combed his hair. He felt giddy with excitement and anticipation as he gazed one last time at himself.

He became quite dizzy as he left the darkness of his room and stepped outside into the bright sunshine. The Bible, a gift from one of his sisters several years before, was heavy in his sweaty hands. He shifted the book from hand to hand and wiped his palms as he walked through the St. Paul's Methodist Church parking lot that sloped down the hill next to his house.

An unmarked police car roared down the hill. Its brakes squealed and Joseph jumped in alarm. He realized he'd been lost in his thoughts. *Pay attention,* he thought.

He watched the officer drive to the south side of the lake, toward the Tallahassee Police Department.

A second police cruiser made an abrupt left turn into the church lot. The officer rolled down his window and turned off the ignition. Joseph noticed the officer reach for a clipboard and realized he had probably stopped to complete his paperwork before his patrol shift ended.

Joseph could see the brand-new TPD building rising above the tree line on the other side of the lake. The department had its own gasoline pumps installed on a lot across the street when the new building was constructed, and the brick structure featured a tall radio tower.

He watched a squad car pull into a two-story building across 7th Street from the TPD. Two uniformed officers came out of the building. He didn't know where to go, so he walked into the new TPD building and asked for Lieutenant Brand.

"No one named Brand works here," the desk sergeant told him. He pointed across the street. "That building is the command center."

The command post had been established in a squat, two-story, yellow brick building. Narrow windows indicated offices every 20 feet or so. A single glass door on the east side of the building was the main entrance. There was an overhang to protect against rain hitting the glass door. The landscaping was neat: the shrubs were trimmed and the lawn was mowed. A grassy knoll east of the building led up to the department's gas pumps. The sun shined brightly on the little hill. It looked like a great place to sit and enjoy the warm sun on a cold day.

Joseph opened the front door and entered a lobby. He walked past a set of stairs to a desk in the middle of the room. He was greeted by a friendly receptionist. Joseph noticed she was quite attractive. Her nameplate identified her as Carol Henson. She was in her mid-20s and had brown hair with a hint of red tint in it.

She greeted Joseph with a smile.

"May I help you?" she asked him.

"Hi!" Joseph felt a bit tongue-tied. *She's really pretty.* "I, uh, I'm here to see Lieutenant Brand."

Carol picked up the phone and pushed some buttons. "What's your name, hon?"

"Joseph."

"Joseph," she repeated into the phone. "Okay." She hung up the phone. "The lieutenant is busy at the moment, but he'll be out soon."

She stood up and Joseph was struck by how beautiful she was.

"Please, have a seat," she said and pointed to some chairs. "May I get you a Coke? Or some coffee?"

"No, no ma'am, I'm fine," he stammered.

"Oh, just call me Carol, honey," she smiled. "And do let me know if I can get you something."

Joseph glanced around the waiting room. He noticed there were half a dozen chairs and several end tables with lamps. There were several other men waiting. Joseph realized they all seemed to be in their mid-20s. Several of the men stood as they waited.

He didn't want to stay in the same room with the others, so he leaned over the desk and spoke quietly to Carol.

"I'd rather wait outside, in the sunshine," he said. "I'll sit on the hill, on the grass."

Carol smiled and nodded as she answered an incoming call.

As he pushed open the glass door, Joseph had a vision of a large, burly man with light hair. He felt disoriented. He had to remind himself where he was and what he was doing.

Something's wrong again, he thought.

He felt like he was dreaming.

Am I asleep?

He glanced toward the window at the men in the waiting room. He wondered if they were suspects. They all looked unhappy.

I could tell the cops none of these guys are the killer.

He walked to the small hill, climbed up a step, and crouched. He opened his Bible to a random page and found he was in the book of Genesis, Chapter 6. It was a good place to start; it seemed to fit. He used the long ribbon attached to the end of the book to mark the spot.

Joseph saw two men come to the front door. The shorter man stood in front of the other and prevented Joseph from seeing the second, larger man clearly. The short man walked toward Joseph and asked him to come back inside the building. His voice conveyed authority. He wasn't a large man, nor did he have light hair. He seemed tense and surly. Joseph did not think this was Brand.

Joseph became increasingly nervous as he followed the officer. His heart pounded in his ears and chest. He breathed deeply to try to control his anxiety, but he couldn't calm himself.

Something is wrong, but what is it?

As he followed the officer, he tried to use his intuition, his sixth sense, to figure out what was happening, but he was worried. He had willingly placed himself under the control of the police, and Lieutenant Brand. He just had to trust what was about to happen.

"Are you Lieutenant Brand?" Joseph asked when they stopped outside of an office. He held his Bible in his hand. The officer turned abruptly to face him.

"Yes, I am," the officer snapped. "Now, do you want to meet with me or not?"

Joseph inhaled and straightened his back. "If you're Brand, then I must speak with you."

The officer looked at Joseph. He had a cold demeanor, and Joseph thought he had a mean face. He felt the cop could lose his temper and lash out at him, perhaps even hurt him.

"Come on," the officer said and continued down the hallway. "This is such bullshit," he muttered under his breath. Joseph heard the comment.

He motioned Joseph inside an office.

"Take a seat," he instructed. "Sit with your back to the door. I'm going to leave it open."

The room was small. There was a window that was about two feet wide. There were no curtains or blinds. A folding cafeteria table and two brown metal folding chairs had been set up in the middle of the room.

Joseph sat down on one of the chairs, his back to the door, as instructed. There was a small stack of papers on the table, face down. The bare walls were painted an off-white color.

Joseph watched people walk past the window as he waited. There was another embankment just beyond the window, and he saw a parking lot behind that. There was a scraggly hedge on top of the embankment. The bushes and trees were stripped of leaves, and warm sunlight poured inside the room.

The officer entered the office and closed the door. He pulled the other chair out from under the table and sat down close to Joseph. He leaned forward and rested his elbows on his knees. His tie dangled between his legs like a pendulum. He stared at Joseph momentarily, then straightened and placed a yellow legal pad and pencil on the table.

"What's your full name and address?" he asked.

"You're not what I expected," Joseph said, fingering the Bible on his lap.

The man leaned back and looked at Joseph.

"Well, now, just *what* were you expecting?" He bobbed his head slightly, as if challenging what the psychic would say.

"I was expecting a large man with light hair," Joseph said slowly.

"Well, you're wrong about that now, aren't you, boy?"

Joseph stared at the policeman. He felt annoyed. He was aware of the sharp contrast between himself, with his long hair and flannel shirt, and the officer's buzz cut and law enforcement attire.

We're from two different planets.

"What's your full name and address?" the officer demanded as he tapped his pencil on the table. "I don't have all day."

Joseph looked into the man's eyes. He gritted his teeth. "Sir, before we go any further, I would like you to read this passage from the Bible, please."

"Okay, son." The officer seized the opportunity. "If I read that part, will you tell me what I want to know?"

Joseph agreed and gave him the Bible, open to Genesis, Chapter 6. He asked him to read verses 1 through 6. The officer began to skim the page.

"Out loud, please, so I know you're really reading the words," Joseph said quietly, never taking his eyes off of him.

The officer read the words aloud, slowly, as if having trouble reading. He moved his fingers under each word while Joseph watched. His speech became faster, louder and laced with impatience as he neared the end of the verses.

"Okay, I've read them," the officer said as he closed the book and handed it back to Joseph. "Now what the hell is your name and address, son?"

Joseph drew a long breath. "You're not going to understand everything I'm going to say to you at first. You must allow your mind to interpret the information later."

The officer looked around the room and shook his head. "Why are you playing games, damn it?" He was frustrated. "Just give me your information and get on with it."

Joseph told the man his name and address. He gave his telephone number and details about his life, including his classes and his roommates.

"I don't understand it," Joseph said after he finished answering the questions. "I was shown someone who was kind and gentle, someone who would listen and understand the messages."

The officer popped his pencil on the pad and leaned into Joseph's face. "Well, you're wrong about that too, now, aren't you? You aren't doing so well, boy. Now, what do you know? I've got more important things to do than to sit here with some damn hippie."

Joseph sat quietly for a few seconds. He was confused. The whole scene *felt* wrong. He considered getting up and leaving. Suddenly, he felt a sense of calmness wash over him. He began to speak.

"I saw a colonial-style house with apartments. And I saw square oaks." Joseph spoke slowly and deliberately.

"Was that the weapon, a piece of oak?" the officer asked.

"Yes, but I saw a *square* oak. The weapon was oak. *Oak* is everything here. I see square oak objects shaped like nunchucks, you know, the Karate weapons, two long square oak pieces about one inch thick, but the ones I'm seeing are not on a string."

The officer slammed his fist on the table. "There are a *million* oak trees in Tallahassee." He broke his pencil in two. Then he took a deep breath.

"Yes, okay, I know what you mean." He motioned impatiently with his hands for Joseph to continue.

"*Square oak* is the key, sir," Joseph said. "Square pieces of oak are important. So are colonial-style apartments."

The officer sighed. Everything in Tallahassee was either named *Colonial* this or *Oak* that. He made a decision to move the questioning forward.

"Can you describe the victims to me?"

Joseph raised his eyebrows. He turned his head slightly, so as to give the officer a good view of what he was about to point to. He raised his right hand and moved it across the right side of his head.

"It was missing. The top of her head was bashed in and missing."

The officer paled and squirmed in his chair.

Joseph continued. "And there were marks on the girls I've never seen before." He rubbed his hand over his breasts. "Their breasts were damaged," he said. "One of the girls had her body ripped open, down here." Joseph pointed to his groin area.

"What about the killer? Was he wearing a hat?" The officer had stopped taking notes. He glared at Joseph and breathed through his nose. Joseph couldn't tell if the officer was angry or excited.

Joseph closed his eyes and tried to find a vision. "He wore a hat. The hat I see is one that is different than people wear now. It is a hat from a long time ago, like from the 1930s. I don't know why I'm seeing that particular hat."

"Well, you're wrong about the hat now, too. You aren't helping us at all, boy. We have more important things to do."

His dismissiveness puzzled Joseph.

"I don't understand," Joseph said. "My visions have never been wrong before."

"Boy, they're wrong as hell now."

The officer got up abruptly and left the room. He slammed the door.

Joseph stood up and walked out of the building. He didn't say a word to anyone he passed, not even Carol, the pretty receptionist. He walked quickly to his house and occasionally looked over his shoulder to make certain no one was following him. He worriedly realized they had his address if they wanted to find him again.

◆❖◆

Ray Stanton, the officer who had pretended to be Brand when he questioned Joseph, found the lieutenant standing in front of the suspect board. Brand finished adding several names to the board before he acknowledged the officer.

"Lieutenant Brand!" Stanton was frantic. "You need to talk with this boy now."

"Yes, Ray, what about?" Brand turned away from the board to look at his subordinate.

"I think we have the killer in the other room." Stanton was nervous and shaky.

"The hippie psychic?" Brand clenched his teeth tightly. "That's our killer? C'mon, you're kidding, right?"

"He knew I wasn't you, sir. The guy kept saying he was supposed to talk to someone else. I think you better talk with him. I swear he's the killer, sir. He just described details only the killer would have known."

"Where is he?" Brand asked gently.

"I left him in the room," Stanton said. "I wanted to get you right away. He has weird-looking eyes, too. I don't know what to think. Maybe he's stoned or something. I'd swear he's high on... something!"

Brand walked out of the room followed by Stanton. They entered the room where Stanton had questioned Joseph. The room was empty.

They exited the building and watched the long-haired hippie disappear down the hill toward the lake.

"There he is!" Stanton pointed. "Shall I get him and bring him back?"

"Did you get his name and phone number?" Brand asked. He turned to go back into the building.

"Yes, sir, I did, but barely. He didn't want to give it to me at first."

Stanton showed Brand the sheet with the information.

"He'll be back, I feel it," Brand said. "If he has something to say, he'll be back."

Brand returned to the room with the blackboard and stared at the names printed neatly in chalk. Stanton followed.

Brand had just hung up with the investigator in Colorado when Joseph arrived. But as luck would have it, one of the suspects he was eager to question had been brought in at the same time. He told Stanton to tell Joseph he was Brand, find out what the kid wanted and get rid of him.

Stanton tried to follow Brand's orders. He was a uniformed officer who had been reassigned to work as a plain-clothed officer on the Chi Omega investigation and report directly to Brand. He was a short man in stature and had adopted a junkyard dog aggressiveness toward police work. He preferred to use heavy-handed intimidation tactics and lacked the friendly, confidential manner used by seasoned detectives.

Brand rubbed his forehead. He had a whopper of a headache.

"Ray, the next time I tell you I don't have time to talk with someone, remind me about this." He lit a cigarette. "I should have never sent you in there. Now, what the hell did he say?"

"He described the victims... and said strange stuff. I don't really remember. I was confused by this guy and the shit he was saying that didn't make sense... making me read the Bible... I don't know what the hell he was talking about," Stanton stammered.

"You say he knew you weren't the right man?" Brand asked.

"He knew. Somehow, that hippie, and I mean he's a *very* strange hippie, knew some shit, sir." Stanton was animated.

Brand dismissed Stanton and went back to the suspect board. He stared at each name on the list.

"Talk to me," he said to the names.

He leaned against a table and picked up a file. He examined it and put it down. He picked up another file and did the same.

He went back to his desk and sat down. He checked his task list of things to get done that day. Few items had been completed. The list had only grown as the day came to a close. Each hour brought more things to do. Brand was weary. It was Tuesday, and he hadn't had a full night's sleep since Friday. That seemed an eternity ago.

The promise he'd made to the victims' parents echoed in his head as he poured himself another cup of coffee. He pulled out an empty pack of cigarettes from his shirt pocket. As he began to crush the packet, he noticed a torn yellow slip of paper. He pulled it loose and opened it.

He read the name he'd written. *Joseph.* He glanced over at the names on the blackboard.

"Okay, son, I'll give you a chance," he said aloud. "Come on back and tell me which one of these sons of bitches did it."

He found another pack of cigarettes in his coat pocket, pulled out one, and lit it. He inhaled, then blew all the smoke toward the suspect board.

Chapter 14: Voices Inside My Head

Joseph heard his roommate Melanie's dog barking at the police cars parked in the church lot as he walked up the hill on the north side of Lake Ella. The cops were busily completing their reports for the day. Joseph skirted the lot and walked along Tharpe Street. He didn't want to call any attention to himself so close to his house.

"Why? Why was Lieutenant Brand so different from what I'd seen?" Joseph muttered to himself. "I don't understand it; I don't get it."

He went into the kitchen and poured a glass of water before he went into his room to play music for an hour or so before his evening practice time at the music school.

He thought about the meeting he'd had at the command post.

What was I thinking? Am I stupid, or what?

He couldn't believe how ridiculous he must have seemed to the cops.

I'm the only one who can help you. He felt his cheeks blush with embarrassment. *Really?*

He realized he was probably the laughingstock of the interagency task force. He felt humiliated by his temerity. He laid down on his bed and tried to take a short nap before going to the campus.

Joseph saw a police roadblock a block beyond the music school parking lot. He was relieved he wouldn't have to be scrutinized by police on his way to practice.

He had booked the practice room for three hours that night, but he had trouble focusing on the music. After an hour or so of fractured practice, he left the piano room and drove over to Poor Paul's Pourhouse on Tennessee Street. He thought he'd relax by drinking a couple of beers and playing a few games of pinball. He was surprised to find one of the employees manning the door and checking ID's. He had never seen that happen at the Pourhouse before. There were only a few customers in the bar that night, and the weekly backgammon tournament had been canceled for lack of players. There were no single women in the bar.

People eyed him suspiciously. The jukebox was silent, and people spoke in hushed tones. Joseph turned around and left without ordering.

Back home, he decided to play a few songs on the guitar and write some poetry to help him relax, but he still couldn't concentrate. After a few pages of doodling, he crawled into bed and stared at the ceiling.

Suddenly, he heard a voice speaking to him. He looked around; he was alone. He closed his eyes and listened.

"See the distance between the attacks? It is *his* distance. Know it. It is *his* distance. Circle it. Tell it. In the colonial apartments. He is an animal. Tell Brand of the animal and his ways in the circles."

Joseph knew he had to try to see Lieutenant Brand again.

Early on the morning of Wednesday, January 18th, Joseph phoned Brand at the task force. He wanted to tell him about his dream. Carol quickly put the call through.

"This is Brand."

"Hello. This is Joseph. Remember I talked with you yesterday about the information I have?"

"Yes, go on."

"Well, I have some more information now."

"Alright, come on in right away."

Joseph thought about his morning classes. "How about a bit later?"

"No, now." Brand was short and to the point.

"Okay, I'll be over in a few minutes."

Joseph slowly hung up the phone, confused more than ever before. He knew he'd just spoken to the right man, but the voice was different from the man he'd met the day before.

He pulled on his brown sheepskin coat and left the house. He walked to the command post, keeping his head down to protect against the cold wind that blew off the lake. When he entered the building, Carol asked Joseph to have a seat.

Several men were sitting in the room. They looked up occasionally and glanced at each other. It was much like the day before, except the faces were different.

A large man with light hair approached Joseph. A meaty hand clasped Joseph's shoulder. "Come on back," he said. The man's neck was squat and thick, like a football player's. His arms were large and powerful. He was a formidable man and towered over Joseph.

Joseph followed the man to the room where he'd been questioned the previous day. The stack of papers was still on the table. He sat on the same folding chair.

"So, son, what is it that you need to tell me?" The man leaned against the edge of the table and lit a cigarette. "You smoke?" he asked as he offered the pack to Joseph.

"Uh, no, thank you," Joseph stammered. "Where's Lieutenant Brand? Where's the other man?"

"I'm George Brand."

Joseph was puzzled.

"No, you aren't. You're not the guy I saw yesterday. Are there two Brands?"

"I'm Lieutenant Brand, son. Trust me." He eyed the young hippie appraisingly. "Nice jacket," he said.

Joseph looked at Brand and began to relax. He smiled at the lieutenant.

"I had a feeling about the other man," Joseph said, "He just didn't seem right."

"Yeah, I know. Ray told me you didn't believe he was me." Brand laughed. "He thinks you may know something about the killer, is that right?"

Joseph nodded.

"Son, would you mind taking those glasses off? I need to see your eyes."

"Yes, sir." Joseph removed his glasses and closed them in his hand. Brand looked into his eyes.

"Look at me directly when you speak, okay?"

"Okay."

"Can you explain to me, now, what it is you think you saw?"

Brand sat down with his back to the window.

Joseph looked over Brand's shoulder and watched several people outside the building through the narrow window. A woman craned her neck to look in as she walked by. He took a deep breath, then began to explain how the information would come to him in bits and pieces. Then he spoke of his newest vision, which described the killer as a territorial animal.

Brand listened carefully but did not take any notes.

"Did the other officer pass along the information I gave him about the square oaks and the colonial apartments?" Joseph asked.

"Yes, he did. He mentioned you saw nunchucks," Brand said. "But I can assure you, the killer did not use nunchucks to hurt those little girls, son." He leaned over and stubbed his cigarette out in the ashtray on the windowsill.

"You know, Lisa Levy was buried yesterday," Brand continued, "and Miss Bowman will be buried today. The other three are still in the hospital, with armed guards, and they're in bad shape. If you have any information I can use to catch the killer before he hurts another girl, I sure would like to hear it."

"Have any of the survivors been hypnotized?" Joseph asked.

Brand thought for a second. "No, why? Will that help us find the killer?"

"I don't know, but you must please try it. It can only help."

Brand agreed.

"You must begin looking in metal containers. Someplace metal and trashy. Maybe the club is in a trash bin."

Brand leaned back a little, disappointed by Joseph's comments. "We've already looked in those places, we've swept the area, several times. It's standard procedure, son."

"What about under the streets?" Joseph watched Brand's eyes.

"Under what streets?" Brand chuckled.

"In the sewer drain systems."

Shit! That was new, Brand thought. He kicked himself for not thinking about checking the sewer drains.

"I don't think we've looked in those yet. What else?"

"Please look at the distance between the attacks, from the sorority house to the Dunwoody house. It is the distance of the killer. It is like a territory to him." Joseph closed his eyes. He wished he could slip back into the vision he'd had the night before.

Brand slapped his hand on the table to force Joseph to remain focused.

"How do you know it was a he?"

Joseph exhaled and shifted in his seat. "The killer is a man. I'm not sure where he lives, but he will live within a specific distance, the same distance from the sorority house to the Dunwoody house. He doesn't live between those two places. If you draw two circles on a map using the distance from one house to the other, and each house in the middle of the circle, making two inter-lapping circles, he will live in or near one of those circles. It is his territory, it is important in his markings. He will do a lot of walking, or stalking, in that area. At night. That's when he hunts." Joseph paused. He was unsure about asking the next question.

Brand lit another cigarette and waited for Joseph to continue.

"If I could touch one of the victim's foreheads, any of them, even the dead ones, I can tap into the mind of the killer easier."

Brand's face hardened as he clenched his jaw. "No way. There's no way in Hell. I can't let you do anything like that."

"Can I touch something? Anything? Please?" Joseph asked. "A piece of clothing one of the victims wore when he touched her? Or even a photograph of one of the girls, or something from one of their rooms after he attacked them?"

"No way. You're not going to touch anything. If you have some power, then you are going to use it right here. That's it. Is that understood? I'm sorry, son, but we just have to do things my way."

Joseph realized the crassness of his request and felt embarrassed. He worried that Brand would think he was a ghoul. Joseph remained quiet as Brand made some notes.

"Is there anything else you want to tell me, son?"

"Just one other thing," Joseph said. "A picture of colonial-style apartments keeps coming to me. Now, I'm not talking about *the* Colonial Apartments because they are too far west of the area. But I'm seeing a colonial-style house, and I think that if you find this house, within the killer's range that I described, you'll find the killer."

Brand wrote something on his notepad, then stood up.

"Alright, now. You go home and think about what this information means. I'll be right here waiting for your next... ah... whatever it is."

Brand smiled warmly and shook Joseph's hand. The two parted at the doorway.

Brand walked into the strategy room and stared at the names on the suspect board. His coffee was cold. He buzzed Carol and asked her to make fresh coffee in all the pots.

Sheriff Katsaris came into the room. "So, what's your report on the boy? Should we add his name to the board?"

"No."

"You know, I heard what Stanton said about the kid," Katsaris said, watching Brand's facial expressions. "I think that boy knows something."

"If you think he's the killer," Brand started, then looked around to make sure the two men were alone, "you're blowing smoke out your ass. I have a feeling about that boy. Something about him is different. You should see his eyes. I need to work with him, Ken, to see where this leads. I told the families I'd get this solved, and he gave me a couple of ideas."

"Such as?"

"He suggested checking the drains and sewers in the area between Chi Omega and Dunwoody. How about we get the cadets back out there today and do another sweep of the area and check the storm drains?"

"Agreed. Set it up," Katsaris said. "What else did hippie boy tell you?"

"He suggested we get the survivors hypnotized to see if they can give us any more information."

"It can't hurt, I guess. Hell, it might even help," Katsaris said. "I'll see if someone can get that doctor on the phone."

"Anything else, Chief?" Brand asked. "I've got things to do, especially now that you're not gonna let me lock up the hippie."

Katsaris shook his head. He had his own ideas about what to do with the psychic. They already knew he drove a green Volkswagen Bug. He had Poitinger place surveillance on Joseph. He wanted Joseph, and his car, tracked.

Chapter 15: Lie to Me

Within 24 hours of the murders, Knight Ridder, publisher of the *Democrat*, offered an initial reward of $2,500 for new information that could lead to the arrest and conviction of the person who killed Margaret Bowman and Lisa Levy. The *Democrat* printed this information on the front page of its issues for two weeks.

Many civic, business, political, and university leaders called emergency meetings to discuss the innumerable problems caused by having a killer on the loose. They agreed that a larger reward should be offered to encourage people with important information to come forward.

Someone, it was reasoned, *had to know who the killer was*.

Four days after the brutal attacks, donations made by the Capital City Bank Group, the City of Tallahassee, and Leon County increased the fund to $10,000. The articles about the growing reward explained how readers could contribute to the fund or call in with information.

The interns working the phones were besieged with calls, not only from people reporting what they had seen, or thought they'd seen, but by people who requested secret code names so they could help solve the case for the police and collect the reward.

In order to control the chaos, the callers were urged to submit their leads through the "Secret Witness Editor" at the *Democrat*. The *Democrat* provided additional guidance: Do not use your real name. Instead, sign the letter with a six-digit number, tear off and keep a corner of the last page bearing the same six-digit number.[5] Thousands of letters flooded the *Democrat*. Callers were asked to identify themselves using their personal numbers. All leads were turned over to the Leon County Sheriff's office.

---

[5] Secret Witness Editor. "Reward is offered." *The Tallahassee Democrat*, Jan. 16, 1978, p. 1A.

```
Look in something metal. Look in metal containers.

See the distance between the attacks? It is his distance. Know
it. It is his distance. Circle it. Tell it.

In the Colonial Apartments. He is an animal.
```

641123

641123

Exhibit 1: A lead with a random six-digit identifying number.

College-aged men who acted strangely in any way were taken in for questioning. One student was brought in to the FSU police because he'd carried a baseball bat into a campus cafeteria after playing in a game. Women thought he was there to attack them.

Another man stood outside Bill's Bookstore and said something about "stupid sorority girls." He, too, was taken to the FSU police for questioning. Some men, including suspected peeping Toms caught repeatedly in areas outside their own neighborhoods, were threatened with arrest.

Calls from thousands of fearful women flooded the hotline. Some called about peculiar neighbors, or having seen strangers wandering outside their apartments or houses. Officers checked out every call, but often found vagrants seeking a warm spot to sleep. The homeless men would be taken to jail for a couple of nights to get them off the streets.

Other women called to report that their boyfriends or husbands had been missing the night of the murders without an explanation. There were at least 100 of these calls. Alibis were checked. Many secret love affairs were revealed, and the investigators became familiar with every working prostitute in Leon County.

Many of the errant men were afraid to talk, and petrified *not* to, for they knew if they couldn't come up with a substantiated explanation they ran the risk of being publicly taken into the command center for further questioning.

Some men offered police officers money, jewelry, or favors to keep their stories quiet and out of the papers. A few of them became emotional and sobbed, telling investigators that if their wives discovered their secrets, they would lose everything in a nasty divorce. This created a dilemma for the officers. How could they tell the wives, waiting for an official police report, precisely what they had discovered?

The officers were advised to be professional.

"Your husband was not involved, ma'am," became their mantra. They offered worried wives and girlfriends no additional information, much to the dismay of most of the women.

A few men refused to talk about their whereabouts and would not provide alibis for the night of January 14th into the early morning of the 15th. They were willing to risk having their names on the suspect board rather than discuss homosexual liaisons or other relationships.

It wasn't long before the heads of the investigation realized the reward money was producing more dead-end headaches than the leads were worth. There were simply too many people involved in the case. These solicited leads were distracting, and cast too wide a net. The risk of someone mishandling evidence, and making a critical item useless in court, increased with the additional manpower needed to investigate the leads. No one wanted to make an avoidable mistake which could result in the killer remaining free to kill again.

After a week or so, most of the reward seekers became frustrated and lost interest. Between the cold weather and the confusion caused by the extensive media coverage, many people began to think that the search for the killer was futile.

But not Katsaris. He was happy for the information; almost all other crimes in Leon County were being solved in the meantime. However, the sheriff knew that without a conviction in the Chi Omega case, he would never be reelected.

Chapter 16: Come Together

Both of the deceased sorority girls were from Largo, Florida. The weather was dark and rainy when Lisa Levy's body was lowered into the ground in Pinellas Park, near St. Petersburg, on Tuesday at Chapel Hill Memorial Park. On Wednesday, Margaret Bowman was laid to rest in the Largo City Cemetery. The same gloomy rain fell on the families and friends who cried and grieved under black umbrellas at their funerals. The services were arranged so their Chi Omega sisters could grieve for them both.

Two detectives from Tallahassee were posted at each gravesite. They quietly snapped pictures of all people attending the funerals. It was a possibility that the killer would attend the burials of his victims. Detectives had also taken hundreds of photographs during the memorial service held Monday evening in the Ruby Diamond Auditorium at FSU.

As the pictures were developed and studied, they were scattered throughout the command post in different unit rooms. New leads were produced from the pictures, leads that needed the cooperation from other state and county law enforcement agencies.

Sheriff Katsaris called the FBI and requested they develop a psychological profile on the killer. The bureau asked the sheriff to send all the information they had gathered so their agents could begin work on the case. Katsaris had his men copy, pack, and express-ship 48 boxes of information to Quantico, Virginia, that same day. The next morning when the FBI received the packages, a team of specialists were assigned to work on the details. Katsaris was promised he'd receive a detailed profile within a few days.

At the same time, the task force began getting calls from psychiatrists and sociologists offering to compose profiles on the killer. This seemed like a good approach. Copies of police and medical examiner's reports were sent to those who requested them.

Word leaked out that the sheriff was seeking advice from psychologists and sociologists to better understand the killer. Soon, the switchboard was flooded with calls from doctors and university professors around the country, volunteering their help. At first blush, the investigators weren't able to distinguish between those who were legitimately trying to help and those just trying to gain a little fame from the situation. Some people who claimed to be working with the sheriff's department released unauthorized and incorrect information about the case to the media.

The few doctors who did help the task force analyzed thousands of photos, hundreds of court-ordered psychological profiles on released convicts, volumes of written reports, and hours of taped interviews. As the doctors produced their reports, the task force rearranged the list into new categories and brought the suspects in for more questioning.

Shortly after Katsaris sent the boxes of information to the FBI, the CBS Evening News received information from the agency which gave a speculative description of the Chi Omega killer. CBS reported it on the air. This thumbnail profile described a man who grew up in a bad family home, who harbored deep hatred for women, and was possibly a high school dropout. The report lacked any significant detail and made just about every 20- to 30-year-old undereducated male in Tallahassee a suspect.[6] The profile, much like the vague description Nita Neary had given the morning of the attacks, did little to narrow the search for the killer.

Katsaris stormed into Brand's office when he learned CBS had aired "his" profile on its national news program.

"I want to rip someone's head off over this," Katsaris said. "It's nothing but the FBI messing with us; it's blatant bullshit disrespect of me and my team. I want the backstabbing, spotlight-grabbing crap to stop. No one has the right to release information without my approval, not even the goddamned FBI."

Brand shook his head. "Ken, they basically just shoved it up our ass. We've got too much to do. Did you listen to that profile? Hell, Nita Neary gave us more information about the suspect than the FBI did. The hell with them."

---

[6] A copy of a draft FBI report would arrive in Tallahassee several days later, almost two weeks after the murders. The official profile was not submitted until mid-February, near the time a suspect was arrested.

"Bullshit on them," Katsaris said. "I've got the hypnotist coming in later. He's going to meet with the girls. We might get more information from this guy than from the G-men."

Katsaris demanded an explanation from the FBI. The bureau officials reasoned that by announcing the profile via an FBI-generated press release, as opposed to one released by the Leon County Sheriff's Department, the killer *might* be intimidated by the FBI's involvement. The FBI officials felt their tactic *could* also help bring forth potential witnesses, who *might* seek protection from the bureau. To Katsaris and the men on the task force, it was a turf war, with Katsaris trying to maintain control of the investigation.

◆❖◆

The morning after the newscast, Joseph called Lieutenant Brand. Joseph had seen the segment on the profile report on CBS. He expressed his disappointment in the profile developed by the FBI.

"Was this the best they could do?" Joseph asked.

Brand was not amused by the call. He explained that the preliminary profile was based on the type of crime and crime scene statistics, and they expected the FBI to send a more detailed analysis soon. Brand didn't admit to Joseph that he thought the report was worthless, too.

He asked Joseph to come in and tell him what he thought the profile should say. The lieutenant wanted to hear for himself the "hippie psychic's" comparison of the killer with the FBI profile.

When Joseph arrived at the command post, Carol buzzed for Brand. Again, the two men went into the same interrogation room. This time, the meeting between them was somewhat more relaxed.

Joseph looked at the table and noticed how the position of the uneven layers of papers had changed a little, stacked in three smaller piles rather than two large ones.

Brand looked at Joseph, studying the young man with his long hair and glasses. He leaned back into his chair and pulled the front two legs off the ground. "What's your profile on the killer? What do you *see*, or whatever you call it?"

"I really don't know what to call it, sir, but I see pictures." Joseph said. "I guess visions, or dreams, those would be the best words."

"Visions? Interesting." He rubbed his chin with his right hand. "You're not doing LSD, are you, son?"

"Ah, no, no sir, I'm not," Joseph stammered.

"Good, then. That would be a problem for both of us." He laughed. "So, Joseph, what do you have for me today?" Brand folded his hands over his large stomach. He rocked himself slightly in his chair and waited for the story.

Joseph had a habit of speaking quickly. This hid a slight speech impediment he'd had since childhood. People frequently had a difficult time understanding him; he often had to repeat himself. But with Brand, he spoke slowly and deliberately as he answered questions.

"The FBI doesn't know what they're looking for," Joseph said. "They have their books. They love their books. But he's not in their books. He will *rewrite* their books."

"Okay, go on."

"He's an all-night type, and he's an animal with a precise territory. He enjoyed the wailing of sirens and the hypnotic flashing lights on police cars and ambulances. He was nearby, that morning, watching the commotion. He craved the excitement. It made him feel very important, like God. He watched all of you work. He knew you were too busy to see him. He knows how to be invisible, like a shadow. He knows how to hide." Joseph had been speaking with his eyes closed. He opened them for a moment, and Brand motioned him to continue. Joseph nodded and closed his eyes again.

"The killer is extremely smart and fools everyone. He *is* the boy next door, the one you want your daughter to marry. Many will be surprised when he's arrested. They'll even say he was raised in a good Christian home; that he's a smart man with great potential."

Brand crashed the front legs of the chair on the floor and leaned forward, inches from Joseph's face. He challenged the psychic.

"How can you say that a guy who could do something like this would be smart, the kid-next-door type that I'd let my daughter marry? I don't think a Christian man did this. This man's a mean, vicious, son of a bitch. He's an animal, no more, no less."

"I didn't say a Christian did this. *People* will say that he was raised as a good Christian. He's a good-looking guy with a charming smile. Women are drawn to him. People like him. That's who you're looking for."

"How do you know all this?" Brand was intrigued by Joseph's profile. He had never heard a killer described in these terms before. "I've never met a killer like the one you're describing. I'm not sure about what you're saying, son."

"He *will* be this way; the way I've described to you." Joseph closed his eyes again. When he opened them, Brand felt a shudder down his spine.

Those eyes, Brand thought. *What's with his eyes?*

"As I said earlier, this guy will rewrite the book on killers."

"Go on," Brand said. He was taking notes.

"He's an all-night type," Joseph continued. "He hangs out around all-night places like Jerry's on Tennessee Street, and he knows how to walk invisibly in the night shadows. He's seen when he wants to be seen; otherwise, he's invisible. I'm telling you, when it is all over, you will read that he was a good child growing up, from a good Christian upbringing. He'll be attractive and witty and fun. He will have hung out in a place like Smoky's, that acoustic bar over on Woodward Avenue. He will like that kind of place. Small, intimate places."

Smoky's was a small beer and wine tavern with one pool table. It offered live classical and acoustic music nightly. It was located several hundred feet from Cheryl Thomas' duplex, and several blocks from the Chi Omega house.

"How are you so sure that the FBI guys, who have been doing this kind of work for years and are experts on thousands of cases, are wrong on this one?" Brand asked.

"I'll bet I'm right," came Joseph's reply. "After all, how useful, really, is that preliminary report? I'll bet not at all."

"Alright, anything else?" Brand was hoping for more information.

"Remember that area I told you about, the circles equal to the distance between Chi Omega and Dunwoody?" Joseph waited for Brand to acknowledge it. "Remember it well. The killer lives within, and moves around, that area. Place your men in that area at night. They will see him. One other thing..." He waited to make certain he had Brand's full attention.

"What's that?" Brand leaned forward.

"Can we drive around the area I have mentioned? I believe that—"

"Nope. No way, son," Brand said. "I don't have time to drive around that area and figure out if you're on some wild-haired goose chase. We have teams doing surveillance all over that neighborhood. You need to stay away from there. If you're caught in the area, for any reason, we're through. Some people may already consider you a suspect, do you understand me?"

Joseph was devastated. "Please, Lieutenant Brand, if you will give me just a half an hour with you, I promise it'll be worth it. I promise we'll see the things I saw in my visions. I haven't gone down there; I knew your men would be there. I didn't want to cause problems. Please, let us ride in your car for just a few minutes."

"I'm sorry, son," Brand said gently and sincerely, "I just don't have 30 minutes to drive around. My job is to run this place. We have too much to do here. I can't just walk out. Understand, I want you to keep helping us. I really do. But, it has to be done my way. That's how we operate here."

They shook hands and left the small room. Carol smiled and said goodbye to Joseph as he left. He thanked her and wished her a good day.

As Joseph headed down the hill again toward Lake Ella, a feeling overcame him. *Only time will prove me right.*

The lake was quiet on his walk home. Police cars were still coming and going, but only one squad car was parked at the church.

At home, Joseph got into his green VW and drove down the hill on Tharpe Street toward the intersection of Monroe. He thought about an apartment complex called the Colonial Apartments. The problem was, that apartment complex was outside the double-circled area he'd been shown. Something about those apartments was important, and he knew he had to see them. They were not within the special security area, so he reasoned that he wasn't breaking his promise to Brand by driving to those apartments and checking them out.

Joseph drove to west Tallahassee and quickly found the Colonial Apartments. He pulled up to the large, red-brick apartment complex and parked his car. He stared at the building. He had no visions or feelings about the place.

He pulled out of the apartment complex, drove to the music school, and practiced piano for a while.

As Brand requested, Joseph avoided traveling anywhere near the crime areas except to go to classes. He even stopped going to the Mecca for lunch.

Chapter 17: Watching the Detectives

The *Democrat* published several articles about violent crimes that were unsolved and similar to the Chi Omega murders. Just months earlier, a young coed, Linda Sue Thompson, had been abducted from FSU's Dorman Hall. She had been savagely raped, beaten, and left for dead in a remote forested area. The *Democrat* writers speculated that the Thompson incident was related to the Chi Omega attacks.

At the same time, the editors of both the *Democrat* and the *Flambeau* had a "new-found awareness" of the escalating problems of violence against women. The front-page articles brought with them a flood of letters to the editors.

Every day, for weeks, the *Flambeau* printed several letters to the editor which debated women and their "provocative ways." The papers were now a political and emotional battlefield involving frightened people and swelling ranks of feminists. The media was in a frenzy over violence against women.

Then, on January 21st, two different but related articles ran in the *Democrat*. One article was about a gruesome murder movie scheduled to be aired on Saturday, January 28th, from 9 until 11 p.m.

The other story mentioned that three of the victims visited a Big Daddy's nightclub, a popular disco on Appalachee Parkway, the night of the murders. The investigators had worked to establish a timeline to trace every movement the victims had made the days before the attack, hoping the information released to the press would help bring someone forward with a real clue to the killer's identity. Had the girls met the killer at the disco?

The Big Daddy's corporation was nervous and displeased with the publicity surrounding this news and quickly issued a statement to the effect that it was *just a coincidence* that three of the Chi Omega victims had been at the bar on that fateful night.

Curiously, the next day, Big Daddy's launched a new radio and newspaper advertising campaign which promised, "You never know who you'll bump into at Big Daddy's."[7]

The inappropriate humor of this commercial enraged many Tallahassee residents and students. Newspaper articles appeared and letters to the editor agreed: people felt this new campaign was in poor taste. It was soon discontinued.

The article about the sorority murder movie announced that NBC programming was not going to pull the movie from national broadcast, regardless of the coincidental happenings in Tallahassee. In the movie, the killer is a psychopathic college student who kills three women in a sorority house. The film had two names. One was *Stranger in the House* and the other was *Silent Night, Evil Night.*

The movie was scheduled to run on two different Georgia channels, Cable 10 from Albany, and Cable 5 from Atlanta, the two NBC-affiliated TV stations available on the cable system in Tallahassee. A third NBC station also on the cable system, based in Panama City, was airing the March of Dimes telethon that night or it would have broadcast the movie, too.

A brouhaha over the upcoming broadcast soon erupted in the papers and lunch counters throughout Tallahassee. An FCC lawyer in Washington, D.C., said that the local cable company, Clearview, was required to carry whatever NBC affiliates were showing. The TV stations confirmed they would air whatever NBC ran in that time slot.

In the movie, the sorority girls were terrorized by threatening phone calls before they were murdered. Sheriff Katsaris pointed out that while the girls at the Chi Omega house received threatening calls, they came in *after* the brutal murders. He also mentioned that none of the victims in the film were strangled or beaten. Katsaris wasn't pleased with the article and realized he should have simply declined to comment.

NBC officials said they were aware of the crimes in Tallahassee but had not planned to delay or cancel the showing. Thousands of people in Tallahassee were infuriated and flooded politicians'

---

[7] "Disco scene is back to normal." *The Tallahassee Democrat*, Jan. 29, 1978.

Continued on next page...

phone lines for hours.[8]

◆❖◆

The first week of the case ended. Katsaris didn't want to see who would screw up next, and he hoped to God it wouldn't be the hypnotist, who had begun working with the survivors. He considered it the worst week of his life.

Then came Tuesday morning.

No one knew how Ken Katsaris would react to the *Democrat* headlines on January 24th. The men in the command post waited nervously to see who the sheriff would take his anger out on.

The article contained an accurate description of the suspect strategy wall, and mentioned the exact number of suspects, 44, currently listed on the command post blackboard.[9] The reporter described in detail how frequently interviews with suspects were conducted, and how many men were assigned to the case. There were detailed histories and occupations of some of the suspects printed in the paper. This information was potentially damaging to the investigation and to the lives of the suspects.

Katsaris was furious when he arrived at the command post. His eyes and face revealed his intense anger over the leak of such sensitive information. "How could this happen?" he demanded. He thought their entire case had been jeopardized. Every man involved in the investigation was outraged.

A special meeting was called.

"I want to know why someone felt compelled to leak the details of this case to the press," Katsaris shouted. "Is this political sabotage? Believe me, I intend to find out."

Katsaris interpreted the newspaper leak as a personal affront,

---

[8] On January 24th, NBC decided not to air the sorority murder movie in the Tallahassee area. It was believed that several high-ranking politicians, including Governor Reubin Askew, used their influence to have the movie blacked-out. Slasher movies and rape became the topics of editorials and letters to the editors. Often Katsaris' name would be smeared somewhere in the middle of these printed comments.

[9] Whiteley, Michael. "Still no firm suspects in murders." *The Tallahassee Democrat*, Jan. 24, 1978, p. 1B

a plot by "good ol' boys" to undermine his new investigatory techniques and strategies.

"I'm trying to work with several different law enforcement agencies to solve this case, but so far, all I have is a major headache," Katsaris yelled, the veins protruding from his neck. "I'm having a hard enough time trying to prove to these other agencies that my Leon County Sheriff's Department is as capable in ability and strategy as any of them. Media leaks have no part in my concept of the modern crime-solving professional."

Katsaris glared at his investigators. He caught the eyes of each man in the room and held their gaze long enough to make the men shrink back into their chairs.

"I want to change the public's perception of us. We're not backwards, old-fashioned, or bigoted. I can't stress enough how important it is for us to be as modern, fair, and as creative as possible... and close-mouthed!" he shouted. "That's the biggest key to solving this case."

He began to pace the room. "I want you men to think, to be creative, and leave no stone unturned. Anything goes, as long as it's legal. If it's not by the book and I find out about it, those involved will answer to me personally."

As Katsaris continued his ranting, he approached the narrow window, looked out, and stopped mid-sentence. He stood at the window as though mesmerized. A photojournalist snapped pictures of him through the window.

His eyes opened wide as he quickly turned around. The blackboard, with all of the names on it, was in plain view of the photographer standing outside. It hit Katsaris like a ton of bricks. The men he had been berating hadn't leaked any information. No one had undermined his authority. He had overlooked a simple and basic fact: the windows were open for all the world to look in and report on what was happening. Even the killer could walk right up to take a look, if he wanted to.

Katsaris turned back to the window just as the reporter yelled "thanks for the great picture," and walked away, chuckling to himself.

Mortified, the sheriff was forced to admit to himself that he was being a total ass. He had to think fast. He had to somehow recover from this embarrassment.

He turned to the men. “The anger I just expressed was justified. Not one of you had thought to cover the damn windows. That’s the point, get it?” He was yelling again. “Oversights like this can kill a case. Now listen to me, and hear me clearly. Leave nothing to chance. Don’t stop until every question is answered. Small details, things like the press and uncovered windows, are killing us, damn it! Small, shit details may seem harmless at first, but they can cause serious damage if unchecked. Do I make myself clear?”

Katsaris continued his tirade for a while longer. He knew mistakes were bound to happen, but he vowed to keep such oversights to a minimum.

Brand quietly asked one of the deputies to cover the windows with pages of the *Democrat*.

By the time the article had been printed, the number of suspects on the command post blackboard had risen to 68. Two-thirds of these new names had been provided by the local mental health offices and the state department of Health and Rehabilitative Services. Brand had asked the directors of these agencies for the names of men thought to have been in the Tallahassee area during the weekend of January 15th. These men had psychological dossiers which seemed to fit the killer’s apparent profile. They were men who had histories of committing crimes against women, many of them quite violent. They were either on work release programs or had been out on weekend passes from the State Mental Hospital in Chattahoochee, Florida. “Overall immersion into the general population” was the name of the therapy technique. It was a popular treatment program at that time.

At first, the state agencies were reluctant to release information about their patients to the police. They did not want to give the information to the police because of the possibility of violating the inmates’ constitutional rights. When officials finally handed the files over, the police discovered that the list of names was much longer than they had first imagined. It alarmed the investigators to learn just how many convicted rapists and sex murderers were on weekend passes or work release programs in

Tallahassee that weekend.

Every man had to be tracked down and questioned. It was a police nightmare. Questioning the men on that list became a top priority, so extra men were assigned to track them down. The investigators knew they had to keep this information absolutely secret. They certainly did not want the residents of Tallahassee to know just how many violent convicts had been allowed to "immerse" themselves into the community that weekend.

By the end of that day, the second floor of the command post had been converted into the media center. This arrangement made it easy to keep surveillance on the reporters. All the out-of-town media reporters used desks and phone lines on the second floor, and press conferences and briefings were generally held here.

It also helped that all of the windows in the investigations rooms were covered and doors were kept closed.

Dozens of reporters sat around upstairs, waiting to get the scoop and the first photos of an arrested suspect. They were starved for a glimpse of the man the sheriff had promised to bring in through modern police work "soon."

Katsaris also knew he had to keep the media out of the investigation, yet be solicitous toward them and keep them on friendly terms. He didn't want them to turn on him during the next election.

At first, the media loved Katsaris' attitude of not resting until the killer was caught. But when no new information or suspects surfaced, media demand for Katsaris diminished. But the sheriff didn't sleep. He had meant what he said. He was a driven man, and he would find the killer.

Chapter 18: Breakdown

The days turned into weeks as the investigation fell into a routine. McDonald's restaurants continued to supply food daily, but the men at the command center were getting tired of burgers and fries, even though they were free. The tips and leads that had flooded the hotlines for the first two weeks slowly tapered off. Outstanding, unsolved cases were closed, but the ongoing mission to find the brutal Chi Omega killer continued.

Morale among the investigators was waning. Lieutenant Brand continued to hold daily early-morning meetings with the investigators directly under his command. He usually stood in front of the suspect blackboard to direct the meeting. Sometimes, Sheriff Katsaris stood alongside Brand. Names on the suspect board were slowly erased. Few new names, if any, were added.

On the afternoon of Friday, January 27th, a meeting was held between the sheriff and his top command post staff, which included Brand and Poitinger, who coordinated the investigative team. During the course of the meeting, the manpower of the task force was slashed from 40 to 13 investigators.[10]

While many of the men reassigned back to their regular jobs felt relieved to be returning to a level of normality, many felt they had somehow failed because they had not caught the killer.

Katsaris reminded the men that because of their hard work and determination, many unsolved cases had been cleared. And because of the increased security in the town, the crime rate had dropped considerably.

The hundreds of hours of overtime put into the Chi Omega case by the appointed task force members, just within the two-week period, had damaged the home lives of many of the investigators. Frightened wives were left home alone, or with children, while their husbands worked around the clock. Many of the investigators came

---

[10] Efron, Seth. "Murder force cut: still no firm leads." *The Tallahassee Democrat*, Jan. 28, 1978, p. 1B.

home solely to shower and sleep, and some were accused of having affairs. The stress of the investigation took a toll on many people in the community, but particularly on the members of the task force and their families.

Lack of sleep, too much coffee and fast food, and frustration over not solving the Chi Omega case were cited as the causes of internal rifts among the law enforcement personnel. Long-simmering personal disagreements erupted openly. Resentment was prevalent and grudges were held.

Reporters were under significant pressure from their outlets to get fresh news, and they spent hours frantically chasing down their own leads. Everyone wanted an arrest. Law enforcement and news people were all feeling disappointed and depressed. Some were beginning to whisper their doubts about solving the case at all.

◆❖◆

Sensing the mood, Katsaris developed an opportunity for some good publicity. He hastily arranged a series of crime prevention seminars in Tallahassee to teach people how to be more aware of their surroundings and cautious about their safety. He felt this would give him to ability to meet more of his constituents while teaching them to protect themselves. He wanted to be a positive presence in Tallahassee. The first seminar was to be held on February 1st.

"Law enforcement can't be on every corner," he reasoned. "It's our role to tell you how to take care of yourselves."

On Monday, January 30th, during his first meeting with the trimmed-down investigative team, Brand decided to try a new approach.

"The killer's name is there on the blackboard. I'm certain we have his name on this list," he said. "Each day, the list grows smaller as we eliminate suspects. It is up to us to find out which name belongs to that piece of shit. We've all made promises to solve this case. So, let's solve it."

Brand took a deep drag from his cigarette.

"Now, I want all of you to take a good, long look at these names and commit them to memory. When you leave here today, keep your ears to the ground and listen for any detail that might lead us to one of these names. Don't be afraid to go back to the beginning of this case and start all over again. You'd be amazed at the opportunities we've missed already. I know we've screwed up some leads and made mistakes, particularly at the beginning, with the crime scenes." He pointed at the names on the board. "I'm not afraid to admit I've made mistakes. But let's do something about this, for the girls and their families. Let's catch this asshole now!"

The investigators reached for a new sense of hope. Some had worn the same suit for days. Each could recite the names on the blackboard from memory. They either chewed gum or chain-smoked. The pressure on them had just increased. With the reassignment of 27 officers, the remaining investigators knew the resolution of the case rested on their shoulders.

As January drew to a close, they were no closer to catching the killer than they had been the awful morning they'd been called to the Chi Omega house, nearly two weeks before. The men concluded the morning meeting and returned to the field. They went back to the grinding routine that would continue for weeks to come.

No one knew how much longer this would drag on, or if the killer would strike again.

Chapter 19: Bad Dreams

Just before the Chi Omega murders, several other Tallahassee women had been attacked and killed. One of these victims was a black woman. She was found in the old part of Tallahassee known as Frenchtown, a black ghetto just north of the FSU campus where drugs and death were common. Someone had clubbed her with a 2" by 4" wooden board and skewered her with a broken broomstick. She was discovered with part of the broom handle protruding from her vagina.

There was no newspaper coverage of the murder, nor was there a visible investigation. This lack of attention angered several of the prominent black community leaders. They demanded the same type of attention and "equal manpower given the white girls" from Katsaris.

These influential black leaders had supported Katsaris in the past election because he had promised better law enforcement for blacks. Now they wanted the black woman's murder solved in exchange for their political support in the upcoming election.

Katsaris responded with relentless vigor. He ordered a dozen men to investigate the Frenchtown murder. At all hours of the night, Katsaris would call the men assigned to the case. "What are you doing? Have you found the killer? Get off your ass and bring the killer in."

Consequently, Frenchtown was crawling with detectives. Informants were given special favors if they helped solve the case quickly. It turned out that a black prostitute was responsible. She had left the Tallahassee area and was arrested in another state for new crimes she had committed, including another murder. She signed a confession while awaiting trial. The black leaders were finally satisfied, and Katsaris was off the hook.

◆❖◆

Joseph looked at the young girl and realized he had hurt her, but he felt no remorse. She was whimpering and sobbing, but the girl was so terrified she had stopped moving. He felt strong, powerful. He had control. No one could catch him.

Pay attention! the voice shouted in this head. *Look at this...*

Joseph opened his eyes and saw bright sunlight. He was covered in something wet and sticky. He was horrified by what he'd seen.

◆❖◆

Katsaris slammed down the phone.

The piece of chewing gum that had been retrieved from Lisa Levy's hair, which held a good imprint of a tooth when it had been carefully removed at the hospital, had been flattened by a postal canceling machine. Someone had placed this piece of evidence, considered one of the few pieces of critical evidence obtained at the crime scenes, into a plain envelope and mailed it to the crime lab in Atlanta with improper protective packing material.

The gum could no longer be matched to teeth impressions of a suspect. Carelessness in handling evidence dealt a serious blow to the prosecution.

Katsaris was furious and heartbroken by the loss of the tooth imprint. Depressed, shoulders sagging, he walked into Brand's office and closed the door.

"I don't know whose head will roll over this shit, but everyone's going to blame me, aren't they?" he asked Brand. "I don't know what to do next to solve this thing. We just keep getting kicked in the ass."

"Yeah, but have faith, Ken. Maybe the hypnotist will come back with a better description for us. We're only two weeks into this case. Something's bound to break our way soon," Brand assured his boss.

"The hypnotist pretty much struck out. Not that I'm surprised," the sheriff said. "He said he may come back to interview Cheryl Thomas, when she's ready, but who knows how long that will be." He stood at the window and looked out, stooped with fatigue. "I need a fucking suspect."

Katsaris took a couple of deep breaths, did a few shoulder rolls, plastered a smile on his face, and left the room. He knew that the only available evidence that could possibly stand up in court were the photographs of bitemarks on Lisa Levy's buttocks and several human hairs shaken from the stocking mask found at the Cheryl Thomas duplex. There were no tests available in 1978 that could conclusively tie the hairs to any one person. There was a small spot of semen on one of Thomas' sheets, but they did not think it came from her attacker.

Bitemarks from a murder victim's body had been successfully used as evidence only once before, in an Illinois case, but never by Florida prosecutors. He thought about his last conversation with Poitinger, who was worried that it would be nearly impossible to convict anyone with the scant evidence they had, without a confession.

In all of Katsaris' frustration over the turn of events, he was curious about Joseph. He noticed how the psychic's name kept popping up in the investigation, but it wasn't yet written on the blackboard.

"Why not?" the sheriff had asked Brand on several occasions. "Who is Joseph? What do we really know about him? Even if he has nothing to do with Chi Omega, do you think he may be plotting something, and think he'll get away with it?"

"No, I don't see that in him," Brand would say each time, shaking his head.

"Joseph might have been a second man in the sorority house that night," Katsaris said one time. "I have a gut feeling about him, George."

That morning, as Brand and Katsaris talked, Carol buzzed the office. Joseph was on the phone. Something had just happened and he wanted to see the lieutenant right away.

"He sounded worried, Ken," Brand said. "He's coming right over now."

"I want to know what Joseph says the moment he leaves," Katsaris said. "He gives me the creeps."

Brand lit a cigarette. "Hey, I'm the one he picked to talk to. I'm the one who sits in that room with him. I don't know what to think half the time." Brand blew a cloud of smoke over Katsaris' head.

"He really tells me some strange shit."

When Joseph arrived at the command center, Brand met him in the reception area. They went into the meeting room together and sat down. Brand asked why Joseph was so agitated.

"I had a dream this morning, and I, uh," Joseph stammered. He cleared his throat. "I was standing on the hill, the one next to the junior high school near Lake Ella. You know, the one by the JM Fields store, the shopping mall?"

Brand nodded. "Yes."

"I stood in the area where the fence is tall, taller than other fences. I looked down at a parking lot below me and saw a van. I had to notice the distance from the van to Lake Ella. This was the same distance between the Chi Omega house to the Dunwoody duplex. Remember, sir, I told you how important that distance is?"

"Go on," Brand said.

"That's how I knew the dream was about the killer."

"Alright," Brand said.

"I could see Lake Ella clearly from where I stood. The trees weren't hiding the lake, like they usually do. Suddenly, I was standing next to the van. The van's back door was open. I grabbed this little girl, who was next to me, and I threw her in the van."

Brand noticed the young man was shaking and trying very hard to remain composed.

"I raped her," he said, so quietly Brand almost asked him to repeat himself. "I think I was about to strangle her or kill her. And I heard a voice calling to me, telling me to pay attention. And the voice yelling at me woke me up. I was so scared because I thought I had hurt the girl. But once I was awake, I knew. I knew I was watching the killer."

Joseph's nose was running. Brand got up and left the office. He returned moments later with a box of Kleenex. He set it down in front of Joseph.

"Thank you." Joseph pulled out a tissue and blew his nose. He held the wad in his hand. "I've never completed sex in my dreams before, you know... made a mess. I've never had that happen until this morning," he said quietly.

"You said there was a girl. Can you describe her to me?"

"I think so," Joseph said. "She was young, like my little sister, younger than the others. She had brown hair. Long. But she's young, not like the ones here. I didn't recognize her."

Brand watched Joseph carefully. He chewed his lower lip.

"Now, Joseph, you mentioned a van, right?"

Joseph nodded.

"Is there anything else you can tell me about it, like the make or model?" Brand asked. "Or the color?"

"It was light-colored, sir, like white, and then it was glowing yellow, everything was yellow." Joseph spoke as if in a trance. His eyes were closed.

"What about the license plate, did you see a number?" Brand asked gently.

"No. No numbers, just the color yellow... yes. Everything was yellow," Joseph said, trying to see the vision.

"The license plate was yellow? Are you sure?" Brand asked.

"Yes, yes, sir, it was yellow," Joseph said. "I think that's important."

"I know that's what you say you saw," Brand said, and leaned back in his chair, "but to my knowledge, there may be only two states that use yellow tags, and they're a long way from here." He tapped an unlit cigarette on the table. "I do know that government vehicles for the state of Florida have yellow tags. Could that be what you saw?"

"Maybe," Joseph said and opened his eyes. "Maybe I saw a state van. Maybe it was stolen or something."

"Joseph," Brand said. "Look at me."

"Yes?"

"Can you please start writing down these things for me?"

"Yes, I can, but I don't know what all this means," Joseph said. "I knew I had to tell you about it."

"And that's good. I'm glad you did." Brand pulled a thick file out from under a stack of files. "I'd like to read something to you. Can you stay a little while longer?"

"Yes," Joseph said.

Brand opened the file and began to turn the pages, one by one. The folder was filled with at least 100 pages of notes and drawings. Joseph recognized Carol's handwriting on message slips. He saw his name on some of them.

"This is our psychic file," Brand said. "We've been getting lots of, ah, *information* from people all over the country. We have letters and drawings that people think will help us catch the killer. I want to show you some of these, and I want you to tell me what you think, or feel, or whatever you do." He laughed. "Some of these folks may be crazy."

Brand held up a pencil drawing of a young man with long hair and horns on his head. "What do you think of this? The artist said that the killer is the Devil." Brand whistled between his teeth. "He drew us a picture so we'd know what to look for." He winked.

Joseph smiled, but didn't see much humor in the drawing.

Brand slowly began to read portions of the letters aloud to Joseph. He did not identify the writers by name. Occasionally, Brand would show another sketch of the "killer" to him. As Brand read the letters, he glanced up now and then, watching Joseph's eyes for a reaction. Nothing he showed Joseph seemed to resonate with him.

Bible quotes were a common theme.

"If, however, the charge is true and no proof of the young woman's virginity can be found, she shall be brought to the door of her father's house and there the men of her town shall stone her to death. She has done an outrageous thing in Israel by being promiscuous while still in her father's house. You must purge the evil from among you."[11]

Variations of this theme, that unmarried girls who were no longer virgins should be killed by the men in the community, was a

[11] Deuteronomy, 22:20-21

message many "psychics" wanted to relay. One passage, "And kill every woman who has slept with a man, but save for yourselves every girl who has never slept with a man,"[12] from the Book of Numbers, came up several times. Many writers insinuated that the killer may have been following instructions from God, or from the Devil, when he attacked the five girls that morning.

It was all quite disturbing and the messages contradicted one another, although the majority of the writers blamed the victims. Some of the notes called the victims Devil worshippers and said the killer was an angel of God sent to "wipe out their wickedness." Still others called the killer an "agent of Satan" and implied the victims had drawn evil to themselves. One message advised the police "*to find the killer, look for the Devil. Satan himself is now in Tallahassee.*"

Joseph made no comment while Brand picked his way through the file. He was visibly troubled and struggled to keep from crying. Brand closed the file and watched Joseph's face for a moment.

"You doing alright?"

"Ah, yeah," Joseph whispered, then cleared his throat. "Yes, I'm okay."

"Is there anything else, son?" Brand asked quietly.

Joseph rose slowly. "No."

The men shook hands as they left the room. "Be sure to write everything down. Those notes are important."

Joseph nodded and exited the command post with his head down and his coat pulled up to partially hide his face. Tears flowed down his face as he walked back to his house.

Sheriff Katsaris waited in the next room for Brand as Joseph left. Brand seemed uneasy as he gave his report on what had just taken place.

"That hippie has just confessed to a rape and murder." Katsaris was elated. "Now all we have to do is find the body. That kid has more going on than you know, George. You'll see."

---

[12] Numbers, 31:17-18

"Ken, you're driving yourself crazy. This boy ain't done shit."

"Work him your way, George," Katsaris said as he left the room. The sheriff was glad he had placed surveillance on Joseph.

Brand started watching for any reports involving vans. He wasn't going to ignore any possibility. He had promised the victims' families that he would do whatever it took to solve the murders.

Joseph walked home slowly. He was troubled by the nightmare and the contents of the psychic file. He wondered how he would write his visions for Brand, and he was apprehensive that others would be reading, and *judging*, what he wrote. He did not want to be associated with the "crazies."

Chapter 20: Little Queen of Spades

A group of clairvoyants and mediums gathered at the psychic Ruth's small house in west Miami during the last few days of January. Ruth had been following the news from Tallahassee closely since the session she'd had with Joseph and his mother, Ellen, in December. Her group held meetings for several days for two to three hours at a time. They were doing *psychic* work on the nationally infamous Chi Omega murder case.

Ruth and her group believed it was time to become involved. "The police need my help," she told her followers.

At each meeting, the group would begin by meditating, clearing their minds, and visualizing Tallahassee and the events of January 15th as reported in the newspapers and on TV. Some knew Tallahassee residents and had spoken with them to see if the *Democrat* had more to report than the *Miami Herald*.

One person was designated to write down all of the comments made during the sessions, and Ruth's observations in particular. Each was asked to concentrate on a single topic, such as the weapon or the killer himself, and bring the visions to the forefront of their minds. Their "clues" would be given to the police.

As they all focused, they began to speak about their feelings and visions. Many reported shadows and glimpses of the killer inside the sorority house. Ruth hoped something would be useful from their sessions and she was excited about the work being done.

The central theme that emerged centered on a crucifix. Members of the group believed a missing crucifix, taken from one of the sorority victims after she was attacked, would lead police to the killer. No other vision seemed as powerful as this single religious article and what it could possibly signify. They described the object as an ornate and unusual crucifix. They believed the killer took the artifact and had it in his possession.

They also believed that if one of the sorority members described the crucifix to a reporter, then newspapers would print a description of it. This description would encourage someone to report anyone who had been seen with this special crucifix to the police, who would then, hopefully, arrest the killer.

During one of the session breaks, Ellen pulled Ruth aside to speak privately with her.

"Ruth, you remember my son, Joseph, whom I brought here last month?"

"Of course, I do," Ruth said. "Is he well?"

Ellen said that Joseph had begun having visions about the murders and had gone to the police. She said that Joseph was nervous about working with a detective and feared he would become a suspect or have his information discarded.

"I'm so happy to hear this," Ruth said. "Now I know who we can send my visions to." She instructed Ellen to call her son and relay the information.

Ellen was excited to work with her son. She called Joseph the next afternoon and told him about the "findings" of the group. Joseph asked if he could speak with Ruth directly. Ellen agreed and gave him Ruth's phone number.

Ruth answered on the first ring. After cordial greetings, she told Joseph he could call her anytime, day or night, if he needed her help. He told the woman what he had seen in his visions.

"Listen, honey," Ruth began, "sometimes it's a person's inexperience or youth that can cause confusion. It kind of blocks you from seeing with your third eye. It's your third eye you must use to locate the killer. Now, Joseph, tell me something."

"What?"

"Why didn't you come to me sooner? You know how much I love your mother. Did you think I wouldn't help you? Listen, baby, I've done years of this kind of work. You should have never tried to take this case on by yourself. You have no idea how dangerous that could be. Did you know it could cost you your life?" Ruth said.

"I've never thought about that," Joseph said slowly.

"Of course you didn't, honey. You don't know what to do."

Joseph thought for a second. "Why are my visions so different from yours? I mean, why do I see apartments and vans and a young girl being hurt, maybe killed, and you just see this crucifix?"

Ruth laughed. "Hey, who said we didn't see other things? Let's just take this one step at a time. My rule is to give information in pieces and not overwhelm them with too much, too fast. You are so close that you feel the direct vibrations. You are in the midst of what has happened and continues to happen. Do you understand?"

"Yes, ma'am."

"This must be so confusing for you. My God, with all that energy flowing up there, it's a wonder you haven't gone absolutely nuts. I mean, the entire country is sending psychic information to your town as we talk. And that can be *very* overwhelming."

Joseph pictured the woman in a brightly colored caftan, waving her arms as she spoke to him.

"I have the years of experience to sort all the information. You're still a baby in psychic terms. You'll learn. That's what I'm here for. Just follow my lead and watch. Okay?"

"Yes, ma'am," Joseph replied.

"Don't worry about this. Just stay calm and we'll work this out together."

She sounded like his mother. Joseph smiled and agreed.

"Now," she said, taking a deep breath, "the information your mom gave you about the crucifix is very important. You must take it to the police right away. It is the key to solving the case. Don't tell them anything else, just tell this to your lieutenant."

"Okay." He noticed that her voice had changed. "But why don't you want to call Brand directly?"

"Honey," Ruth said with surprise, "I never call the police, they call me. I'm famous for this kind of work. I've helped people all over the country and even some people in places around the world. Now, don't question the way I work." She was stern. Her motherly tone of voice was gone.

"Please, Ruth? Please call Lieutenant George Brand, the detective who's handling the psychic information? I'll give you his number. He's a real nice gentleman and he can be trusted."

"The police call me, Joseph, I do not call them. Now you tell your friend that I'll be happy to speak with him and we can solve the case. But he has to call me. That's how it works. *They* have to ask *me* to help them."

"I guess this means you won't call Brand?"

"Listen to me!" Ruth exploded. "Quit playing around with your abilities and concentrate on what we're doing here. I'm *very* powerful. I'm renowned for my skills. So do as I say, understood?"

"I understand."

"Good. Now, if you can't get the police to call me, then you'll have to be my message bearer."

He realized that the demanding old woman wanted him at her beck and call. She wanted to manipulate him for her personal gain. He felt uncomfortable with this arrangement and regretted calling her.

"Honey, you there?" Ruth asked, her tone soft again.

"Yes, I'm here."

"You're quiet. Is everything alright?" she asked. "Just hear me and your mother out. I have great powers you don't even know about. Just do as I say and watch what happens. Now, you'll help me, okay?"

"Okay, I'll talk to Lieutenant Brand for you," Joseph said.

When he hung up, he called the command post. He was put immediately through to Brand. He explained the situation about Ruth and what she had told him about the crucifix.

"Now, Joseph, I'm sorry, but I *am* going to put you in the middle of this situation," Brand chuckled, "because I'm *not* going to call her. If she's got something to say, she needs to pick up the phone and call me." He laughed so loudly Joseph thought he could hear the man from across the lake.

"Just write that up for me," Brand instructed.

Ruth and Joseph spoke on numerous occasions over the course of the next few days, in both the mornings and the evenings. The old woman pressed Joseph for information from the police about the investigations.

"Joseph, I need you to do something important," she said one morning.

"What's that?" He was suspicious.

"I need you to get an article into the paper. Tell them about the crucifix and ask them to put an article out there that asks people to look for the crucifix."

"How am I going to do that?" He'd never spoken to anyone from a newspaper before.

"Find a reporter, or someone in the news business," she instructed, "and have them call me. I can crack this case if you'd just get something in the paper about my visions."

Joseph was worried about exposing himself as a psychic. "Ruth, can we keep the reporters out of this?"

"No, it's publicity in the paper and on TV that creates the most business for people like us. I make my living by giving readings and performing other psychic services. When the papers print my name, my clientele grows. That means my income goes up, too."

Joseph was silent.

"Do you understand?" she asked.

"Yes, I do."

"Good. Now listen: I'm taking you under my wing and teaching you the business. Watch and learn, and I'll teach you how to network your powers. You know, Joseph, I don't do this for just anyone. I'm doing it because I love your mother. She's one of my closest friends."

"I understand. But of all the things I want to do with my life," Joseph said carefully, "charging people for giving psychic readings is *not* one of them. I just want to make music and write. I want to go to school and not be bothered with other people's problems. I'm happy to tell a story or sing a song, but other than that, I don't want to *perform* for anyone."

"I don't think your mother would like to know you're talking to me like this." Ruth's voice turned cold and hard.

Old witch. Joseph had a flash of an old, ugly, lonely woman who hid behind a character she had constructed, like an actress in a play. He wondered if, were he to die suddenly, Ruth would charge his mother to raise his spirit from the grave. He'd had enough of this. He ended the conversation and hung up the phone.

Later that day, his mother called and asked him to call some reporters and try to work Ruth into the investigation.

"Mom, I'm sorry, but I just can't do it, not even for you," Joseph said. "Ruth is in this for money. She doesn't care about people or the victims. She just wants glory and notoriety. And money. This is a big ego trip for her. This is how she earns her money."

"I don't believe that," Ellen said. "Are you sure it's not *your* ego getting in the way? Is there anything wrong if Ruth makes a living with her talents?"

"Mom, if I'm able to get someone to write a story about Ruth and the visions of the crucifix, they might insist on using my name. They might even print a photo of me. I don't want anyone to know who I am. Hey, you guys are safe in Miami. I mean, you and Ruth are 500 miles away. No one's going to come get you there. The killer's here, where I am, in Tallahassee."

"Alright, Joseph, I see your point," his mother said. "I'll speak with Ruth."

Ruth called Joseph a few minutes later. "Listen honey, nothing's going to happen to you."

"How do you know?" Joseph demanded.

"I'm in total control now. I know everything that's going on," she said in her most comforting voice. "I've already foreseen good things for your helping me. Now, remember when we spoke in Miami last month?"

"Yes."

"And I told you that I saw you doing a great deed? Right?"

"Yes."

"Well, what I saw as your great deed was you telling a reporter what I need you to tell them. That's your real deed. You should be honored that you're helping me solve the case. You must realize that I'm the only one who can solve it."

"Why is my mind telling me different things?"

"Trust me, honey," Ruth said in a soothing voice, "I'm a lot older, a lot more experienced, and mine is the only voice you should listen to now." She paused. "It's your confusion that won't allow my thoughts to transfer to Lieutenant Brand. That's why he won't call me. Your confusion is blocking my ability to work with him. Now, just stop messing everything up. You're too inexperienced to control the lieutenant's mind. Obey your mother and do as I ask."

"Call Brand yourself."

"No!" she shouted. "I told you, *they* call *me*. If you get my words right, they'll call me. Now just write exactly what I tell you and you'll see how I operate. I'm just like a doctor, honey. Do as your mother and I ask."

Ruth dictated a statement to Joseph. She made him read it back to her. Once he had it right, she told him to give it to Brand.

"This is very powerful, Joseph," she said. "He'll call me as soon as he hears it." She slammed down the phone.

"Fucking yenta," he said. He called Brand and read Ruth's statement.

"Really?" Brand said. "What a pain in the butt. I'm not calling her, son. And don't call me back with any more of her crap. She's not the only person in the world who can solve this case. I believe you said the same thing." He snorted. "Tell her George Brand said she can kiss my ass."

Joseph determined he was finished with Ruth as well. He was relieved.

Chapter 21: Between a Rock and a Hard Place

Florida State University operated on the quarter system in 1978. February was the time to study for mid-term exams and finish class projects that were due. During mid-terms, students often organized into study groups. It was a great way to work and socialize at the same time. Guys would try to get the best-looking girls in their classes into their study groups. Every group then tried to get the smartest kid in the class to join them. Study group nights often turned into party and date nights.

All of the campus dormitories and the two off-campus student housing buildings had meeting rooms that lent themselves well to these study parties. Most of the time, everyone would pitch in and order pizza and beer. Often, someone brought marijuana. No one cared, as long as everyone stayed under control and some actual *studying* occurred.

Several days after his nightmare and the telephone conversations with Ruth began, Joseph was invited by Joan, a classmate, to work on a project at Dorman Hall. He planned his schedule to finish his afternoon piano practice early so he would be there on time. He knew the dorm was on the other side of the campus, near the corner of Woodward Avenue and Jefferson Street.

Woodward Avenue ran north and south, splitting the campus in two. Jefferson Street ran east and west along the southern edge. It also ran in front of the Chi Omega house.

Where the two roads met on the northeast corner of the intersection, there was a large, dusty parking lot with enormous, timeworn oak trees draped with Spanish moss. Just east of this lot was Dorman Hall, a dormitory for women. It was a couple of blocks west of the Chi Omega house and a few blocks north of Cheryl Thomas' duplex on Dunwoody Street.

Joseph was to meet Joan at Dorman Hall at 6:30 that evening. Joseph arrived a few minutes early and had to wait outside. Since the murders, visitors were not allowed into any campus dormitory without an escort.

Prior to the murders, anyone could walk in the front door of any dormitory until 11 p.m. Sometimes, doors were propped open with cinder blocks to allow effortless entry all night long. Unsurprisingly, this practice ended with Chi Omega. Dorman Hall, in particular, was close to the crime scenes and some viewed it as an area of interest for the killer, especially since it had been the location of the Linda Sue Thompson abduction the previous May.

When Joseph knocked on the front door, a large, black security guard peered out at him. The guard opened the door a couple of inches and asked to see Joseph's student ID card. Joseph took his card out of his wallet and handed it to the guard. After recording Joseph's name and ID number onto a sheet held on a clipboard, the guard compared the photo to Joseph's face.

"Hey man, who are you here to see?" he asked in a deep Southern drawl.

"Joan, in this room." Joseph showed the guard the girl's name and room number he'd written on his notebook.

The guard then wrote the name and room number next to Joseph's information. "Wait here a few minutes." He locked the door and Joseph remained outside.

He returned a few minutes later and handed Joseph his ID card.

"Sorry, but you have to wait outside. She's not in her room."

The sun was setting and the air was cold and clear as Joseph waited on the steps in front of the dormitory.

Dorman Hall was a large, eight-story building with wide concrete steps. Along the east side was a large meeting room that projected out from the main building. A long, wide sidewalk ran down to the street where it met the main sidewalk that completely surrounded the FSU campus.

Each room had a large window that provided a floor to ceiling view. People walking by could see into the rooms, and some students taped life-sized pictures of movie stars on the windows to create the illusion of people looking out.

Nearby the dormitory was an apartment building, a big church, a handful of old rental houses, several sorority and fraternity houses, and two student hangouts: the Sweet Shop and Sherrod's Nightclub. Most of the older buildings were surrounded by thick vegetation and oak trees.

Joseph sat down and watched the traffic. The unpleasant conversations he'd had with Ruth replayed in his head. He was done with her, no matter what his mother said. But never far from his mind was the nightmare. The vividness of the dream about the little girl haunted him. *Who was the girl that was raped and, probably, murdered? When was she going to show up? Was she already dead, killed by the Chi Omega maniac? Could her death be prevented?*

Joseph drifted into a near sleep and visualized vans driving by the front of the dorm. Every other vehicle seemed to be a cargo van or a passenger van. Joseph watched as a van stopped in the dusty parking lot to his right. A black man grabbed a woman who stood in the lot, shoved her into the van, and took off quickly. As his dream continued, he saw two of his friends, Ron Blount and Ron Bradshaw, drive by in opposite directions. Blount, a black man, drove a VW van, and Bradshaw, a white man, drove a Dodge van.

Joseph opened his eyes and looked around the street. There were no vans anywhere. It was quiet. His heart pounded and his breathing was ragged, as if he'd run a long distance while he sat on the steps. He was very cold, and his leg had fallen asleep.

He got up and gingerly limped around in a circle to wake up his leg and warm himself. Suddenly, alarms went off in his head. The men he'd seen in the vans kept flashing before his eyes. They had something to do with the murders. He had to tell Brand.

When Joan appeared, Joseph asked if he could use the phone. She pointed to a phone booth in the lobby and told him to dial "9" to get an outside line.

Joseph dialed and watched Joan as she chatted with the guard. The phone rang a couple of times and Brand answered.

"Lieutenant Brand," Joseph started, "something weird just happened to me."

"What is it, Joseph?" Brand asked calmly.

"I had a strange dream that was really spooky. I mean, it was like the dream I had the other night, only different." Joseph leaned on the telephone booth wall, pressing the top of his head against the wall to support his body weight.

"Come on, boy," Brand urged. "Tell me what you saw."

"I saw a van. A man got out of the van and grabbed a woman. He wasn't gentle to her. She was hurt. And then I saw other vans with two friends of mine in them. They were driving by. One was black and the other was white."

"The men or the vans?" Brand asked.

"The men. I don't remember what color the vans were."

Joseph knew the colors and makes of the vans that belonged to his friends, but he did not want to implicate them.

Brand wanted more detail. "Do you know the names of the men in the vans, son?"

"Yes sir, I do."

"Well, what are they? Who was in the vans?"

"I don't know how to tell you. They're friends of mine. I don't know what this all means."

"Tell me, son. I promise it'll be okay. Just tell me. If it was important for you, it's important for me. Now tell me their names." Brand spoke softly.

"The black man is Ron Blount. He's a musician friend of mine. The other is Ron Bradshaw. I go to school with both of them. I really don't like this, sir. I'm not trying to get anyone in trouble. I don't think they did anything." Joseph did not feel comfortable giving out names to the cops.

"Joseph," Brand said, "I know you care, but you think this means something. Where are you, anyway?"

"Dorman Hall," Joseph replied.

"Son of a bitch, you're where?" Brand yelled into the phone. Joseph heard Brand's chair legs drop to the floor.

"Dorman Hall," Joseph said again. "Why?"

"What are you doing there?"

"I'm here to work on a project for a mid-term. Isn't that alright?" Brand's reaction made him feel even more anxious.

Brand calmed himself down. "Yeah, that's fine. Did you know that a girl was kidnapped from Dorman Hall?"

"No. Oh, my gosh. I didn't know."

"It was in the paper a few months ago, and it's been mentioned again since Chi Omega. Do you remember now?"

Joseph thought for a second. "Maybe. But I didn't know that a van was used during the kidnapping."

"Joseph," Brand said, "we believe it was a van that was used. What kind of van did you see the black man driving?"

"A Volkswagen van. It was yellow, too, like Ron's VW."

"Which Ron?" Brand fired back.

"Ron Blount, the black man."

"Son of a bitch," Brand said. "You might be onto something, boy. I've always thought there could be some kind of connection between this case and the earlier one. She was kidnapped from there, beaten, and left to die in a park. Do you feel there's a connection?" Brand's tone of voice was hopeful.

"I don't know, um, I really don't know what the vision means. I don't like the fact that my friends are involved. It has to do with the killer, though. That's all I know. I have no idea if it means anything about the other kidnapping."

"Can you come by tomorrow and see me?" Brand asked.

"Yeah," Joseph answered, "of course."

"Write it down, and I'll see you tomorrow."

Joseph hung up and walked out of the booth. He felt that he had betrayed his friends and didn't know why. Maybe they were murderers and maybe they weren't.

After the study session, Joseph went to the music building to practice but he couldn't concentrate. The latest vision about the vans possessed him now as strongly as the dream he'd had of the little girl's rape and murder.

He leaned forward on the bridge of the piano and rested his forehead on his arm. He watched his long hair dangle down, touching the keys and tickling his arm as he turned his head from side to side in deep frustration.

The fear of implicating his friends hung heavily over him. He knew they liked to smoke and sell pot, but that was nothing to the cops now. Catching the killer was their goal. Joseph's intention was to help the police stop the killer before he acted again. He hadn't foreseen that he would be incriminating his friends in the process.

Joseph quickly left the small practice room. He could hear the music of a guitar nearby and recognized the performance style of his friend Ron Bradshaw. He leaned against the wall and listened to the guitarist. He thought how his life had been so innocent just a few weeks ago. Weary, he slid down the wall, slumped to the tile floor, and held his knees.

Ron Bradshaw came out for a break and a drink of water. He noticed Joseph on the floor. Ron was an easygoing kind of guy. His big, white teeth split his thick, light-brown beard. His wavy hair was a dark auburn and long, nearly touching his shoulders. It was uneven and raggedy, like he cut it himself. Ron stood over 6 feet tall and had broad shoulders. His arms were long and muscular and he had long, thick fingers. Joseph often wondered how he could play the guitar so well with such large fingers.

He had a slight speech impediment and a goofy-sounding laugh. When he spoke, he sounded like he was drooling. It was weird to hear him sucking up words. Sometimes, he had to apologize for the spittle that sprayed when he spoke.

"Hey, Joe," he greeted.

Joseph stood and they shook hands.

"You got any more of those atomic brownies?" Ron was referring to the Thanksgiving party where potent marijuana brownies had been served. When Joseph didn't respond, he said, "Hey, what's bothering you, man? Why the troubled look?"

Joseph smiled weakly. "Just some personal problems I'm having. Nothing I want to talk about."

"Is it women problems or school?" Ron asked.

"Neither, really. Just some shit I need to work through."

"Well, better you than me. See you." Ron went back into his cubicle and continued practicing.

"Yeah, Ron, better me than you, too," Joseph whispered. With a heavy sigh, he got up and walked over to Poor Paul's Pourhouse.

Perhaps a couple of beers will make me feel better, Joseph thought.

Chapter 22: Visions of the Night

Meeting George Brand was either a calming experience or a frightening one, and that depended upon which side of the law a person was on. Brand's demeanor could quickly generate confidence, as long as one had a cooperative attitude toward him.

He was a funny man with a storehouse of jokes, but he was also a large man who could easily intimidate the worst criminals.

At times, he was a difficult man to read. He was adept at concealing his thoughts with a practiced, almost bored, blank expression. He was an excellent poker player and used this skill to great effect. He was a third-generation resident of Leon County, and he had no intention of living or dying anywhere else. He called women "ma'am" and opened doors for them. He was deferential and respectful to all people, as long as they treated him with the same regard. He was the consummate Southern gentleman.

Joseph enjoyed the manners of the enormous man. He had come to trust the lieutenant.

On the gloomy, overcast morning after the Dorman Hall vision, Joseph arrived at the command post. Carol greeted him with her usual friendly courtesy. She let Brand know Joseph had arrived. When Brand came out to get him, Joseph noticed he seemed *lighter* somehow.

The two men sat in their usual room at the table with the same piles of paperwork.

"What's up?" Brand began the conversation. "You have something new to tell me, don't you?"

"Yes, I do," Joseph said, "but I'm not sure I'm comfortable with everything I need to tell you."

Brand leaned back in his chair, hard. He frowned. Joseph was speaking more cryptically than usual.

"I experienced dreams that have my friends in them. I don't like that. It's not my way to include people that I don't think are involved. I don't want to tell you about my friends. I don't know why they came up last night." He took his glasses off and absently cleaned the lenses with his flannel shirt. "Am I making any sense?"

"I think so." Brand leaned forward and looked directly into Joseph's left eye. He knew now that Joseph was blind in his right eye.

"I have a note for you." Joseph handed it across the table to Brand.

Brand studied the note. It had two names on it. The first thing he noticed was that both names had the initials "R.B."

"What do you think the vision you had yesterday meant?" Brand asked. "Did you know of the Dorman Hall incident before?"

"The one mentioned in the papers?" Joseph didn't know quite what Brand meant.

"The papers didn't know the real story. Last May, a female FSU student was kidnapped from Dorman Hall, beaten all to hell, and left to die in a park on Springhill Road. A dog found the girl hidden under pine straw, half naked. Based on folks we interviewed and some tire tracks we found near the girl, we thought someone in a VW van had kidnapped her. What color are these two men again?" Brand folded the note and palmed it.

"One of them is black and the other is white. The black man is clean-shaven and owns a VW van. The white one has a full beard. It's thicker than mine." Joseph rubbed his rough chin.

"How do you get these visions? I mean, how do you know what you know? Can you explain this to me? Is there something that helps you do this better sometimes than other times?" Brand waved his hand absently. "I mean, what sort of condition are you in when you have these... insights?"

Joseph was unsure how to answer. He didn't know if Brand was asking him if he got drunk or smoked pot before he had his insights. Truthfully, neither of those substances seemed to trigger a vision. Joseph was beginning to believe he was receiving mystical messages from God.

He hesitated for a moment, trying to figure out how to explain. "In the Miccosukee Indian language, Tallahassee means seven holy hills. The entire area has great spiritual value to the Miccosukee people. It is this aura of spirituality that holds most of the community together now in the aftermath of the murders. Even the Muslims regard Tallahassee as being of great importance, almost a shrine, because it contains within it the holy name 'Allah.'

"In our realm, the dead souls rarely speak to the living. It's better that way because it is forbidden for the living to contact the dead. But there is no commandment forbidding the dead from contacting the living," he said. "I think it's okay for us to receive special messages from the world of the dead, like what we are doing now."

"So, this is where you get your visions from? The world, or the realm, of the dead?"

"Yes, that's what I'm saying. And sometimes, I see someone who I know is dead, and they smile at me. Especially in the grocery store."

"What!" Brand was amused. "I've seen a lot of dead people in my life, hundreds probably, but I've never seen one smiling at me in the middle of Albertson's. Now, what the hell are you talking about? Shall I add you to the crazy file too?"

"No, sir, I'm not crazy. Not like those people. You've seen violent deaths, like murders, or people killed in car accidents. You've never seen the death of a person who lived in the grace of God, someone who gave up the ghost to the light of God."

Joseph's assertion was not quite true. Brand *had* seen violent deaths: murders, accident victims, fatalities caused by unusual circumstances, and unexplained deaths by the hundreds. But he'd also seen generations of friends and family members who had died peacefully. Their death masks were different from those who'd passed unexpectedly. The thought of people dying badly struck a chord of sadness within him. He chose not to correct the young man. *He'll have plenty of sorrow in his life.*

Joseph smiled shyly and avoided Brand's eyes. He felt self-conscious about speaking so candidly with the lieutenant.

"Do you have anything else for me?" Brand asked.

"No," Joseph said.

As they walked out the door, Brand asked Joseph, "I'm curious about something. Did you notice that both men have the initials 'R.B.' in their names?"

Joseph stopped in his tracks. "That's it!" he exclaimed. "*That's* the message I was meant to see: not their names, but their *initials*. The name of the killer will include the initials 'R.B.'"

"Well, since they both have these initials, are you sure these men aren't somehow involved?"

"I don't know. I'll have to think about it. Besides, a black man didn't commit the Chi Omega murders." Joseph walked backward toward the command post door as he spoke.

"Yes, but in the Dorman Hall case, we know a black man did it," Brand said. "Maybe your friend was involved in that. Go home and think about it. Let me know. I'm curious to hear more about that."

Brand watched as Joseph pushed open the door with his back, then spun around, leaving with a bounce in his step.

Brand was glad he didn't have to deal with magical thinking very often. He just wanted to sit down and have a shot of bourbon with his friends and forget the whole damn world for a while. He glanced outside. The wind had picked up and the sky was beginning to darken. A cold front was pushing into the area. Lots of rain meant more accidents and pool hall fights. He knew that no one would be enjoying a bourbon that night.

Brand stepped into the conference room and looked at the suspect board. There were no names with the initials "R.B." on the list.

The closest matching name had the initials "T.B."

Chapter 23: I'll Be Watching You

Two days after the Dorman Hall vision, the weather cleared. It was early afternoon. Joseph had just returned home from school. He went outside into the back yard with his friend Melanie's dog, a German Shepherd named Lady. He worked with her nearly every afternoon, training her to heed his hand signals.

That afternoon, Lady was preoccupied and didn't want to follow his commands. She kept growling and barking, despite him trying to distract her. Joseph looked around a couple of times but he didn't see anyone or anything unusual. He and Lady made a circuit of the yard, and then he saw them. Two men stood in the covered walkway between the office area and the chapel of St. Paul's Methodist Church. The men had radios in their hands, and were talking and glancing over at the yard where Joseph and the dog were playing. The men apparently assumed they were concealed.

Joseph stood completely still for a moment, unsure of what to do. He'd promised Brand some more notes. He considered putting Lady on a leash and leaving the house to deliver the notes to the command post. He'd use that as opportunity to sneak up on the men to let them know he was aware of them.

It'll be great sport. Lady can growl at the cops.

He bounded up the back stairs of the house, and then stopped suddenly. He turned and looked back at the church.

Cold chills ran through his body. He smelled burning marijuana coming from his house. He realized in that instant that his actions with the police had jeopardized the lives of his roommates. He had drawn the scrutiny of the cops to his home, and this really worried him.

The phone rang. He was startled and hit his knee on the door. "Shit," he said as he limped into the kitchen and answered the phone. The caller was a mutual friend of his housemates. He wanted to know if anyone wanted to buy some pot.

Panicked, Joseph wondered if the phone was tapped. It was a bad situation for all of them. He quickly told the caller, "Look, hang up and don't call us, any of us, for a while. The cops are hanging around our house, man. They park their cars right next to us in the church parking lot. I hate to say it, but my house is no longer a cool place to hang until this murder thing blows over. Shit, we're only a few blocks from the command post. Things are pretty hot right now." He hung up and walked back to the dining room.

"God," Joseph said out loud. *What the hell did I just say?*

Joseph sat down and typed what he thought was his last written note. He wished Brand luck with the investigation, but said he was finished working with the lieutenant. He was ending the relationship that could compromise the futures of his roommates and himself. There would be no more phone conversations with Ruth or communication with Brand.

When finished, he folded the note and grabbed Lady's leash. He went down the stairs and opened the gate. He signaled Lady to heel, and they began the walk to the command post.

At the edge of the parking lot, Joseph glanced over to see if the two men were still there. They were gone. A lone squad car sat in the parking lot, the officer writing his shift report. The lake glimmered in the bright sunshine.

Joseph stuck his head in the doorway and asked Carol if he could speak with the lieutenant. He waited outside the building with Lady and continued to give her commands.

"Is that your dog?" Brand called to Joseph.

"Oh, hey, hi," Joseph said. "No, she's my roommate's dog. I'm training her."

"She sure is pretty. I like to train dogs too."

"I brought this over for you," Joseph said and handed him the note. "I think this is it."

Brand took the note but was puzzled. "For today? Is this it for today?"

"No, sir. I think I've given you all I can. If you find the van and the colonial apartments, then you'll soon find the man with the initials 'R.B.' He'll be your killer."

"Are you feeling alright?"

Joseph took a deep breath and shrugged his shoulders.

"Okay," Brand said.

The men shook hands and each went their own way. Brand stopped by the door and watched Joseph and the dog walk away.

Inside the command post, Brand read the note. He folded it and set it down on the desk. Someone had left a BOLO report for him.[13] A white Dodge van had been reported missing from the audio/visual department at FSU.

That's a state vehicle; it'll have a yellow tag.

Brand requested that he be notified instantly if the van turned up anywhere. He requested a two-man team of investigators to begin pulling traffic and incident reports. They were to look for someone with the initials "R.B."

---

[13] B.O.L.O. is an acronym used by U.S. law enforcement as shorthand for an all-points bulletin, and stands for the phrase "Be on the lookout."

Chapter 24: Games Without Frontiers

Blink. Blink. Blink.

Joseph wasn't quite awake when he saw the eyes looking for him. He fought the impulse to jump out of bed and flee. Instead, he remained in bed with his eyes closed. He was angry now and wanted to fight back. He watched the brown eyes blinking and scanning, blinking and scanning. The killer was looking for him again.

Mentally, Joseph set up mirrors around him. He positioned the mirrors facing outward so the killer would only see his own reflection, keeping Joseph hidden from view.

He was safe, but only for now.

He knew that if the killer saw him, he would find him.

The command post grew quiet as the search for the killer neared the second week of February. Tips tapered off and the hotline rang less frequently. Leads, deemed unlikely during the first and second weeks of the investigation, were reviewed and run to ground.

Joseph was only one among many who claimed to receive messages in the form of dreams or visions. Brand studied the notes in the file and decided which ones should be scrutinized. Some of the "psychic" leads were hoaxes designed to prank the officers who investigated them. But each demanded inspection. It was possible the killer was playing a game.

One of the most memorable leads came in an envelope postmarked from a little town just north of Tallahassee. The writer said the message was urgent, and gave directions to an area where investigators would find a plastic garbage bag. Inside the bag, they would find the bloody clothes the killer had worn when he attacked the girls at the Chi Omega house and the Dunwoody duplex.

Larry Clark, a red-haired, heavyset deputy, was dispatched to check out the claim. He drove north on U.S. Highway 319 for 36 miles to the Thomasville, Georgia line. From there, he was instructed to turn around on US 319 and drive 5.6 miles back toward Tallahassee. It was a heavily forested area, but the letter said there were markers that would lead him to the bag.

Clark arrived at the specified location and radioed in to the command post that he was leaving his patrol car. As he stepped out, he saw an orange arrow spray painted on the shoulder of the road. It pointed into the woods.

He followed the arrow. It led to another. He moved further into the woods, his hand on his holstered service gun. A bird flew out of a bush near his leg, startling him. He unsnapped his holster. The forest floor was dry, and each step he took was accompanied by loud, crackling sounds. If someone was lying in ambush, he'd be an easy target.

He saw a third arrow. It pointed to a clearing. A bloody plastic bag lay in the middle. It was lumpy and appeared to be filled with something dense. Clark thought the bag might possibly contain body parts and clothing.

He returned quickly to his patrol car and radioed in his discovery. Brand instructed him to cut open the bag with his pocket knife and look inside.

When he did, a sickening stench hit him full in the face. Dismembered pieces of a small body oozed slowly out onto the ground. He turned to the side and threw up.

"Oh fuck, oh shit, it's a dead kid... someone's killed a little kid. Oh shit, shit, shit. I hate this shit!"

Clark braced himself and leaned in for a closer look. A wave of relief washed over him when he saw it was not human. Someone had skinned and dismembered a medium-sized dog. The carcass was severely decomposed.

His relief was replaced by anger at the sick bastard's idea of a joke.

"You're a stupid fucking asshole!" he screamed into the forest.

He cursed the case and the psychic's note the entire way back to Tallahassee. On that day, he hated being a deputy, but he would tell the story for many years to come.

◆❖◆

With the chief investigators running out of answers, the men under them were asked to reanalyze all of the information and evidence they'd gathered. Maybe, just maybe, an important detail had been overlooked during the previous reviews. There were still names on the suspect board. They needed to find the men they had not interviewed and bring in a few that needed to be questioned again. It was time to either rule them out or rule them in.

While reexamining his own case notes, Brand also studied his file on Joseph. He noticed that Joseph did not date his letters, and realized that the only dates ever recorded were on the telephone messages taken by Carol Henson.

Joseph's "farewell" note was final; there would be no more to follow. He also said that in his latest vision, something would happen "soon."

◆❖◆

Poitinger reminded his officers to keep an eye out for green VW Bugs. Katsaris believed that Joseph had been playing a game with Brand. Most of the names on the board had been cleared, and while Joseph's name had never been written on it, Katsaris kept him on his private list. So did Poitinger.

Because there had not been any more assaults, the speculation among the townspeople and the students was that the killer had moved on. Many, including some of the investigators, thought he'd left Tallahassee. Routine bar fights and volatile domestic arguments comprised the majority of the calls law enforcement officers responded to during the weeks following the Chi Omega attacks. These altercations were strangely comforting to the weary police officers. Life, it seemed, was back to normal.

◆❖◆

Owners of the local bars, nightclubs, and restaurants were relieved as students returned in large numbers and spent lots of money. Lively coed crowds shared pitchers of beer, and wine and liquor flowed freely again. Women exchanged smiles with men. The thousands of students making small talk in bars brought the entertainment scene back to life in Tallahassee. Live bands began to play and the dance floors filled with crowds. The students were back and having fun. Three weeks after the murders, Tallahassee was a normal college town again.

But talk and speculation about the killer and what had happened to the victims was an inevitable topic of conversation. It seemed most students had heard details of the attacks, in particular the mutilations of the victims.

The subject of the mutilated bodies would always come up. Everyone had heard rumors of the gruesome details. Most of the stories were expectedly exaggerated but close to the truth. Talking about the unsolved crimes seemed to make people feel better. It also served as a cathartic release and a reassurance of protection for one another.

Despite the imagined horrors with no suspect yet in custody, most students forgot about their fear of strangers. While many women continued to go out at night in groups, some began again to go home with guys they met at parties or in bars, as was typical for the 1970s. Women once again threw caution to the wind and began sleeping with men they didn't know.

One night, Joseph ran into one of his friends, Gary. They'd met through a female roommate who had dated Gary briefly. The roommate was gone, but Gary occasionally showed up at Joseph's to hang out.

Gary was a theater major at FSU, but the joke was that he was really majoring in women. He was a good-looking guy with long brown hair and a well-groomed beard. He had the body of a track star, which he had been in Pensacola, and he had the Southern accent of that Gulf Coast town. Gary was a go-to person at FSU: whatever you needed, he knew how to get it... exam papers, drugs, and girls.

Gary found himself with a stunning young woman who seemed interested in him, but she had come with a friend and they did not want to ditch her at the bar. Gary saw Joseph playing on one of the pinball machines and thought his friend was the answer to his prayers.

"Hey, Joseph!" Gary yelled above the rock 'n roll band. "You alone?"

"Yeah, what are you up to? How've you been?" They shook hands and Joseph continued with his game.

"Just hanging out," Gary said, "but I need a favor and I'll make it worth your time and trouble."

Joseph lost the game and picked up his beer. He moved out of the way as another young man inserted a quarter and began a game.

"What do you need," Joseph asked.

"I've got kind of a problem tonight. See, I met this girl, she's a knockout, but she's here with a friend. They walked over here, across campus, and my girl doesn't want to leave her friend alone, and her friend doesn't want to leave yet. I'm on foot too."

"So you want me to hang out with her, then take her home?"

"That's the idea, man."

"Sure, I'll be happy to. I haven't talked with a new girl for weeks."

Gary reached into his shirt pocket and pulled out a neatly rolled marijuana cigarette. He put it into the pocket of Joseph's plaid flannel shirt. "There you go, man. Thanks for helping me out."

"No problemo," Joseph said. He made certain the joint was pushed down into the bottom of the pocket. He did not want it hanging out for everyone to see. "You want to introduce me?"

Gary led Joseph to a table where two women were drinking beer and talking. One of them looked like she did some modeling. Joseph had seen her around campus. She had waist-length brown hair and blue eyes. Her friend, the one Joseph suspected would be his date, was chubby with short red hair and freckles. She was cute, but not his type.

"Joseph," Gary said, "I'd like you to meet my friends, Anna and Mary Alice."

Joseph shook hands with the girls and sat down with his beer. He wondered how long it would be before Gary and Anna left him alone with Mary Alice.

One song played on the jukebox and the four made small talk. A second song came on and Gary stood up. "We're gonna get some air, man."

"Will you be okay?" Anna said to Mary Alice as she stood and slipped into her fur-lined suede jacket.

Joseph looked her up and down. *Man, Gary has all the luck.*

Mary Alice nodded. "I'll be okay." She looked at Joseph. "Right?"

Joseph smiled at Mary Alice. "I'll make sure you get home safe and sound. I've got my car here, so you can ride in style." He laughed. His car was anything but stylish.

Gary and Anna left, and Joseph sat back down at the table across from Mary Alice.

"Would you like another beer?" he asked. "I'm going to get one..."

"You really don't have to," she said. "I didn't mean to be dumped on you. I know I was in their way. You don't have to do this."

"Please have a beer with me," Joseph said. "I really haven't spoken to anyone new in weeks. Life has been pretty lonely since the murders."

He went to the bar to order the beers. He looked at the stools near the television and saw the one he'd sat on during the Super Bowl, when he first learned of the Chi Omega assaults. A lot had happened to him in the weeks since that night.

He ordered a pitcher and returned to the table. They made small talk and danced a couple of times. The band was not very good, but they were loud and played songs by the Rolling Stones, The Beatles, Jackson Browne, Fleetwood Mac, and the inevitable anthem of the South: Lynyrd Skynyrd's "Free Bird." The dance floor was jammed with students dancing wildly. Long hair flew around the room. It was a normal Tallahassee night, the first since January 14th.

Joseph noticed the pitcher was nearly empty. "Another?" he

asked.

Mary Alice looked around the room and her face became somber. "No," she said. She reached across the table and touched Joseph on the arm. "Listen, Joseph, I'm pretty psychic. I think the killer is back in Tallahassee now. He may even be close by. I think we should get out of here."

Joseph was momentarily surprised by what she said. *Another psychic?* He wondered if he should reveal his visions to Mary Alice.

"You know, I felt that today as well," Joseph said. "I mean, just today I had that same thought, that he was back in Tallahassee." He couldn't believe his openness. He rarely spoke about his visions with anyone.

"It's weird," she said. "I can't believe we're having this conversation, can you?" She pulled her jacket up around her shoulders. "I feel a little creepy talking about him here."

"Me too." Joseph got up from his seat across the table and sat next to Mary Alice. "I couldn't feel him for quite some time. He didn't seem to be here anymore. And then this morning, I knew he was back."

"It's too scary here. I feel him here, somewhere near. Would you like to go back to my place and play backgammon?" she asked.

Joseph looked around. A tall man with a long, sharp nose and dark-brown, wavy hair sat at the bar, nursing a beer and staring at the dance crowd. He was alone. Alarms began ringing in Joseph's head.

He reached for his beer and finished it. "Sure, I'd love to play some backgammon. Can you control the dice, too?" he asked jokingly.

"Most of the time," she said, a challenge in her voice. She finished her beer and said, "Come on, let's go."

Joseph looked back at the bar for the man he had seen. The bar stool was empty. He was gone.

The air was freezing when they exited the warm bar. They walked briskly to Joseph's green VW and stayed in the lot for a few minutes, waiting for the car's heater to warm up. Mary Alice directed him to her place on the other side of the campus. It was just west of the Chi Omega house and northeast of Cheryl Thomas's Dunwoody Street duplex.

Joseph parked and they walked up the exterior stairs to her apartment on the second floor. They rushed inside to escape the cold.

Mary Alice's apartment was furnished with third-hand wooden tables and a tie-die décor. The living room was filled with potted plants and boards placed on cinder blocks that served as bookshelves. The shelves were filled and there were books strewn on tables, chairs, counters, and even the floor.

Someone is a serious reader, Joseph thought.

A door led to the hallway, which opened to a bedroom and a bathroom. Mary Alice and Anna shared the one-bedroom apartment.

There was a small couch in the living room. It was pushed against the wall behind a coffee table. A bean bag provided another place to sit. A TV set and stereo were perched on a stand next to the wall that separated the main room from the kitchen area. It was a small apartment, but it *felt* comfortable.

Mary Alice removed her coat and Joseph laid his across a kitchen chair. She asked him into the bedroom, where they sat on the floor. She wanted to share some of her pot with him.

As they smoked, she talked about her boyfriend who lived in Gainesville. She explained that he couldn't make it to Tallahassee that weekend and she was afraid to be alone. She told Joseph that she was often alone in the apartment, as Anna had numerous boyfriends and spent many nights away. Mary Alice's boyfriend had come to Tallahassee right after the murders and stayed with her for nearly a week, but he had to leave to get back to school.

The room was filled with brightly colored glass ornaments, mostly of animals, and she had a mug collection from all of the towns she had ever visited. She showed Joseph a few of her favorites.

Mary Alice pulled out a backgammon set from under her bed. They went into the kitchen and set up the board on the small dining table. The garbage can overflowed with empty beer bottles, paper plates, and pizza boxes. She said if it bothered him she would take it out to the dumpster. Joseph said he'd take it down when he left.

They played a dozen or so games of backgammon. Joseph won most of them.

"I usually win," Mary Alice said. "You're pretty good."

"I am tonight. One more game, okay?" He began setting up the board.

Mary Alice looked up from the board at Joseph. She began to shake as if she were having a seizure.

"What's wrong?" Joseph asked. "Oh, my God. Are you alright?"

Mary Alice was crying. "I really don't know who you are," she said, "and all of a sudden I'm really scared. And, what's wrong with your eyes? They seemed normal, but now they're really weird."

She jumped up and grabbed a baseball bat.

"You need to leave. Right now," she said.

Joseph stood up slowly. On top of the beers he'd had at the bar, he was stoned. His glass eye always closed up when he drank too much or got high, and he swayed as he got to his feet. He stood by the table and steadied himself.

"Stay away from me, please!" Mary Alice screamed. She pushed herself against the wall as far from Joseph as the room would allow.

"Please, Mary Alice. I'm sorry I've frightened you." He swallowed. "I have a glass eye," he said, looking at her with a mortified expression. "When I drink or get stoned, it can close up and make me look really strange."

He took his glasses off and tapped his prosthetic eye with the frame. The clicks resounded throughout the room.

Mary Alice covered her mouth. "Oh, I'm so sorry. I didn't realize. Oh, my God, I didn't mean to freak out like that."

She put the baseball bat down and walked slowly toward him. She put her hands on his arms and started rubbing them to comfort him.

"I guess I really embarrassed you, didn't I?" she said softly, still rubbing his arms and hands. "*I'm* embarrassed."

"It's okay, really." He backed away from her, picked up his jacket, and began to put it on. "I'm sorry I scared you... I think I'll head on home."

"Please don't go, Joseph. I'm really sorry."

"I've had too much to drink, and then we smoked the pot. If I don't go now, I'll pass out right here," he said. He felt gloomy at the way the evening had turned out. "It's late. It's almost 3 in the morning."

Mary Alice offered to let him sleep on the couch, but he declined. He knew he had to leave the apartment. She apologized once more as Joseph gently kissed her on the cheek and left.

He drove slowly past the Chi Omega house.

The killer is back.

He had suspected it since he'd had the dream of the killer's eyes, and now he was certain. Mary Alice had confirmed it for him.

Joseph drove home carefully, under the speed limit but not too slowly. He came to full stops and used his turn signals. He didn't want to get pulled over and have to explain his condition to anyone, *especially* to Brand.

Once he was safe at home, Joseph went immediately to his room. He stripped off his clothes and flopped into bed. The room spun as he closed his eyes.

Chapter 25: Darkness on the Edge of Town

Joseph opened his eyes and looked around the room. He was still slightly drunk from the night before and clearly not ready to take on a new day. His mind wandered for a few moments and then he began trying to remember something.

What day is it?

He thought back to his activities of the day before. He tried to piece the puzzle together. He knew something important had happened, but he could not recall what it was.

"Oh, shit. What a night."

He crawled out of bed. As he brushed his teeth, he had a quick vision of the lone man seated at the bar. He dressed quickly and headed around Lake Ella toward the command post. He nearly ran there. He jerked open the glass door and hurried to Carol's desk.

She smiled and said Brand was already on his way. She'd seen Joseph coming and had already buzzed him.

"Why do you look so worried?" she asked.

"I had something strange happen to me again. I need to tell Lieutenant Brand."

The reception area was empty for the first time. Usually, there were at least a few people sitting around, but this time Joseph was alone with Carol. He noticed packing boxes taped and placed near the door.

"Come on back," Brand said, pointing into the interrogation room. "Carol, hold all my calls, please."

"Yes, sir."

Brand was standing, waiting to close the door behind Joseph. He pointed to the chair in front of the covered window. It was the first time Joseph had sat with his back to the window. Brand sat on a folding chair, legs spread wide, and leaned it back on its rear legs.

"What's up? I haven't heard from you for a couple of days,"

Brand said. *I wasn't expecting to hear from you again*, he thought.

"I have something important to tell you," Joseph began slowly. "I was with some friends last night at a bar on Tennessee Street. They were psychic friends, people like me. They confirmed what I was feeling."

"What's that?"

"The killer's back in Tallahassee. He had left. Now he's back." Joseph looked at Brand with a troubled expression.

Brand came to attention. He rested his massive arms on his knees. He stretched out his thick neck and squinted. "Are you sure?" he asked.

"Yes, sir," Joseph answered. "He left town. He went someplace else. He was gone, and now he's back in Tallahassee, somewhere close to where I told you to look for him. You *must* put your men back out there to keep an eye on the neighborhood and watch the bars again. You'll see him if you do. You'll have him in your hands. Put your men back on the streets."

Brand sat quietly for a moment. "I don't know if that's possible."

"You must! He's back in town. He's just as I told you, an all-night person, good-looking, clean-cut." Joseph became more forceful. "I don't know how to make this any clearer to you. He left town and came back. Please put your men back out there. You'll catch him if you do."

"Alright, I'll see what I can do," Brand said. "Look around you, though. See those boxes?"

He pointed to several empty packing boxes in the corner and Joseph nodded.

"Son, the command post is closing down over the next few days. Most of the investigators have gone back to their regular duties. It'll take an act of God, or the sheriff, to put investigators back onto the streets."

"But you haven't caught the killer yet. Have you given up?"

"No. But we don't need this building and we certainly don't need the media hanging around. We're getting back to real life. If you need to see me, call this number."

He jotted down a telephone number on the edge of a piece of paper. He tore it off and handed it to Joseph.

"You'll need to call before you come by from now on, just to see where I am." Brand stood. "Anything else?"

"Yes, soon, real soon, we'll have him. I feel it," Joseph said. "He's here now and I am close to knowing exactly where he is. You'll have him soon."

"I sure hope so," Brand said, opening the door for Joseph. "Call me if anything else comes to you. And please remember to write things down."

Brand remained in the doorway. He leaned against the door frame. His arms were folded against his chest.

"I don't like to write these things down. I prefer to tell you in person," Joseph said, walking backward down the hallway.

"Okay, whatever works for you." He watched Joseph leave the building.

Carol said goodbye to Joseph as he left.

"I think I'm about to become very unpopular around here," Brand said to her.

"Why's that, George?"

"Because I'm going to increase the surveillance again. Get the sheriff and Jack Poitinger on the phone."

"Yes sir," Carol said. "What's the message?"

"Ask them to meet me here as soon as possible."

By the time Katsaris and Poitinger arrived, Brand had outlined a surveillance strategy.

"These last few names on the board are here because we don't know where these men are. I have some new information that the killer may have left town but has come back. If this is the case, I think we should put some men in the area and see if we can find him."

"The hippie told you this?" Katsaris asked. "I don't know, George. I don't know if I want to pull assets and put them back there just so your hippie psychic knows how easy it is to manipulate us, especially you."

"But what if he's right?" Brand said. "What if the killer has come back and is going to strike again? We're closing the command post and reducing manpower back to pre-Chi Omega levels, and some people have been quite critical about this. If there's another attack, the mayor, the governor, and the president of FSU are going to come after you and hang you in the middle of the student union."

Poitinger laughed, but he knew they had no other choice than to put teams back in the area of the Chi Omega house. "I think George just called the next play, Ken. How do you want to lay it out?"

"Well, sir," Brand said, pointing to the diagram he'd drawn on the board next to the remaining suspect names. "If we increase surveillance in two areas, about one mile surrounding the Chi Omega house, and then around Dunwoody, I think we'll catch this guy. We're going to have to stop everyone going back into the neighborhoods, make them show ID, and wait for the killer to make a wrong move."

"Are you talking about a 24-hour roadblock?" Poitinger asked. "We're going to pick up a lot of drunk kids coming home from the bars."

Brand nodded.

"Do we still have some residents who haven't been interviewed?" Katsaris asked. "We could put a team in there, early evening, and have them knock on some doors."

"I think there are a few," Brand said. "I'll check on that. We can use that as our cover for putting more people in the area, at least during the day and the evening. I want the night teams manning checkpoints for IDs, but I want the majority of the men to keep a low profile by hiding in the bushes."

The three men laughed.

"Maybe if we're really lucky," Brand cut in, "we might see the killer stalking his next victim."

Katsaris smiled grimly. "Let's do it, then."

The three task force leaders knew they would need tremendous manpower to make a workable security net that would trap everyone entering the target area. The dragnet was placed in the areas around the Chi Omega house and the Dunwoody duplex. Brand used the distance suggested by Joseph during their first meeting. He extended the circumference by several blocks in all directions. The surveillance would begin immediately.

Later that evening, Brand briefed the officers assigned to the watch. "Every person seen in the area will be stopped and checked. Everyone, whether they're on foot or on a bicycle or in a car, must show identification. If they don't, hold them until they can produce proof that shows who they are. You are to document every person you stop."

"Females too?" one officer asked. "Or just the men?"

"Ask the women if they're okay, where they live, and if they need help going home. It's okay if they don't have ID. But they shouldn't be out alone, and if they are, they need to be taken home by an officer, for their safety. The Chi Omega attacks and the kidnapping at Dorman Hall occurred around 3 a.m. That time may be crucial for us. Our killer knows how to make himself invisible, especially at night when people are most vulnerable. Look for him in the shadows. Everyone is a suspect. We have one week to catch him."

"And watch for green Volkswagens," Poitinger said.

The men who knew about Joseph laughed.

Chapter 26: Look At You Look At Me

The visions Joseph had experienced since the Chi Omega attacks continued for nearly a month. Many he could not decipher, but he saw the eyes looking for him nearly every time he closed his own. He questioned his sanity because of these hallucinations and wished he had someone he could speak with about what he was experiencing. Except for Ruth, whom he refused to deal with, Joseph could think of no one he could trust other than Brand.

He stood in front of a large picture window and watched a thunderstorm as it rumbled through the town. A crack of lightning flashed, accompanied by a boom of thunder so close it rattled the window. Joseph closed his eyes.

The eyes of his visions found him and looked directly at him. They blinked, then stared into his own.

Terrified, Joseph wanted to open his eyes to stop the vision.

He heard a voice whisper to him.

Look.

He forced himself to look at the killer. Joseph saw the face for the first time.

The killer was a white man. He was older than Joseph and had light wrinkles beginning to form around his eyes. He had a long, sharp nose. He was clean-shaven. He wore a knitted ski cap. He had dark-brown hair and dark-brown eyes.

The killer stared back at him.

The two men were so close that they could have been sitting across from one another in a restaurant. They were *telepathically* linked. Joseph knew now that the killer was a powerful psychic.

This realization scared the shit out of him.

What if the killer can see my face?

Joseph broke the vision. Rain pounded furiously against the window. He was freezing. He went to the kitchen to call Brand.

When Carol answered, he told her that he needed to see Brand. She told him to come on by and that they were still at the command post.

"Tell him I saw the killer's face."

He grabbed his coat and an umbrella. The rain fell in a steady drizzle. The day was dark and cold; the walk around the lake was disquieting. He walked quickly along the eastern shore to the command post. He turned around from time to time to make certain no one was following him. The glassy surface of the lake was dimpled with millions of spreading circles.

The command post was warm inside and Carol smiled when he walked in. "He'll be right with you," she said. "Please sit down. May I get you some coffee?"

Her kindness nearly made him cry. He wished he could hug her because he felt so alone and so lost.

Brand motioned to him from the hallway, by the door to their customary meeting room. Joseph entered the room and sat down in his usual chair. The room was empty except for the folding table and two chairs. All of the file folders were gone. In their place were several square Polaroid instant camera photos turned face down.

"Do you have something for me?" Brand asked.

"I saw his face. I had a vision of his face. If you show me some pictures, I can pick him out. Right now. Please, let me try."

Brand looked at Joseph for a few seconds. "Okay." He picked up one of the photos from the table and showed it to Joseph.

"Is this the face you saw?" Brand asked.

The photo was of Ron Eng, the Chi Omega houseboy. Eng was another musician friend of Joseph's.

"I didn't see a mustache," Joseph said and squinted at the photo. "This is not the killer, but it's close. The face I saw is close to his, but older."

Brand threw the photo on the table. "That's just what the girl said. Anything else?"

"Yes," Joseph said. "The person in this photo doesn't have a 'B' in his last name."

"How do you know the killer's last name begins with the letter 'B'?"

"Because it does." Joseph was confident about this. "Remember the vision of the two Rons with the vans? 'R.B.' You put that together, and once you did, we knew the initials of the killer."

Brand nodded.

"Did you know that I know Ron Eng?" Joseph asked.

"I figured as much." Brand smiled. "Shit, Joseph, Eng's a musician and he goes to school with you. You probably know most of the musicians in town, don't you?"

"It seems that way," Joseph laughed.

There was a sharp rap on the door and it was pushed open. Joseph turned around and caught a glimpse of Sheriff Katsaris.

Brand was immediately on his feet toward the door. "Wait here," he said to Joseph.

Joseph sat alone, reflecting about the face he'd seen and the photo of his friend, Ron Eng. He was upset that Eng's photo had been shown to him. He knew that Ron was innocently tangled up in this terrible tragedy because he worked at the Chi Omega house and looked like the killer.

"What's the kid talking about?" Katsaris asked Brand.

"He's telling me what the killer looks like and I'm showing him some photos," Brand whispered.

"Any luck?"

"No, not yet, but he said the guy will look like Eng, only older, without the mustache."

"We know that already. He's wasting your time. Rough him up a little. Let's see if he's just trying to play games with us or if he's trying to cover something up, like a body."

"Yes, sir," Brand said.

Brand quietly entered the room and stood behind Joseph. The psychic turned around and looked at the lieutenant. Brand crossed the room. He was no longer friendly; he was cool and professional.

"Joseph, look at me," Brand commanded. Joseph did as he was told. "Did you kill someone?"

"No. No, sir." Joseph was shocked by the question. His jaw suddenly hung slack and a knot twisted in his stomach. He stared at Brand and waited for the cop's next move.

Brand clenched his jaw and his fists. It was the first time Joseph had seen him angry.

"Are you sure?" Brand asked. "Are you certain you haven't killed someone?" Brand slammed his fist on the table. Joseph nearly fell off his chair.

"No, no. I didn't kill anyone. I could never kill anyone," Joseph said.

"Are you sure you didn't kill someone and dump the body somewhere for us to find?" Brand asked.

The room was spinning. Joseph felt unbalanced, like he was drunk. "No, sir," he managed to say.

"Are you aware that you are a suspect?" Brand asked in a quieter voice. "One of our prime suspects?"

"I thought maybe someone might think that." Joseph's tongue was thick and he was talking through a bad case of cottonmouth. "But not you. I didn't think you would think I was a suspect."

"Why are you really doing this?" Brand said, raising his voice again.

"To help." Joseph could barely breathe.

"What did you think would happen if we found what you gave us? Telling us to set up roadblocks in a certain area?" Brand stared at Joseph. "You're a smart boy, aren't you, like the way you described the killer?"

"But I didn't do anything."

Brand was questioning him like the cops had found something.

"Where were you the night of the murders? I've never asked you that before." Brand sat back in his chair, thumping his fingers on the table. "Can somebody alibi you?"

"Oh, God. I have to think," Joseph stammered. His memory

was blank. He could barely remember where he was before he came into this room, much less what he'd done a month ago. "I don't really remember... I... ah... I'm not sure..."

He wanted to get up and run out of the room but he didn't think his legs would support him.

"This isn't looking good, is it?" he asked.

Brand remained quiet.

Joseph understood the situation. Brand had just been asked to interrogate, then arrest him. It was time. Brand had stopped asking questions. Joseph was paralyzed. He had known the possibility of arrest but had never really believed it would happen.

Am I going to be arrested?

He took a deep breath and swallowed. "Now what?"

"Son, go home. When you can remember where you were that night, call me, okay?"

Brand stood up and reached into his shirt pocket for a cigarette.

"Yes, sir," Joseph said. He stumbled to his feet.

Brand moved past Joseph and opened the door. He stepped into the hallway, shook his head, and mouthed the word "No." He turned and walked away without saying another word to Joseph.

Several men watched as Joseph quickly left the command post. Carol watched silently as he walked out.

Joseph walked home in the rain. He worried that he was going to need a lawyer and thought he should call his father. He knew his father would be furious that he had gone to the police in the first place and he didn't want to be on the end of that call. He thought of calling his mother, but he didn't want to worry her, or have Ruth, that *yenta* spiritualist, involved again. Raindrops splattered his glasses. Or were they tears? He was devastated.

Once home, he went to his room and laid down on his bed. "Oh, God!" he cried out. "I thought I was helping." He began to sob. He wondered when the cops would pick him up and his picture would run in the *Democrat*, or worse, on national TV news.

The phone rang in the kitchen, shocking him back to reality. It was his housemates' friend again, wanting to sell some marijuana. Joseph told him not to call until further notice.

Joseph felt like an idiot. He knew his phone was probably tapped.

They could get me for possession and bury me under the jail for the murders.

He tried to remember where he'd been the night of the murders, but he couldn't. He remembered hearing about the attacks during the Super Bowl, and that was a Sunday. The murders happened late Saturday night, he reasoned. He tried to recall that particular Saturday night and Sunday morning, but little came to mind.

He picked up the phone and called Brand.

"I was home the night of the murders, playing my guitar. I forgot where I was and what I was doing that night. I don't normally go out on Saturday nights. You scared me back there. I couldn't remember."

"Yeah, I knew you'd say something like that. I just wanted to hear it from you," Brand said in a friendly voice. "Joseph, listen to me. You're not in any danger and you're not in any trouble. You hear me?"

Joseph thanked the lieutenant and hung up.

A few days later, Joseph left one more message for Brand. The command post was closed and he had to use the number Brand had given him the week before.

"You'll have the killer in the Leon County Jail by Monday," he said.

Chapter 27: Simple Twist of Fate

The next day, Jacksonville Police Detective James Parmenter called the Leon County Sheriff's Department about an incident that had happened to his daughter, Leslie, two days earlier, on February 8th.

Detective Parmenter told investigators that a man with brown, wavy hair driving a white Dodge van had tried to lure his daughter into the van. The 14-year-old was walking home, waiting for her older brother to pick her up on the way.

As she crossed the K-Mart parking lot adjacent to her school, a man pulled up in a van, wearing what looked like a fireman's jacket with some kind of tag or emblem on it. He told her his name was Richard Burton from the Jacksonville Fire Department. The man wore dark glasses, a three-day-old beard, and his clothing was disheveled. His behavior was suspicious. He asked Leslie where she was going and if she was a student at the middle school next door. Leslie stopped in her tracks and did not respond. The man told her that she needed to come with him.

Because of the rainy weather, Danny Parmenter, Leslie's older brother, had gotten off work early. He did construction work for a company his father owned an interest in. When he arrived at the shopping center, he saw Leslie talking to the stranger. He knew immediately that something was wrong.

Leslie saw her brother and anxiously beckoned him to her.

Danny parked his truck behind the van, approached the man, and challenged him.

"Can I help you?"

Danny was a tall and muscular man. He loomed over the stranger. He was not friendly.

The man looked at him and calmly replied, "Nothing, my mistake." He climbed into his van, rolled up the window, and quickly drove off.

Danny was shaking with anger as he and his sister drove after the van. He managed to write down the van's license plate number before losing it in traffic. Later, Danny gave the tag number to his father.

Two days passed before Detective Parmenter found the time to call the Leon County Sheriff's Department. He gave the license plate number to Detective W.D. Phillips.

Phillips followed up on the tag. He informed Brand that the tag belonged to a Randy Ragan who lived near Cheryl Thomas's Dunwoody Street duplex. Brand felt certain the van in Jacksonville was the stolen FSU van and that the driver was the Chi Omega killer. He was struck by the name the killer gave the girl: Richard Burton. *R.B. again.*

He had Phillips check out Ragan. Phillips discovered Ragan had reported the tag missing. The FSU van was now officially listed as stolen.

Brand asked to be notified about missing persons reports, especially those involving young teenaged girls. Late in the day on February 10th, a report came in about a missing 12-year-old Lake City girl. She had been abducted from a junior high school. Brand's stomach turned over with pain.

"I believe there's a connection between the Chi Omega case and this one." Brand handed W.D. Phillips the Lake City wire report. "It's a report of a teenage girl missing since yesterday in Columbia County."

The news spooked everyone on the task force.

That night, just before he headed out for his nightly surveillance duty, Brand put out a statewide BOLO for the van. The Jacksonville and Lake City reports indicated to Brand that the killer was headed west, back to Tallahassee.

Lieutenant Brand always said that surveillance work is similar to duck hunting. You sit in an area for hours, sometimes freezing cold or wet from rain, your nerves wired on hot coffee and cigarettes, waiting for something to happen. Much of the time, nothing does.

Brand spent several hours in the watch area each night during the week of the special surveillance and checked the reports in the morning.

The officers assigned to the surveillance quickly became familiar with the local residents. They learned everyone's name and face. After several days, they knew many details about the residents in the area of the Chi Omega house. Two of the officers joked that they could write a best-selling book about the sex life of one prominent local politician.

The monotony of surveillance was broken one night when a black man was stopped in a car. When he was asked to show his driver's license and car registration, the man placed his hands on the ceiling above his head and began to scream: "I ain't got no gun, I just stole the car but I didn't kill no girls!"

Officers were startled and drew their guns. Because the man was shrieking hysterically, they couldn't understand what he was saying. Once they calmed him down, they realized what he was trying to tell them.

The man wouldn't get out of the car until the officers promised they wouldn't shoot him or rough him up. The officers were laughing so hard they could hardly make the arrest. They got him out of the car and he offered no resistance.

That week, more than 20 crimes were solved before victims reported them committed. Often, the police would find a thief walking down the street with merchandise in his hands, or spot someone loading a TV or stereo into a car without being able to provide a reasonable explanation or proof of ownership.

Then, on the night of February 10th, and later in the early morning of February 11th, significant reports were filed by two officers who had been working the dragnet.

Around 10:45 p.m. on February 10th, Tallahassee Police Officer Roy Dickey, sitting in his patrol car, watched a man walking east along St. Augustine Street. Dickey could see the man was wearing blue jeans, a red vest, a blue cap, and tennis shoes. As the man passed under a streetlight, he looked at the patrol car. Dickey could see the man's face clearly. They locked eyes. Something about the guy *seemed* wrong to Dickey.

Dickey started the car and followed the man as he turned left and headed north on Dunwoody Street. The man disappeared between Cheryl Thomas's duplex and the house next to it. Dickey did not see the man again that night. He turned his report in at the end of his shift at midnight.

On the very next shift, Leon County Sheriff's Deputy Keith Daws was working in an unmarked Chevrolet Chevelle in the surveillance area on the corner of Jefferson and Boulevard. At around 1:45 a.m. on February 11th, he reported over the radio that he had spotted a man trying to break into a green Toyota sedan.

Deputy Daws eased his car up to the Toyota and stopped just as the man opened the car door. The man had a set of keys in his hand and turned around to see who had pulled up alongside him.

"Hey, there," Daws said. "What brings you here this evening?"

"I'm just getting my textbook out of my car," the man said.

"Where's the book?" Daws asked.

"It's in the car, on the other side, up on the dashboard."

Daws looked into the car with his flashlight and saw a book and a bunch of papers on the floor. He also noticed a license plate from a car. He asked the man to hand it to him.

"Please open the door," Daws asked the man. He noticed that the man had no wallet in his back pocket. "Where's your wallet?"

"I, ah, just came down from my place on College Avenue to get my books. I didn't think I'd need ID for that. I couldn't park over by my place; no spaces."

"What's your name?" Daws flashed his light in the man's eyes, getting a good look, both front and side, of the man's face.

"Ken Misner," the man answered calmly.

"Mr. Misner, where did you get the license plate on the floor of your car?"

"I found it. I just haven't had the time to turn it in yet. I guess you can take it now. It wasn't the most important thing on my mind, you know with mid-terms and stuff."

Daws reached into the car and picked up the plate. "Mr.

Misner, please place your hands on the roof of the car and don't move."

When Daws reached into his car to grab the radio hand piece, the man took off running and jumped a fence.

Daws was surprised by the man's reaction. Everything the man had said made sense, except that Daws thought he looked older than the typical FSU student. The dispatcher came back with the report on the license plate. It had been reported stolen the day before and belonged to a Tallahassee man, Randy Ragan. Someone driving a van with that plate had tried to kidnap Leslie Parmenter in Jacksonville on February 8th.

The deputy filed his report with a complete description of the man who ran from him and the stolen license plate. The report was picked up, along with Roy Dickey's report, by Lieutenant Brand in the morning.

Brand found a listing for Ken Misner in the city telephone directory. He instructed Daws to go to the residence and speak with Misner. The man Daws found was not the guy he'd seen fooling with the Toyota. Misner told Daws he had lost his wallet with all of his identification the week before.

Brand was certain the two officers had come face to face with the killer. He theorized that if they had seen the killer, perhaps the van was nearby too.

"Daws, did you see a white Dodge van in the vicinity when you talked with the mystery man?" Brand asked.

"Yes. There was a white Dodge van parked just behind the Toyota."

"I put out a BOLO last night on a white Dodge van. Why the hell didn't you notice it?" Brand wanted to know.

"Well, sir," Daws said, "the man had been fooling around with the Toyota, not the van, so I never looked at the van... I didn't see the BOLO."

A team of deputies went back to the area and searched for the van. It was gone. Brand and the rest of the officers worried that the killer had put another stolen tag on the van and disappeared.

Brand couldn't believe the killer's luck. Fellow officers questioned how he had known to put a BOLO on a van. They wondered if he was psychic.

When Katsaris came in that morning, Brand told him of the sighting and how a deputy had the killer in his hands. "The surveillance worked. The son of a bitch, we almost had him."

Katsaris was skeptical. "You *think* we had him?"

"I'd bet my badge on it, Ken," Brand said. "I've got a guy who ran from Daws in the surveillance area. He had a stolen tag in his car, a tag that came back as being on a van involved in a near abduction of a teenaged girl in Jacksonville. He disappeared."

Katsaris didn't say another word and left.

Brand now knew the killer was smart, good-looking, and elusive. This was different than the profile given by FBI psychologist Dr. Howard Teten. The official profile had just been delivered the previous day and they had released it to the media. Coincidentally, the report appeared in the *Democrat* that morning.

Teten described the killer as a semiskilled worker who probably did not have any formal post-high school education. Brand disagreed with this analysis. He didn't know how much education the killer had, but he knew the assailant was smart.

Teten also believed the man was a loner and a patron of local bars, had a dominant mother, and lived alone. He concluded he could be wrong about the profile, though. He hadn't kept score of how often he was wrong or right.

Katsaris agreed with the FBI profiler. "The profile lets the sheriff's department know we're on the right track."[14]

---

[14] Whiteley, Michael. "Profile of a loner drawn in killings." *The Tallahassee Democrat*, Feb. 11, 1978, p. 1A.

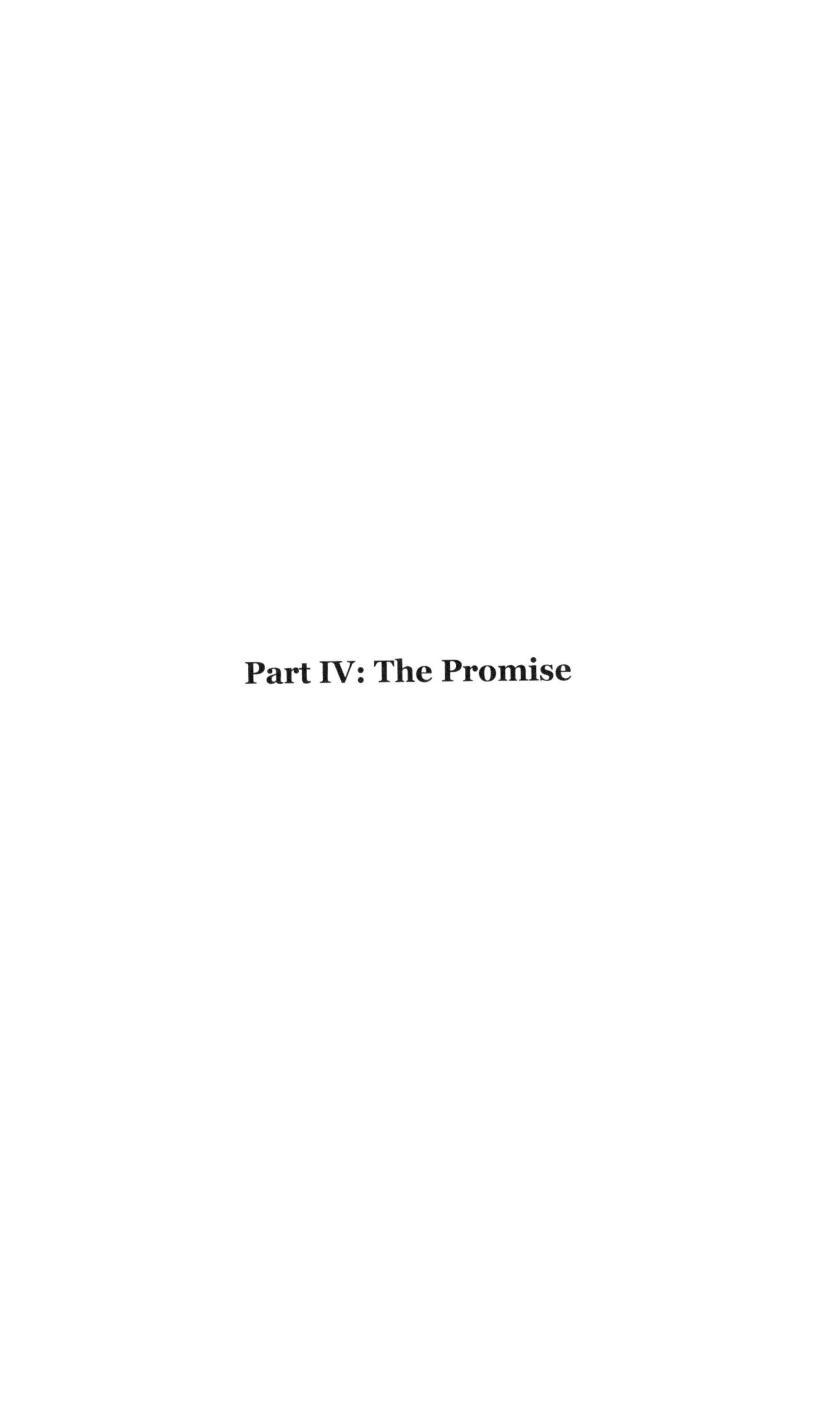

Part IV: The Promise

Chapter 28: I Fought the Law

The week of surveillance was over and the command post was closed. There were four names on the suspect board. A mystery name, Kenneth Misner, had been discovered, but he'd vanished. There was little left for the team of investigators to do but keep a watch on the remaining top suspects.

On Monday, February 13th, George Brand sat in his office at the sheriff's department in the Leon County Courthouse. He had the psychic file out and read through it again. When he got to Joseph's note concerning the dream about the van, he remembered their discussion about yellow plates and the comment that perhaps they should look for a stolen state van.

Brand called Steve Bodiford in his office. "Steve, I want you to call all the state agencies and see if any of them had any white vans missing that have turned up in the last few days."

"Yes, sir," Bodiford answered. "Anyplace special I should start?"

"Yeah, there was a van reported stolen from FSU about a week ago. See if it's come back."

Bodiford left Brand's office and called Captain Steve Hooker of the FSU police to ask him if they'd had any missing vans show up in the last couple of days.

Hooker was surprised. "Yeah, we found one less than an hour ago. It was stolen from the audio/visual department. Why?"

"You're kidding," Bodiford said, surprised. "Where is it now?"

"Over at the football stadium to get it cleaned up. It was filled with dirt and trash, but no other damage."

"No! Don't touch it. It might have been involved in a kidnapping and maybe the Chi Omega murders. I'll be right over. Make sure no one else touches it." Bodiford hung up the phone and ran into Brand's office. "George, Hooker said they found a missing van at FSU less than an hour ago. I'm going over there now to get it."

"You're shitting me." Brand smiled. "Take Bill Gunter with you and get the van over to FDLE for processing."

Steve Hooker was waiting for Bodiford and Gunter at the stadium. The three men examined the van together.

Bill Gunter jumped into the driver's seat and drove the van to the FDLE lab. Bodiford called the lab to let them know they were on their way with a van they believed was used in a kidnapping by the Chi Omega killer.

At the FDLE, Bill Gunter signed the van over to the crime lab and left. The actual processing of the van's contents would begin the next day.

◆❖◆

The same morning Bodiford located the van, Ricky Garzaniti reported his orange VW stolen. The night before, Ricky had stopped by his ex-wife's house to pick up his daughter. When he walked into the house, the movie *Gator* starring Burt Reynolds was playing on TV. Ricky stayed to watch it. When the movie was over at 11 p.m., his VW was gone. One of Ricky's friends suggested that maybe the Chi Omega killer had stolen it. They all laughed at the thought.

◆❖◆

Working late that night and still excited over finding the van, Brand thought about the mystery man, Kenneth Misner. He found it odd that the man seen during the surveillance was fooling around with a small sedan. The stolen license plate found by Deputy Daws was from a Volkswagen.

Acting on a hunch, Brand pulled the reports on all small cars reported stolen in Leon County in the past two days. He then put out a statewide BOLO for the cars, especially Garzaniti's stolen orange Volkswagen. Perhaps the killer had a fondness for small cars.

Brand tried to concentrate on his other cases that needed attention after four weeks of neglect. Every time the phone rang, he hoped it was a law enforcement agency reporting they had caught someone driving the stolen orange VW. Brand's hope dwindled as the hours and days passed and the exhaustion of the past four weeks took over.

◆❖◆

At around 10 p.m. on February 14th, Pensacola patrol officer David Lee woke up with a slight hangover. He'd been drinking beer earlier at a poolside party given by Officer Barbara Potts. She had invited all of the officers who worked the graveyard shift to her apartment complex for a Valentine's Day party. Lee had joined his buddies around 9 a.m. when he got off duty and stayed until late afternoon.

Lee took a handful of aspirin and jumped in the shower. He decided that if he wasn't feeling any better in a few minutes, he'd call in sick. Just before he had to leave for work, he picked up the phone and called his shift commander.

"Hell no, Lee, you're the fourth one calling in sick tonight. I can't let you stay home," the shift sergeant said. "Unless you're dying, you're coming in."

"Three are sick?"

"That's right, and with only three other officers tonight, we're spread too thin. Get your ass in here."

Lee hung up the phone. *Son of a bitch. I should have called in earlier.*

He felt nauseous, but managed to pull himself together. It was a weeknight, and he knew it should be a quiet patrol shift.

David Lee had dark hair, green eyes, stood around 6 feet tall, worked out at the gym regularly, and weighed close to 190 pounds. He was a 6-year veteran of the Pensacola Police Department and knew just about everyone who lived and worked in his patrol areas of 7 and 8, on the west side of Pensacola.

Beat 7 was considered one of the roughest sections of town. It was a large ghetto with black night clubs, drug dealers, and illegal gambling. Lee had been treated at the hospital several times for minor injuries suffered while working that area. Beat 8, also known as Brownsville, was a business district.

At 1:30 a.m. on February 15th, Lee was cruising his patrol car in the Brownsville area. He was making a routine sweep of storefronts on Cervantes Street when he noticed an orange Volkswagen pulling out from behind Oscar Warner's restaurant with its headlights off. Lee knew the restaurant closed around 10 p.m. and he was familiar with all of the employee vehicles. His initial thought was that a burglary had just taken place.

Lee pretended to ignore the VW. He passed the car and continued on for a couple of blocks. He wasn't sure if he'd seen one or two men in the small car. Lee made a U-turn, cut off his headlights, and parked his patrol car. Soon, he saw the VW again, now with its headlights on, proceeding west on Cervantes Street, also known as U.S. Highway 90. Lee followed the VW with his cruiser's headlights off.

The VW turned left, drove two blocks, made another left behind a used car lot, and pulled to a stop. As Lee made the second left, the driver saw the darkened patrol car and took off west on Cervantes Street again, then quickly turned north on W Street.

Turning his headlights back on, Lee pulled up behind the VW and decided at that point to question the occupants. As he called in a 10-29[15] on the tag to the dispatcher, he also turned his overhead lights on.

The VW sped up to 70 miles an hour.

What, are you stupid? Lee thought. He knew those small engines could sustain 65 mph, at best. He laughed to himself. He knew the little manual VW could never outrun his Ford LTD cruiser.

"Just pull over, buddy," he said.

The radio crackled as the dispatcher informed Lee the license tag was reported stolen. Lee now turned on the sirens. The driver of the VW refused to pull over. The high-speed chase lasted nearly 3 miles and took them out of the city limits into Escambia county, out of his jurisdiction.

When the VW finally pulled to the side of the road, Lee maneuvered his patrol car in a standard felony traffic stop position,

---

[15] Police scanner 10 code, 10-29 is shorthand for "Check for wanted."

behind and to the left. He called in his location to the dispatcher for backup.

"We're shorthanded, you'll have to go it alone," the dispatcher informed him. "We've only got three men on patrol. I advise you to proceed with extreme caution."

"10-4," Lee acknowledged.

As he stepped out of his cruiser, Lee drew his revolver and pointed it at the driver. He ordered the driver out of the VW.

"Step out of the car. Step out of the car, slowly, slowly."

The man opened his door and got out of the car. "What's wrong, officer?"

"Just keep your hands where I can see them," Lee said as he watched the inside of the VW. Something was in the front seat that looked like a person slumped over. Lee was concerned that a person could be either hiding in the car, or injured.

"Hey, you, in the car, get out and place your hands where I can see them," Lee directed to the front passenger seat.

The driver lowered his hands below the window, out of Lee's sight. "What's wrong, sir? What's wrong? There's no one in the car."

Lee noticed a TV through the rear window, along with several suitcases and bags. With his gun still pointed at the man, Lee ordered him to step out in front of the VW. "Stand in front of the car. Who's in the car with you?"

"No one. I'm by myself." The driver moved to the front of the car.

Lee leaned down to take a closer look inside. He kept his gun trained on the driver. The passenger seat overflowed with clothing casting shadows throughout the darkened car. No one else was in the car.

Lee could now see the man in the headlights. He pointed the gun at the man. "Lie down, now, face down on the pavement. Do it."

The man laid down flat on his stomach with his arms outstretched. Lee kept his gun aimed on the man. He stepped around and placed his knee in the middle of the man's back, grabbed his left arm, and snapped a handcuff on the man's left wrist.

"What did I do wrong?"

The man seemed genuinely surprised to be handcuffed and on the ground. Lee's mind then flashed on an incident that had happened a couple of days earlier, when a state trooper shot a man who was reaching into his coat for his wallet. Maybe the stolen tag hadn't been pulled off the hot sheet yet and this was a big mistake. Lee knew sometimes it could take a couple of days to remove recovered cars from the National Crime Information Center computer.

Suddenly, as Lee shifted his weight to gain a better grip on his suspect's untethered wrist, the man turned to the side and knocked his legs out from under him. As Lee fell to the ground, the man rolled over on top of him. Lee fired a warning shot into the air. The traffic stop had turned into a very serious situation.

The man jumped up and ran off. Lee leapt up and fired another warning shot, aiming at a nearby building. He wanted to make sure he knew where the bullet went. Lee used his shoulder-mounted radio unit to call for backup.

"Dispatch, this is Officer Lee in pursuit on foot after suspect. Requesting backup now."

The words "Officer requesting backup" crackled in Lee's ears as he sprinted after the suspect.

"Halt or I'll shoot!" Lee screamed. "Halt or I'll shoot!"

The man turned left at the first intersection. When Lee turned the corner, he saw the man running, but turned slightly, looking back over his shoulder. A metallic object in the man's left hand glinted in the streetlights. Lee was certain the man had a gun and was about to shoot him.

"Drop it!" Lee screamed as he leveled his gun at the fleeing suspect.

In his panic, Lee forgot that the third shot in the chamber was a .357 Magnum load. It was standard for officers to load their .357 Magnums after two .38 bullets. That way, an accidental discharge or intentional warning shot would not go through one house or building into another dwelling. If two shots were discharged, then a firefight was in progress and maximum penetration was desired.

As Lee pulled the trigger, the loud explosion of the magnum cartridge surprised him and snapped his hands back.

The suspect lost his balance on the sandy sidewalk and his feet slid out from underneath him.

"Got you, you son of a bitch," Lee yelled as approached the man sprawled face down on the sidewalk. "God, that load was loud enough to wake the dead!" His ears were ringing from the last shot. His heart was beating rapidly.

With the revolver still in his hands, Lee knelt over the man and looked to see where the bullet had struck. He placed his hand on the man's shoulder to turn him over. "Now where's your gun, and where's the wound?"

In a lightning-fast move, the man jumped up and grabbed Lee's arm, pulled him to the ground, and grappled for the gun. The two men wrestled, rolling over and over on the ground in a life or death struggle.

"Help! Help me, someone please!" the man began to yell.

"You're under arrest. Now stop! Stop or I'll kill you!"

Lee was screaming in the man's face, only inches away.

As they rolled in the grass, the owner of the house they were fighting in front of came out to see what was going on. He started yelling at Lee. "Don't you hurt that man, Officer!"

Being about 20 pounds heavier and stronger, Lee broke free of the man's grasp and smashed the butt of his gun against the side of the man's head as hard as he could. The blow stunned the man for a split second, just long enough for Lee to maneuver into a better position.

Still struggling as hard as he could, the man broke free again, but Lee quickly kicked the man's legs out from under him and straddled him, using his weight to subdue him.

Lee put his gun to the man's head. "Move and I'll blow your brains out. I mean it, move and you're dead. I'm mad as hell and killing you won't bother me a bit." Lee finished cuffing the man and then turned toward the homeowner standing next to them. “And you, sir, get back in your house, now!”

The homeowner retreated into his house and watched the scene unfold from one of his windows.

Now captured, the man was motionless, but talking. “Please kill me. Please kill me.”

Lee was surprised by the statement. *This man hasn’t done anything he should want to die over*, he thought. *Mostly*.

Lee’s shoulder radio crackled to life. Clayton Ard, a plainclothes officer, had discovered Lee’s abandoned cruiser. He was worried and called for additional backup.

Lee was winded and sweating. It was an unusually warm February evening. The sky was clear and the lights were bright. He looked around as he caught his breath. He pulled the suspect to his feet.

“Get up. Let’s go.” He spoke into his radio. “This is Lee. I’m alright. I have a suspect under control and I’m bringing him back to my car now.”

He looked up as two marked units from the sheriff’s department pulled up.

“Need some help?” one of the deputies asked as he stepped out of his vehicle.

“Thanks, I’m okay.”

When Lee got the man to his cruiser, he patted him down to make sure there were no hidden weapons. With his hand on top of the suspect’s head, Lee maneuvered the man down into the cage in the back seat and slammed the door closed.

The two sheriff’s units left the scene as Lee and Ard walked over to the VW. Its door was open and its lights were on. A wad of credit cards sat on the floor behind the driver’s seat, in plain view. Lee picked them up and counted 21 of them. Mixed in with the cards were three female FSU student ID cards.

“Son of a bitch, Clayton, look at this shit.” Lee was amazed. “These are from Tallahassee. I think we’ve got ourselves a suspect for the Chi Omega murders.”

"What's that?" Ard pointed to a cup.

"It's from Big Daddy's." Lee shook the cup. "It still has ice in it."

"You'd better read him his rights," Ard said as he got in his car to leave. "He's hot as hell. Better call Tallahassee, too."

Lee found a wallet and a small black book with the name "Kenneth Misner" written in it, along with a birth certificate and a Social Security number. The Florida driver's license had the same name on it: "Kenneth Misner."

After locking up the VW, Lee walked back to his cruiser and read the prisoner his Miranda rights. "Do you understand these rights, sir?"

"I wish you'd killed me," was all the man would say. "I wish you'd killed me."

Every fiber in Lee's body warned him that this man was dangerous. While serious, assaulting an officer was not significant enough to want to die over. Neither was driving a stolen vehicle. As he drove to the station, Lee watched the suspect through his rearview mirror as the prisoner repeated over and over, "I wish you had killed me."

"Were you going to swap tags at that car lot?" Lee asked, knowing that if the man had made the swap, it might have taken weeks before anyone would have noticed the tags missing. Had he spotted the VW several minutes later, its new tag would have come back clean instead of stolen. Lee felt lucky he had seen the man when he did.

"I just wish you'd killed me," repeated the prisoner and fell silent.

When they arrived at the station, the man turned to the sergeant on duty and asked, "What rank is this officer?" indicating Lee.

"Patrolman. Why?"

"Well, he should get a promotion after this."

The sergeant looked at Lee quizzically. "Looks like it got rough. We better get him some treatment. What did you hit him with?"

"The butt of my gun," Lee said grimly.

"What's your name?" the sergeant asked. Lee handed the sergeant the prisoner's wallet and black book.

"Kenneth Misner," the man replied. "I want to talk with a priest. I know my rights. I want to see one now."

After booking, fingerprinting, and photographs, a shackled and guarded Kenneth Misner was taken to the local hospital and treated for bruises to his face.

Chapter 29: Wanted Man

Rather than wait for the morning shift, Detective Norman Chapman was called in to process Misner and the stolen car. The duty sergeant felt that the credit cards and student ID cards were suspicious enough to warrant special attention.

Lee began to worry about what might be considered excessive abuse to his prisoner. He had fired his weapon three times and he knew he'd have to face a board of inquiry. When he got home later that morning, Lee was tired and fretted that his suspect might turn out to be a terrified man who had panicked during a routine traffic stop. Lee *had* approached the car with his gun drawn.

Around 5 a.m. that morning, Pensacola time, Detective Chapman called the Tallahassee Police Department to say that they had a man in custody who had 21 credit cards, all of which had been reported stolen from Tallahassee, and three FSU student ID cards belonging to young women. The Tallahassee police referred the case to the FSU Police Department, since most of the credit cards had been reported stolen from purses in Sherrod's, the nightclub next to the Chi Omega house.

Immediately after Misner was processed and booked into the Pensacola Jail, the duty sergeant called Father Michael Mooney. It was 5:30 a.m. when Father Mooney arrived. The two men spoke confidentially for several hours. The police had microphones in the room, but for some unknown reason, they did not record any of the conversation.

After the session with Misner, the detectives wanted to know what Father Mooney had learned, but the priest told them he couldn't do that. Mooney walked out without ever telling anyone what was said that morning.

By 9 a.m. Tallahassee time, Chapman contacted the sheriff's department with the same information and spoke with Steve Bodiford. "We have a prisoner over here who claims to be Kenneth Misner from Tallahassee. We picked him up last night driving an orange VW, with a Leon County plate, both stolen. He resisted arrest and had in his possession 21 stolen credit cards, along with three female student IDs. We thought you might like to question him."

"Hell yes!" Bodiford said. "Let me get right back with you."

It's the Chi Omega killer, he thought. *It's the killer!*

He ran down the hall into Brand's office and told him about the call.

Brand's face lit up. "I want you and Don Patchen to drive over there immediately and interrogate this man."

"You got it," Bodiford said and ran out the door.

Brand called Katsaris with the news. "Ken, we just got a call from Pensacola. They arrested a man using the name 'Kenneth Misner.'"

Katsaris thought for a second. "That's the guy Daws saw during the surveillance, isn't it?"

"Yep. And he was driving that orange VW I put the BOLO out on."

"Son of a bitch, that's the best damn news I've heard in a month," Katsaris said excitedly. It had been four weeks to the day since the attacks had occurred. "Who are you sending to check him out?"

"Patchen and Bodiford."

"This is great. Get me the *real* Ken Misner now," Katsaris shouted. He had a big smile on his face.

When Misner arrived, his confusion was apparent though he was amused to hear that he had been arrested in Pensacola. By now, they all reasoned that the person in Pensacola was probably the man who had taken his wallet.

Misner, a former FSU track star, was a 29-year-old long-distance runner for the Atlanta Track Club. An Olympic hopeful, he had just finished third in the U.S. track and field meet in Montgomery, Alabama. He confirmed to the police that his credit cards, along with his apartment keys, had been stolen a month earlier. He had received a suspicious phone call from an FSU employee who did not identify himself, asking to verify his name and Social Security number. Misner refused. He also confirmed that there had not been any burglaries at his apartment.

"What I want to know is, why is this guy doing this to me?" Misner said. "It's crazy. And it's going to be terrible if he really does turn out to be the Chi Omega murderer."

On February 16th, the *Democrat* printed a humorous article describing how Misner was in two places at once.[16] The real question lingered: Who was the mystery man in Pensacola?

Steve Bodiford and Don Patchen went home to pack their suitcases. Later that afternoon, they arrived in Pensacola and met with the prisoner who called himself Kenneth Misner.

Bodiford and Patchen conducted a tape-recorded interview which lasted into the night. They confronted the prisoner with the information that they knew he wasn't really Kenneth Misner. They had already spoken with the real Kenneth Misner in Tallahassee. Because the prisoner hadn't had any sleep, they cut the interview short. They resumed the interview early the next morning, before his scheduled first appearance in court.

Several hours passed before the prisoner admitted he wasn't Kenneth Misner, but he refused to give his real name. His public defender had the identifying name on all the paperwork changed to "Mr. X."

After his arraignment on charges of driving a stolen vehicle and assault on an officer, Mr. X requested to make a phone call to Millard Farmer, a staunch Atlanta ACLU attorney who was considered by many to be one of the best criminal defense attorneys in the country. Farmer sent one of his junior attorneys, located in Florida, to see Mr. X.

Bodiford sent several mug shots of the mystery man back to Tallahassee by Greyhound bus, the quickest way to send information across the state at that time. When the photos of Mr. X were shown to Deputy Daws, the officer recognized him as the

---

16 Whiteley, Michael. "Man arrested in Pensacola while he was in Tallahassee." *The Tallahassee Democrat*, Feb. 16, 1978, p. 1A.

man he had stopped on the morning of the 11th who claimed to be Kenneth Misner. Officer Roy Dickey also identified Mr. X as the man he'd seen the night of the 10th while sitting in his patrol car near Cheryl Thomas's Dunwoody Street duplex.

The interviews continued until Mr. X, with his attorney, agreed to give his real name only if they'd let him use the telephone WATS line for an hour.[17] The detectives refused unless he gave them his real name first. It was Wednesday evening before the man conceded and finally provided his name.

"My name is Theodore Robert Bundy," the man said haughtily.

"Ted Bundy. Okay, Mr. Bundy, where do you come from?" Bodiford asked.

"You don't know? I'm Ted Bundy." He waited for Bodiford to recognize his name. "You don't get it, do you?"

"Get what, Mr. Bundy?"

"I'm a famous guy. I'm the most cold-blooded son of a bitch you'll ever meet. I'm on the FBI's Most Wanted list." Bundy relaxed into his chair. "We're in the boondocks here, aren't we?"

"Well, I'm sorry, Mr. Bundy," Bodiford laughed.

"Please, call me Ted."

Bundy was visibly disappointed. He had been almost jubilant as he announced his name. Now he seemed deflated. Bodiford had the Pensacola Police Department call the local FBI office and pull Bundy's rap sheet. The FBI agent said he'd just received several wanted posters on Bundy that day in the mail. He brought them over right away. The detectives fingerprinted Bundy a second time, then compared the prints to those on the FBI posters. The prints matched.

A few minutes later, at 7:30 p.m., Brand's beeper went off while he was attending Ladies Night at the Lion's Club. Steve Bodiford was calling to report the news that they now knew the man's real name. Brand asked the dispatcher to have Bodiford call

---

[17] Wide Area Telephone Service (WATS) was introduced in 1961 as a specialized form of long-distance flat-rate service that businesses used to allow people to contact them toll-free. WATS became the basis for the toll-free 1-800 numbers still in use today.

him at the Holiday Inn on West Highway 90.

"Hey George," Bodiford said excitedly. "We've finally got the suspect's real name. You ready?"

"Hold on, let me get something to write it down with." Brand grabbed a pad and pen off the clerk's desk. "Okay Steve, what's his name?"

"Theodore Robert Bundy."

As Brand wrote down the suspect's name, he whispered "Son of a bitch!" under his breath as he circled the initials "R" and "B."

"Steve, who else knows the suspect's real name?" Brand asked.

"Me and Patchen. Some of the Pensacola officers. The FBI agent. But no one else, not really."

"Great, get me several mug shots of Bundy. Send them on the Greyhound." Brand was elated. "I think we got a break here. Keep it quiet for now. That could mean the difference between making a good case and letting him walk." Brand breathed deeply with relief. "How's your money holding out?"

"You gave me enough, but send more if you can." Bodiford felt good. "This Bundy guy is a real oddball. He was disappointed that we didn't know who he was. On top of that, he only wants to talk at night. Wait 'til you hear the interviews. He's one disturbing individual."

"You don't say? Wish I could be there with you." Brand snapped his fingers. "Bundy, Bundy, no shit. Dee Phillips has a file on Bundy."

"You're fucking with me."

"Nope. His name's been on the suspect board since the beginning. Colorado escape artist. Keep him locked up tight." Brand hung up and stared at the name. "'R.B.' Theodore Robert Bundy. You son of a bitch."

Brand called the Leon County Sheriff's Department and asked the dispatcher to find W.D. Phillips. The dispatcher had Phillips signed off at a local restaurant, the Brown Derby, dining with his wife. He wanted Phillips to meet him right away with the file.

Before the wire services got hold of the suspect's identity,

Captain Jack Poitinger took several of the file photos of Bundy, along with photos of several other men who looked like Bundy, and flew in a private plane to Muncie, Indiana, where he showed the pictures to the sole Chi Omega eyewitness, Nita Neary. Without hesitation, she picked Bundy out from the several mug shots placed in front of her. Poitinger flew back to Tallahassee minutes after meeting with Neary.

He then drove to Pensacola to interview the suspect. After listening to hours of the suspect's recorded interviews, Poitinger was convinced that Bundy *was* the Chi Omega Killer.

◆❖◆

Bundy had memorized Misner's biographical information to the point where he knew everything about him. Bundy, 31, had seen Misner one day near the FSU campus and followed him. They were close in age, and Bundy wanted to stay in Tallahassee. He needed credible ID, so he obtained a certified copy of Misner's birth certificate and used it to acquire a driver's license with his picture and Misner's name. The newest telephone directory was published with two separate listings for Ken Misner. One was for the real Misner, the former FSU track star and Olympic hopeful; the other listed Misner's name with his former coach's address and telephone number. Bundy used the latter address on the duplicate license.

While he did not have enough cash to pay rent for February, it appeared that Bundy had planned to stay in Tallahassee for a long time. His plans changed when the police ratcheted up their surveillance operation during the fourth week of the investigation.

Before releasing the suspect's name and the photos to the press, the Leon County Sheriff's Department showed the mug shots to Leslie Parmenter, the girl who had been approached in the K-Mart parking lot across from her Jacksonville school. She immediately picked out Bundy's photo from the set of mug shots, as did her brother.

The press picked up the Bundy story only hours after Neary had identified the man as the person she saw leaving the sorority house early in the morning on January 15th.

The next day, Bundy's picture appeared on the front page of

the *Democrat* and newspapers across the nation. The papers reported that Bundy was a "key suspect" and wanted in four states in connection with the rapes and murders of 36 young women between the ages of 19 to 24. The 31-year-old Bundy was considered the prime suspect in the murders of eight young women in Washington state alone.

Many Tallahassee residents came forward to identify Bundy once they saw his face in the papers. Some knew him as Chris Hagen, a quiet resident of the Oaks Apartments, a rooming house close to the Chi Omega sorority. The witnesses were able to provide investigators with enough information to piece together Bundy's activities during his time in Tallahassee.

One woman in Pensacola came forward and said she'd danced with Bundy at Big Daddy's and had considered going home with him, until her roommate talked her out of it. She realized she was lucky to be alive.

Another man reported he'd helped pull Bundy's VW out of some deep sand just outside of Pensacola late in the afternoon of February 13th. Everyone who dealt with Bundy couldn't believe how sincere and convincing the man was. Neighbors described him as friendly and helpful. He was charismatic and charming.

As he pulled up to the Oaks Apartments, Brand noticed that the decorative pillars outside were square shaped. The building had been an old colonial-style home that had been converted into a boarding house. He also noted that it stood exactly within the area Joseph had predicted. The Chi Omega house was equidistant between the Dunwoody Street duplex and the Oak Apartments.

Reporters thronged the perimeter of the building. Some were preparing to air their reports on national news programs. Several reporters asked Brand for a comment. He waved them away as he entered the building.

Helen put a quarter into the slot of the newspaper machine and opened the door to pull out a copy of the *Democrat*. She folded the paper and tucked it under her arm. She entered Manny's, a local Greek diner, and took a seat in an empty booth. The waiter brought her a cup of coffee and a glass of water.

"Good morning, Miss Baxter," he said. She smiled. "Same breakfast this morning, or something different?"

Helen took a sip of coffee and looked at the waiter. "No, just the usual," she said and pulled out the paper.

The headline screamed "Murder suspect comes here."[18]

She looked at the photos arrayed across the top of the story. "Oh, my God," she said aloud. "Oh, my God!" She touched the third photo in the lineup.

She read the article quickly, and ate her breakfast of eggs over easy, potatoes, and toast. The waiter kept her coffee cup filled.

When she left the restaurant, she drove to her friend Betty's apartment. She brought the paper with her. She knocked on Betty's door.

"Good, I caught you," Helen said as Betty opened the door. She was in her pajamas.

"Helen! What a surprise," Betty said.

"There's something I want you to see." Helen opened the folded paper. "They caught the killer. Here. Look at this photo." She pointed at one of the shots of Bundy. "Recognize this guy?"

"Wait, wait." Betty pulled her long hair back from her face. "I don't have my contacts in." She squinted at the photos.

"Oh, my God, that's the guy from the restaurant, isn't it?"

"Yes," Helen said. "It is."

The women talked about the last time they had gone out together: Helen and Sharon, Betty and Adrienne. They had met up at the Subway Station, a pizza and beer restaurant on Tennessee Street on Friday night, January 13th.

Friday the 13th, they had all joked.

The four girls had all lived in Osceola Hall, a private dormitory, the year before. They caught up on their classes and finished a

---

[18] Gussow, David. "Murder suspect comes here." *The Tallahassee Democrat*, Feb. 19, 1978, p. 1A.

pitcher of beer with their pizza. They were sorting out the bill when the waitress appeared with another pitcher of beer.

"No, that's not for us," Adrienne said and waved the waitress away.

"Yes, yes, it is," the waitress said and placed the pitcher on the table. She also set down a small vase with a carnation in it. Each table had one, but she brought a second. "Guy over there sent it to you."

All four girls looked over to a lone guy seated at a two-person booth. He smiled and waved. The girls all invited him to share the beer with them. He grabbed a chair from another table and pulled up to the girls. He positioned himself between Sharon and Betty.

Helen was a little miffed. She thought she was the prettiest girl at *that* table, but she soon understood the guy was attracted to Betty. She was truly "the girl next door," with her wholesome good looks and her long brown hair. As far as Helen knew, Betty had not dated anyone at FSU and did not have a boyfriend.

They all talked with the guy. He was slightly older than they were. He had dark, wavy hair that poked out from underneath a knitted ski cap. He wore a heavy knitted sweater, like those seen in ski towns. He had dark eyes and an inviting smile. Helen thought he was cute. So did the rest of her friends. He said his name was Vance Irack and that he was a student at Tallahassee Community College, training to become a paramedic. Helen tuned him out as he spoke with Betty.

After they finished the pitcher, he asked Betty if she wanted to go dancing with him that evening. She considered his offer, thanked him, and declined. She just wanted to go home. She was cold. He offered to escort her to her apartment.

"Where do you live?" he asked.

She ignored him and shrugged into her coat. "Thank you for the beer," she said. "I have a school project I need to work on."

On the way home, the other girls had chided her for not going dancing with the guy.

As it turned out, Betty's decision not to go dancing with him probably saved her life.

Betty looked at the photos in the *Democrat*. "That's the guy from the Subway Station," she said, and pointed to the same photo Helen had.

"Yes," said Helen. "And he wanted to take you dancing."

◆❖◆

Brand met the crime technicians inside the house. The room Bundy had occupied had been so thoroughly cleaned there seemed to be no proof that anyone had lived there for a month. There wasn't a single fingerprint to be found.

The detectives found Bundy to be a nocturnal, quiet, highly intelligent, good-looking, and territorial predator with a distinctive modus operandi. Bundy submitted to over 40 hours of taped interrogations by Bodiford and Patchen while he was held in the Pensacola Jail. Bundy only agreed to interviews at night and insisted they be conducted in areas where he could see the moon.

He chose his words carefully and deliberately, a skill no doubt learned in law school. Bundy never admitted to committing violent crimes such as kidnapping, rape, or murder.

When asked about why he liked VWs, Bundy said it was because they got good gas mileage. He also liked how easily he could hotwire them and remove the front seat.

"Why was that important?" the investigators asked. "Did you remove the seats to store the bodies of the women you killed?"

"I use the cars to carry cargo," Bundy replied obtusely. He liked to pick up his "cargo" in one state and move it to another. He laughed when telling the investigators how this crossing of state lines created jurisdictional confusion between law enforcement agencies in the different states.

When asked about the credit cards, Bundy freely admitted he stole them. But when Bodiford and Patchen asked him direct questions about his involvement in the attacks at the Chi Omega house and the Dunwoody duplex, he would not answer.

"Hey, guys, I like you. I don't want to start lying to you," Bundy said cryptically when they tried to cajole him into answering questions about the January 15th butchery.

By this time, Bodiford and Patchen had spoken with Lake City detectives working on the Kimberly Leach abduction. They had run out of leads and had not yet found the 12-year-old girl.

"Just keep looking, you'll find what you're looking for," Bundy said.

"Where's Kimberly's body?" they asked. "Why don't you tell us where she is?"

"It's too horrible," Bundy answered. He was not yet aware the police had found the van.

Once they were certain they had their suspect, Sheriff Katsaris and Jack Poitinger began the process of transferring Bundy from the Pensacola Jail to Leon County. Pensacola Police Chief Bill Davis thought it was a good idea too, but the county prosecutor, Curtis Golden, wanted to keep Bundy and try him in Pensacola. When Davis pointed out that the jail was old and Bundy was a known escape artist, Golden still protested. However, Police Chief Davis didn't want to be known as the man who allowed Bundy to escape again.

Katsaris gladly assumed custody of Bundy.

◆❖◆

When Bodiford and Patchen brought Bundy to the Leon County Jail, Katsaris was there to meet him. So was the media.

"Now that you're in my jail, you're going to play it my way," Katsaris said gleefully to Bundy.

Bundy flashed a big smile to the cameras. "We'll see," he said. A battle of egos had commenced.

The detectives watched this display of arrogance and worried that the opportunity to obtain a confession from Bundy had vanished. They had established a rapport with their suspect and felt that Bundy had been close to confessing to them in Pensacola.

When Katsaris asserted his power over the intelligent and crafty Bundy, he challenged Katsaris to convict him. The possibility that an actual confession might have been obtained by the cautiously treading detectives was lost in the clash of personalities between Ted Bundy and Ken Katsaris. Each would not concede to the other.

Katsaris made front-page headlines and was interviewed by reporters from the national television news programs. He basked in the spotlight. Katsaris felt confident his team would put a case together that would convict Bundy. The sheriff was certain that a conviction would give him a landslide reelection. His ticket to victory was now safely locked up in the Leon County Jail.

◆❖◆

After the van was processed by the FDLE crime lab, Brand had it driven to see if gas receipts from the stolen credit cards matched the amount of gas used. Officer Bill Gunter and a couple of men drove the van around the city on Capitol Circle, a truck route which completely encircled Tallahassee. They put in the amount of gas noted on the receipts and when they used up the gas, they had driven nearly 700 miles. They knew with certainty that the gas bills paid using the stolen credit cards tallied accurately against the Jacksonville, Lake City, and Tallahassee trips.

The investigators still wondered, *Where else had he driven?*

Fibers and shoeprints found in the van by Hinson and Stephens positively matched the clothing and shoes Bundy had in his possession when he was arrested. Adding to this evidence were the testimonies of eyewitnesses along his presumed routes who were able to associate Bundy and the white van with the disappearance of the Lake City girl, Kimberly Leach. Additionally, bloodstains found in the van matched the blood type of Leach.

While trying to account for the 700 miles of gasoline, investigators tried to tie Bundy to the disappearance and murder of a University of Florida coed. Her body was found in the Austin Cary Forest just miles north of Gainesville. The investigators were unable to establish a link to Bundy.

Still, the Leon County prosecutor wasn't as optimistic about the case as the sheriff's men. The attorney still had no hard evidence. Without a confession from Bundy, the case would be too close to call.

WANTED BY THE FBI

INTERSTATE FLIGHT - MURDER

THEODORE ROBERT BUNDY

DESCRIPTION

Born November 24, 1946, Burlington, Vermont (not supported by birth records); Height, 5'11" to 6'; Weight, 145 to 175 pounds; Build, slender, athletic; Hair, dark brown, collar length; Eyes, blue; Complexion, pale / sallow; Race, white; Nationality, American; Occupations, bellboy, busboy, cook's helper, dishwasher, janitor, law school student, office worker, political campaign worker, psychiatric social worker, salesman, security guard; Scars and Marks, mole on neck, scar on scalp; Social Security Number used, 533-44-4655; Remarks, occasionally stammers when upset; has worn glasses, false mustache and beard as disguise in past; left-handed; can imitate British accent; reportedly physical fitness and health enthusiast.

CRIMINAL RECORD

Bundy has been convicted of aggravated kidnaping.

CAUTION

BUNDY, A COLLEGE-EDUCATED PHYSICAL FITNESS ENTHUSIAST WITH A PRIOR HISTORY OF ESCAPE, IS BEING SOUGHT AS A PRISON ESCAPEE AFTER BEING CONVICTED OF KIDNAPING AND WHILE AWAITING TRIAL INVOLVING A BRUTAL SEX SLAYING OF A WOMAN AT A SKI RESORT. HE SHOULD BE CONSIDERED ARMED, DANGEROUS AND AN ESCAPE RISK.

FBI/DOJ

Exhibit 2: Theodore Robert Bundy's FBI Wanted poster.[19]

---

[19] Ted Bundy's FBI Wanted poster. FBI.gov. https://goo.gl/MSIveV. Accessed Mar. 31, 2017.

Exhibit 3: Theodore Robert Bundy at the Leon County Jail.
(photo courtesy of Leon County Sheriff's Office)

Exhibit 4: Theodore Robert Bundy at the Leon County Jail. (photo courtesy of Leon County Sheriff's Office)

Exhibit 5: Theodore Robert Bundy and Sheriff Ken Katsaris.
(photo courtesy of Leon County Sheriff Office)

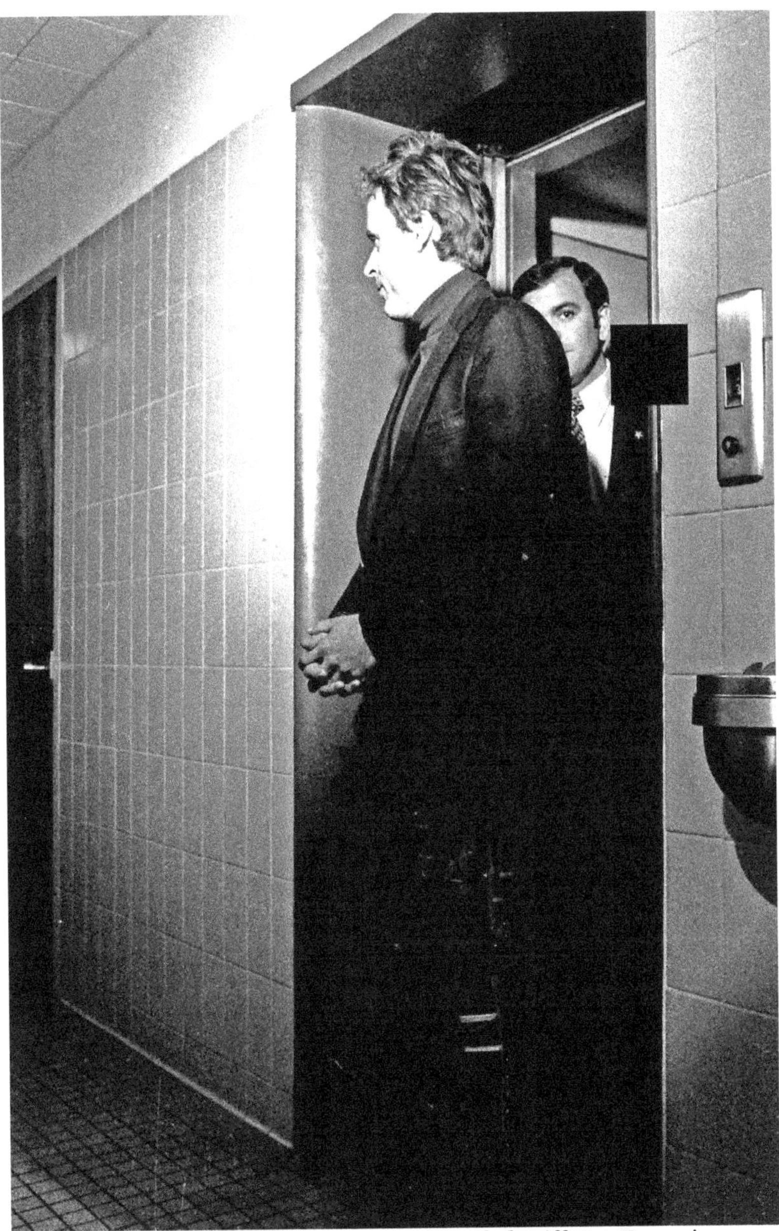

Exhibit 6: Theodore Robert Bundy and Sheriff Ken Katsaris.
(photo courtesy of Leon County Sheriff Office)

Chapter 30: Fish in the Jailhouse

On Friday, February 17th, the *Democrat* ran a small picture of Bundy, grinning, on its front page. The caption under the photo said he was being held in the Pensacola Jail and the article provided details describing his possession of a stolen vehicle and resisting arrest.[20]

As soon as Joseph read the newspaper and saw Bundy's picture, he called Brand. This time, the hotline telephone number rang directly at the Leon County Sheriff's Department. Carol answered the line for Brand's office and asked who was calling. Joseph identified himself and she put him through to Brand.

When the lieutenant picked up the phone, Joseph immediately told him that the picture of the man on the *Democrat*'s front page was the man he'd seen in his vision.

"Did you know I'm psychic too?" Brand chuckled.

"How so?" Joseph asked.

"I just told some folks that when Bundy's picture ran in the paper you'd be calling me," Brand laughed into the phone. "Come down to the sheriff's department in the Leon County Courthouse building. There's some people who want to meet you."

"Yeah, that would be great, I'll see you soon." Joseph hung up the phone.

He drove his green VW Bug to the Lewis State Bank parking garage just off Monroe Street in downtown Tallahassee. The sun was bright and warm as Joseph walked toward the courthouse. He wore his usual straight-leg jeans, flannel shirt, sheepskin coat, and tennis shoes.

The sheriff's department was located on the second floor. The hallways in the courthouse were wide with high ceilings and marble

---

20 Whiteley, Michael. "Suspect wanted in 4 states." *The Tallahassee Democrat*, Feb. 17, 1978, p. 1A.

floors. Light streamed through the large glass windows.

The building was crowded. Uniformed officers crisscrossed the floor from all directions, carrying boxes of files. Small groups gathered to gossip. Joseph felt their eyes on him as he walked down the hall. One deputy stopped Joseph to ask him what business he had in the building.

"I'm here to see Lieutenant Brand," Joseph said.

"Is he expecting you?"

"Yes, sir, he is."

The deputy pointed down the hallway toward two glass doors. A large green sheriff's star with the Florida state seal identified the office.

The receptionist was sitting at her desk to the right of the door. Joseph walked up and asked for Lieutenant Brand.

"And who shall I say you are?" she asked.

"Joseph."

"Joseph who?"

"Just Joseph. Trust me, Lieutenant Brand will know." He smiled at her shyly.

"Sir, please have a seat and I'll call him."

Joseph sat in the green padded chairs with his back to the glass wall and faced the doors he'd just walked through. He looked around the reception area as he waited. He noticed the door to Sheriff Katsaris' office to his right, just a few feet away. Next to the door was a large photo display of all of the previous sheriffs of Leon County.

On the wall to the left side of the glass doors were current law enforcement public relations posters with slogans like "Be Safe and Aware, Ride Your Bike Safely." There were two more chairs under the posters. There was a table to Joseph's left that had a display of marijuana, cocaine, amphetamines, and heroin under glass.

He glanced up from the drug display and noticed Carol as she walked into the reception area. Carol smiled warmly when she greeted him and asked him to follow her. They turned a corner and walked to the end of the hall. Brand's office was across from the elevators.

Brand was at his desk rearranging papers when Joseph walked in. The burly officer glanced at him, walked around the desk, and shook Joseph's hand firmly.

"Welcome to my hole in the wall," Brand said. The room was small with no windows. Light came from an eight-foot fluorescent fixture on the ceiling. There were two chairs placed in front of a utilitarian wooden desk.

The walls were painted a shade of beige and were unadorned of artwork or certificates. Two bookshelves, one to the right of Brand's desk and one behind the chairs, were the only other pieces of furniture. They were mostly empty.

The desk was littered with papers, pens, and a couple of framed photographs. It was the first time Joseph had been privy to any part of Brand's private life. He leaned forward to get a better look at the pictures on the desk.

"When I saw the picture of Bundy in the paper," Joseph said, "I knew you had the right man. I recognized him from my vision. It was exactly like I saw him, except his eyes were blinking in my vision. I'm happy you guys caught that asshole."

"We've got that piece of shit just where we want him, locked up in our jail." Brand beamed. "I don't think we're ever going to have to worry about him again."

Joseph remarked that he had never seen Brand looking so relaxed or happy.

Brand reached for his phone and spoke softly into it. "You got a minute?" he asked Joseph.

The young man nodded.

"Sheriff Katsaris is on his way here to personally thank you. You've done fine by everyone."

They heard footsteps coming down the hallway. There was a quick rap on the door.

"Come on in, Sheriff." Brand stood up. Joseph moved to stand, but Brand motioned for him to remain seated.

Joseph turned around and looked at the doorway. He saw Sheriff Katsaris. Two uniformed deputies stood behind him.

Katsaris was grinning from ear to ear.

"Sheriff Katsaris, this is Joseph, the psychic, who helped us," Brand said. "He's the one who gave us some key things to look for: the van with the state tag, the initials, and the surveillance area."

"You did a great job, son," the sheriff said as they shook hands. "We couldn't have done it without you. Thank you for your help."

"You're welcome, sir," Joseph said.

Katsaris continued to grasp his hand. "I've got a question for you, son," Katsaris said. "How do my chances for reelection look?"

Joseph removed his hand. He looked the sheriff straight in the eye. "Better, much better now, sir."

Katsaris' smile vanished and was replaced by a stony gaze. He had wanted Joseph to tell him the next election would be a landslide victory for him. Instead, Joseph said his chances of winning the election were a disappointing "better." His prize for solving the Chi Omega murders was a lukewarm endorsement.

With a brief goodbye, Katsaris turned and walked quietly down the hall. The two deputies followed him. "That hippie can kiss my ass," he muttered. "I'll show him who's really psychic."

Joseph stayed with Brand for a moment longer. He was unsettled by the sheriff's abrupt change in demeanor. He looked at the lieutenant.

"I wish he hadn't asked me that," Joseph sighed. "Any other question would have been fine."

"Don't worry," Brand said and shook his head. "You did good." Brand was no longer surprised by the sheriff's capacity for conceit. "The best way to get out is to use the door next to the elevator. Just go down the stairs."

They shook hands.

Joseph left the building and found himself in the courthouse parking garage. As he searched for the street level exit, he noticed Sheriff Katsaris walking toward his car.

Katsaris opened the trunk of his car. An arsenal of guns was neatly packed in the trunk. The sheriff turned, acknowledged Joseph, slammed the trunk shut, got into his car, and backed out of the space quickly. As he sped off, his tires squealed loudly and echoed throughout the garage.

◆❖◆

Joseph was relieved the investigation was over and hoped he would never see the eyes of the killer again. He decided to treat himself to a late lunch. He parked in the lot next to the theater school and walked over to the Mecca.

As he entered, he saw his friends sitting at the booth just like he'd hoped. He got into the line and Clyde joked with him as he loaded extra French fries onto a plate.

"Hey, Joseph," Tracy yelled in her gruff New York accent, "you wanna join us?"

Joseph laughed and yelled back, "Where am I going to sit?" He handed some cash to Clyde and grabbed his lunch tray.

Tracy pushed everyone closer together. "Come on, we've got room for you."

People at all of the tables were debating about Bundy. Some people thought he was being framed for the murders, that he was a *convenient* suspect. *Was he the real killer?* Joseph listened to the conversations.

"What are you grinning about, shithead?" Tracy asked.

Joseph noticed that the students seemed relaxed, happier.

"I don't know, maybe it's nice to see my friends now and then." He took a bite of his sandwich.

I'm just glad this shit is over and I didn't get arrested.

"Where have you been, anyway?" Tracy asked. "I haven't seen you around in ages."

Joseph smiled. "I had to catch the killer."

"Oh, bullshit! You are the biggest space-case I know. 'Had to catch the killer,' give me a break. You shit, you." Tracy picked up some fries from his plate. “I swear to God, Joseph, if there was a bullshit contest, you’d win without any problem.”

Everyone at the table laughed. Several people got up and headed back to the music building.

“How’s the opera coming along? Still working on it?” Tracy asked.

“I’ve come up with an underlying main theme,” Joseph said.

“Oh yeah, what’s that?”

“It’s about this guy who has dreams that come true. But sometimes, dreams are really nightmares. Nightmares that come true.” He took another bite of his sandwich. “What do you think?”

“Oh, I like it,” Tracy said. “What are you going to call it?”

“Something biblical, I think.” Joseph stared into space. “Yeah, you know, I was thinking maybe... I don’t know.” He felt self-conscious. He changed the subject. “How’s your recital piece coming along?”

The conversation switched to music classes and their upcoming student recitals. Just like normal. Just like life before the Chi Omega murders.

Life was like that sometimes, Joseph mused.

Chapter 31: Down to the Wire

One of the concerns of a high-profile criminal case is dealing with people who are confessors. For whatever reason or motivation, people will admit to crimes they did not commit. This is one of the reasons investigators withhold a few vital clues from the press, because they need to be able to quickly weed out the phony claimants.

Shortly after the news of the Chi Omega murders broke, several men visited the command post and confessed to the killings. None of them, however, could offer any information other than what had been printed in the papers. The confessors were disappointed when they couldn't prove they were the assailants.

One of these confessors was a quiet man who lived alone a few blocks from the FSU main gate. Initially, the investigators considered him a possible suspect. He rented a room in a boarding house on College Avenue, which was very close to the Chi Omega house and the Oaks Apartments where Bundy had resided. The man seemed earnest and lonely. His version of the murders was also incorrect. He *wanted* to be the killer, yet his story didn't match what the police had found at the crime scenes.

Immediately after Bundy was arrested in Pensacola and identified as the top suspect for the Tallahassee crimes, the confessor committed suicide by hanging. He left a cryptic handwritten note that read "Chi Omega girls, I'm sorry."

According to Brand, the suicide and the note "creeped the shit out of the whole investigative team."

Without hesitation, Brand moved quickly to negate the dead man's possible tie-in to the murders. Moments before pathologist Dr. Thomas Wood performed an autopsy to determine the exact cause of death, as per state law, a local dentist and his assistant were called in to make impressions of the dead man's teeth for comparison to the bite marks on Lisa Levy's body.

Neither the dentist nor his assistant had ever taken dental impressions from a corpse. Initially, both had been eager to assist the investigation, but the reality of the situation quickly set in. Brand hid his amusement at the anxiety of the dental practitioners.

Rigor mortis had set in. The confessor's jaw was frozen in a death mask, which made it impossible to do the dental work. The jaw had to be broken to get a good set of impressions.

The coroner, Dr. Wood, was present for the dental impressions and asked his assistant to break the necessary bones. The loud crunching and snapping sounds of the jaw being broken shocked the dental assistant, who collapsed to the floor and had to be carried to a nearby room. The dentist made the dental impressions without her help. This was "as strange as investigative police work ever gets," Brand later recalled.

The dental impressions did not match the bite marks made by the killer. Still, Brand and the investigative team puzzled over what the confessor had meant in his suicide note.

Even though the dental impressions eliminated the possibility the dead man had committed the Chi Omega murders, some still wondered if he was linked in some way. Was he a second man working with the killer? As the investigators researched the possibilities, nothing surfaced that connected the man to Bundy or to the victims.

Investigators worried that the news of the confessor and his suicide would impede the confession they felt Bundy was about to make. They needed Bundy to confess and they did everything they could to keep the news of the suicide out of the papers. They didn't want Bundy trying to pin the blame on someone else.

Soon after Ted Bundy was incarcerated in the Leon County Jail, the *Democrat* began publishing articles that linked him to at least 22 unsolved murders, and as many as 36 in Colorado, Oregon, Utah, and Washington.[21] There was additional speculation that

[21] Efron, Seth, "Bundy-links to murders unjust?" *The Tallahassee Democrat*, Feb. 21, 1978, p. 1A.

Continued on next page...

Bundy had been in the wrong place at the wrong time.[22]

Bundy's arrest was colossal news nationally. Leon County prosecutors knew the barrage of media coverage could make seating an impartial jury impossible. Bundy was a showman and he wanted to be in front of the cameras. He requested access to the press to tell people he was innocent of the charges he was sure were to be levied against him. Katsaris denied his requests for daily press conferences.

Nationally renowned Atlanta criminal defense attorney Millard Farmer and his Team Defense Project stepped in to advise Bundy. One of the agency's lawyers had met with Bundy in Pensacola and planned to help him put together his defense in Leon County. Farmer felt there was a rush to judgment by the sheriff's department, spurred on by the FBI.

"They are creating an image over him. They just go ahead and say they've got the Chi Omega killer because of his background," Farmer said.[23]

Challenged by Farmer, Katsaris admitted that they did not yet have enough evidence to indict Bundy for the five Chi Omega attacks. However, Bundy had been charged in Leon County with stealing the orange VW he had been driving in Pensacola, and investigators were building cases for the stolen credit cards and the theft of the green Toyota.

Katsaris quietly told Brand that he wished he'd allowed Eddie Boone and the FDLE to take the lead on the tech work at the scenes that night. It was now rumored that Eddie Boone planned to run against Katsaris in the 1980 election cycle. Katsaris knew he had to solve the murders and obtain a conviction or he wouldn't stand a chance being reelected.

As investigators pushed hard in Tallahassee to build a criminal

---

22 Whiteley, Michael & Seth Efron, "Bundy-always in the wrong place." *The_Tallahassee Democrat*, Feb. 22, 1978, p. 1A.

23 Efron, Seth. "Murder link unjust." *The Tallahassee Democrat*, Feb. 21, 1978.

case against Bundy, a team of FDLE agents were working overtime in Lake City, Florida, where 12-year-old Kimberly Leach had vanished without a trace. They knew that a man driving a white van had lured the little girl from her junior high school on February 9th. Kimberly had been missing ever since.

The receipts found in the van were shown to the restaurants and gas stations in the Lake City area along the route followed by the killer. A credit card receipt found in Bundy's possession when he was arrested in Pensacola was for a Lake City motel. Whoever used the card had checked in on February 8th and checked out early February 9th, the morning Leach went missing. Agents showed clerks and waitresses photo lineups that included Bundy. His photo was identified.

The technical team from the FDLE had been able to make detailed impressions of the shoeprints found inside the stolen FSU audio/visual van. They then carefully removed the several inches of dirt and debris that covered the rug on the floor of the van and identified the types of vegetation embedded within the flotsam and jetsam, along with the soil's acidity. The leaves belonged to several species of plants that only grew around the Suwannee River State Park area, west of Lake City.

Search crews, including several on horseback, began sweeping the Suwannee River State Park. On April 7th, six weeks after she disappeared, the body of Kimberly Leach was found under an abandoned hog shed. She was still wearing the football jersey with the number 83 that she had worn to school the day she disappeared. Some of her clothes were lying next to her.

FDLE investigator Terry Bondurant arrived on the scene with Lynn Hinson and forensic photographer Frank Lanzillo at 3:35 on the afternoon of April 7th. They were met by special Jacksonville FDLE agents J.O. Jackson and Jim Taylor. They hiked on foot to the hog shed.

The FDLE technicians dismantled the hog shed before they began the removal of Leach's body. The wood and metal was hauled away to be inspected inch by inch in Tallahassee. Lanzillo took hundreds of photographs.

The medical examiner, Dr. Lipkovic, supervised the removal of the remains from the area. He cut off both of Kimberly's hands and gave them to Lynn Hinson, who took them to Tallahassee Memorial Hospital to have them X-rayed and enhanced for fingerprints to compare with the many prints taken from Kimberly's notebooks and personal belongings.

Her purse contained a brush, several pieces of Bubble Yum gum, an opened tube of Blistex, a bottle of perfume, and a mirror. Her wallet contained one dollar and 15 cents, numerous photographs, and her school identification card. While Lynn Hinson cataloged the items found at the scene, she couldn't help but notice that the little girl had loved flowers. Many of her possessions were decorated with them.

Along with her hands, Hinson took back to Tallahassee Kimberly's scalp and hair, shoes, clothing, eight teeth found on the ground under her head, an earring, and bags of soil samples.

At the autopsy in Jacksonville performed by Dr. Lipkovic, parts of Kimberly's body were removed for further study. Her skull was given to Dr. Clark V. Marshall for dental identification.

Dr. Lipkovic believed Kimberly had been raped and strangled in the van, and killed during intercourse. He couldn't explain the origin of a one-inch wide bloodstain found in the back of the van.

Hundreds of cotton and synthetic fibers microscopically detected in the carpet from the Dodge van were collected and examined. Several matched the fibers from the football jersey Kimberly was wearing at the time of her abduction. Various fibers also matched clothing discovered in the VW Bug Bundy was driving when arrested. Several fibers found on Kimberly's clothes matched exactly with fibers from the coat Bundy was wearing when he was arrested. A knife was found in Bundy's VW. The scrapings from this knife did not match any of the evidence found in the van or on Kimberly's clothes and body.

The night of the arrest, Bundy was wearing a new pair of dress shoes he had bought earlier that day with a stolen credit card. A pair of tennis shoes found in the VW was matched to the shoeprint from the van.

Although Brand was not working on the Leach investigation, he followed it closely. He was intrigued by the similarities between

Kimberly Leach's abduction in Lake City and the failed attempt to lure 14-year-old Leslie Parmenter into a white van in Jacksonville. Both girls attended junior high. Brand shuddered when he thought about Joseph's nightmare vision that described a junior high school, a van, and a young girl with long brown hair.

◆❖◆

Several days after Leach's body was found, Columbia County Sheriff Glenn Bailey paid a visit to Sheriff Katsaris. Brand was asked to join them in the conference room.

Bailey wanted Katsaris to transfer Bundy into his custody at the Columbia County Jail. Katsaris smiled broadly and refused. According to Brand, Bailey was riled by Katsaris' refusal to discuss moving Bundy from the Leon County Jail. Brand said the sheriff told Katsaris, "Let me have Bundy in my jail. I promise you that son of a bitch will never make it to court."

Bailey was adamant that *Southern* justice prevailed for the Leach family. He begged Katsaris for Bundy. Katsaris refused.

"You son of a bitch. Your ego is too big for your britches," Bailey yelled. "I'll see to it that you'll never get reelected. Law enforcement men in the South know how to treat each other. You don't deserve to be one of us."

"Tallahassee is the new South," Katsaris said evenly. "The old days of lynch mobs and conveniently attempted *escapes* for exacting justice are gone. When and if you need Bundy for trial, then and only then will he spend any time in your jail."

Bailey was incensed. He slammed the door and left the building.

"Can you believe that shit?" Katsaris asked Brand.

"Ken, just watch your ass. You sometimes make enemies with that big smile of yours."

Sheriff Katsaris was proud that he had Ted Bundy caged up in his jail. Bundy was a prized trophy, a notorious serial killer who was on the FBI's Most Wanted list. He referred to Bundy as his "favorite prisoner" during a political event. That remark would not be forgotten.

◆❖◆

As the case against Bundy was slowly building, Katsaris understood that they did not have any substantial evidence against him. He knew the key to convicting Bundy was to match the teeth marks on Lisa Levy's body with Bundy's. The state attorney's office agreed. "We've got nothing without dental impressions from Bundy. We can't win without them."

The jailers served Bundy apples, gum, and other foods he'd have to bite into. Guards were tasked with retrieving Bundy's uneaten food, all of which was examined for usable teeth marks. They tried not to alert Bundy to their motives, but no matter what they fed him, they couldn't get a clear set of dental impressions.

Brand mentioned to Katsaris that a basic health examination could be their best solution. "Let's say we take Bundy to the dentist for a checkup. That's not unusual. We pretend that it's a standard procedure for all long-term prisoners in the Leon County Jail."

Katsaris and Poitinger agreed this was a great idea. They worried that if Bundy learned they were planning to take dental impressions, he might smash out his teeth or grind them down on his cell bedposts. They decided Bundy was not to be told until the morning of the exam, and that he would be told only that he was scheduled for a medical exam.

Captain Poitinger spent three weeks drafting a search warrant for Bundy's mouth, which outlined the necessity of dental impressions.

Poitinger knew he had to establish a credible probable cause for the search. He gathered every known bit of information about Bundy and wrote it into the warrant. He traced Bundy's life as far back as childhood in Washington state, and later his adult life in Colorado. When he finished the draft, the warrant was taken to the state attorney's office and reviewed. The attorney general's office then analyzed the document for discrepancies and loopholes.

The morning after the search warrant was approved, Bundy was told he was going to the doctors for a routine checkup.

"We don't want any complaints about not taking good care of the sheriff's 'favorite prisoner,'" Brand grinned at the suspect.

"That's right, Georgie," Bundy beamed. "You'd better take good care of me. You know, when I get out of this place, I think I'll hire you guys to be my chauffeurs. Shit, when I sell the movie rights, that alone will make me rich. I'll pay you guys double what you're making now. I'm a real nice guy to work for, you'll see."

As Bundy was being shackled and placed into a transit van, Brand quietly left the prisoner escort team and drove across town to the Tallahassee Regional Airport. Forensic dental specialist Richard Souviron had been flown in from Miami to conduct the special search of Bundy's mouth. On the way to the office where Bundy had been taken, Brand briefed the dentist on the suspect and what was needed. He gave the dentist a copy of the warrant.

The men who escorted Bundy were excited to be driving him to the doctor's office. They were keyed up, aware that Bundy was about to get the surprise of his life.

The escort officers drove Bundy to a dental office on Thomasville Road. The deputies were ordered to quickly strap Bundy into the chair and to restrict his head movement. They signaled when they were finished.

Immediately, Katsaris, Assistant State Attorney Juan Goodwin, detectives Bill Gunter and Steve Bodiford, Brand, and Dr. Souviron crowded into the exam room. They all smiled broadly at the surprise they had for Bundy.

Captain Poitinger read the subpoena to Bundy. The suspect squirmed in his chair with disbelief.

Brand leaned toward Katsaris. "For a second there, Ken, I thought Bundy shit in his pants."

"Now, Mr. Bundy," Dr. Souviron said as he sat on a stool next to the exam chair. "You can cooperate, or I can use this little machine on you to make these impressions. Which do you prefer?"

The machine and dental tools were handled in a way that made them look like they would hurt. Bundy did not want to be hurt, so he agreed to allow Dr. Souviron to make the impressions.

"Oh, by the way, do you care if I wash my hands, or can I just proceed?"

"You can wash your hands," Bundy said.

It took 45 minutes to obtain Bundy's teeth impressions. Everyone but Bundy was elated.

Several days after the impressions were obtained, Bundy, acting as his own attorney, subpoenaed Brand for a deposition. The question and answer session was held in Bundy's cell at the Leon County Jail.

Brand answered each question slowly and with as few words as possible. Brand knew that Bundy considered himself a gifted attorney, but he also knew Bundy had dropped out of law school in Utah. Brand was not going to make this easy on Bundy.

"What happened on the morning of January 15th, 1978?" Bundy asked the lieutenant.

"I got up," Brand said.

"Then what did you do?"

"I sat on the edge of my bed."

"And then what did you do?" Bundy asked, becoming annoyed.

"I looked for my pants."

"You're going to give me a hard time, aren't you, Lieutenant Brand?" Bundy was irritated. "I can keep you here all day, you know."

"Look, Teddy baby, if you're on some fishing expedition, then just get on with it."

"I know you know big things. I can tell. You know things that will help me," Bundy said. "I can feel it."

"Then either ask me now, or let me out of here." Brand maintained his poker face. He sat back in his chair and watched Bundy lose his composure.

Bundy was intimidated by the large lieutenant. He was unable to keep his thoughts or feelings together. Frustrated, he ended the deposition.

♦❖♦

Almost daily, Bundy was taken from the Leon County Jail to the courthouse. The sheriff's department and the courtrooms were on the same floor. Each time Bundy stepped out of the elevator, he was in front of Lieutenant Brand's office.

One day, Bundy came out of the elevator and saw Brand smoking a cigarette.

"Hey, Georgie baby," Bundy said.

"Hey, Teddy baby," Brand said sarcastically, without a hint of friendliness in his voice.

Bundy smiled. "You still don't like me, do you Georgie?"

"Teddy, baby, it's worse than that," Brand said. "I'd like to take out a rusty knife, cut off your head, and shit down your throat. That's what I'd like to do to you. Hell, I'll bet I could sell the movie rights to that and get rich."

Bundy's smile disappeared. He paused momentarily, then shuffled slowly down the hall to the courtroom, his leg shackles clanking.

Several weeks later, Brand, along with W.D. Phillips, was assigned to escort Bundy down in the elevator. The two officers were chatting about how they both had left their guns behind. Of course, Bundy couldn't help but join in the conversation.

"If I were going to try to escape, now's the time," he joked.

Brand turned to Bundy with a wild look in his eyes.

"Please try to escape. I'd love the opportunity to beat the living shit out of you. I'd even take a suspension for using too much force. I'd like a vacation on account of you. Better yet, let's leave you in the middle of Monroe Street and see how long it takes before someone recognizes your ass and runs you over a few times."

Bundy never tried to engage Brand in conversation again.

As a result of the Chi Omega murders, Katsaris was able to obtain funding to modernize the Leon County Sheriff's

Department. This had been one of his campaign promises and was an important factor in his election. The modernization plan included building a larger, modern facility on Thomasville Road.

New investigation techniques had been developed by the task force, and some were incorporated into the curriculum at the FBI Academy. These included the dental techniques and the command post operation designed by George Brand. This command center approach was used in Atlanta to catch the mass murderer Wayne Williams.

Katsaris was proud of his men and especially of himself. He had achieved his goals. During this period, Katsaris recruited bright young men and women from colleges and universities. He offered better pay and training in the most advanced and sophisticated investigative procedures. He was building the finest sheriff's department in Florida.

The bright side of this was shadowed by the reaction of some of the men. They weren't all that honored to be working under Katsaris.

Many veteran deputies, in quiet, private conversations, expressed their dismay over Katsaris' ego. They didn't like his immediate seizure of jurisdiction of the Chi Omega house and Dunwoody duplex in those first early-morning hours after the murders. Many felt more exact evidence may have been gathered if the technicians from the FDLE had been allowed access to the rooms. Hopes for a conviction now hinged solely on the bitemarks and the impressions of Bundy's teeth. Skeptics blamed Katsaris and his personal conflict with Eddie Boone for a lack of usable evidence.

◆❖◆

When the grand jury delivered the indictments of Bundy in the two Chi Omega murders, Katsaris called Lieutenant Brand into his office.

"Okay George, should I call the press before or after I give Bundy his papers?"

Closing the door behind them, Brand said, "Ken, if you read those papers on TV, you're screwed for sure. Now, if I were you, I'd read it to Bundy, then call the press and tell them you're happy to announce the grand jury's decision."

Katsaris thanked Brand for the advice, but he didn't heed it. Katsaris called a press conference. He decided he would read the indictment to Bundy on live television.

On July 28th, 1978, television cameras captured the grinning sheriff as he read the long and detailed indictment to the thin, manacled man. Bundy, ever-conscious of cameras and publicity, smiled and cracked jokes about the sheriff as Katsaris read from the documents in his hands.

When Katsaris finished reading, he handed the indictments to Bundy. The suspect mugged for the cameras as he shredded the indictment into tiny pieces and let them fall to the ground. "That's all you're going to get, an indictment," Bundy said.

The citizens of Leon County watched the antics of an egotistical sheriff who relished the spotlight turn a somber occasion into a circus. Many criticized the sheriff for not respectfully and quietly handling the levying of charges against the man accused of committing the most heinous and brutal crimes in Tallahassee history.

As a result of the media hype generated by both Sheriff Katsaris and Ted Bundy, a motion for a change of venue was filed by Bundy and his public defenders. No one in the sheriff's department or the state attorney's office liked the fact that Bundy and Katsaris were engaged in running a media circus from the courthouse building. The battle that raged between the state attorney's office and Bundy's defense team cost the taxpayers millions of dollars and resulted in the move of the trial from Tallahassee to Miami, much to Katsaris' chagrin.

Many reporters and photographers found Bundy charming, and a few wondered if he perhaps had been a convenient arrest and the real killer was still on the loose. The actions of the sheriff colored these opinions, and many people openly wondered if Katsaris had rushed to charge Bundy to prop up his chances for reelection.

The sheriff tried to keep information about the case from the press, but this alienated the journalists. The achievements Katsaris made in Leon County law enforcement were rarely covered in the newspapers. The good work of the deputies was overshadowed by problems with the Bundy case and the vanity of the sheriff. Few would remember how Katsaris had turned the Leon County Sheriff's Department into a first-class law enforcement agency.

◆❖◆

During Bundy's trial in late July, 1979, a woman named Carol Ann Boone suddenly appeared every day in the Miami courtroom and sat next to Louise Bundy, the defendant's mother. Ms. Boone had moved from Washington state with her teenaged son to lend support to Bundy. She said she was his fiancé, and was convinced and outspoken of his innocence.

Ms. Boone was particularly upset by the testimony given by Pensacola Patrolman David Lee about his apprehension of Bundy. Ms. Boone went to Lee's motel room just past midnight after he testified. She was hysterical as she pounded on the door and yelled for him to allow her into his room. Lee, woken from a deep sleep, wore only his underwear when he opened the door a crack. Boone tried to force the door open.

"Why are you doing this to my Ted?" she screamed. "Why are you lying about the man I love? Why are you doing this? You know you're just making all of this up."

"Lady, get out of here and leave me alone," Lee insisted. "I'm just doing my job."

"You're all just pigs trying to kill my Ted. You son of a bitch." She spat at him.

"Lady, get out of here before I get ugly," Lee said. He was troubled by this madwoman and he briefly visualized his gun in its holster in the drawer of the nightstand. She was not able to get into his room, nor would he fully open the door to her. She eventually gave up, but continued to yell and scream as she walked down the hallway.

On July 24th, 1979, Ted Bundy was convicted of the Chi Omega murders after the jury deliberated for seven hours. The bitemarks he had left on Lisa Levy's body were a definitive match to Bundy's teeth.

His trial had been the first ever broadcasted live on public TV in the state of Florida. Bundy represented himself during the trial. He was a media darling, and it seemed the public could not get enough of his courtroom antics. Carol Boone and Louise Bundy wept as the verdict was read. One week later, he was sentenced to die.

Chapter 32: Closing Time

After the convictions, Katsaris was ridiculed repeatedly in the newspaper. He was even accused of trying to tamper with the jury. Katsaris defended his actions as part of his rights and duty as sheriff to have a discussion with the jury.

On Thursday, August 30th, 1979, a front-page article in the *Democrat* stated that Sergeant Lynn Freeman had accused Sheriff Ken Katsaris of placing his service revolver on a table and making threatening remarks to Freeman during a meeting that took place around April 1st.[24]

"I hope what you have to say, Sergeant, isn't bad enough for me to shoot you over," Katsaris allegedly said.

"Although it was done in a joking manner," Sergeant Freeman wrote in his resignation letter to Katsaris, "I shudder to think what might have happened if the pistol discharged as it did while you were working for the St. Petersburg Police Department. I venture to say that Lieutenant Dale Wise would have been killed or seriously injured..."

The gun in question was an antique Old West six-gun. It was mounted on a plaque. When Freeman sat down in front of the sheriff's desk, the gun was on the table and pointed at him.

"I'm a little nervous with that gun pointing at me," he said.

Katsaris turned the gun. Lieutenant Dale Wise joked, "Hey, don't point that gun at me, either."

Katsaris picked the gun up and slammed it down on the other side of the desk so that now it was pointing at George Brand.

"I swear I'm voting for you, Ken," Brand said, playing along and raising his hands in the air.

The men laughed over the gunplay, but the article made it look

---

[24] Peterson, Jonathon. "Deputy quits, assails sheriff." *The Tallahassee Democrat*, Aug. 30, 1979, p. 1A.

as if Katsaris had threatened and nearly killed his deputy.

The elections were still a year away and Katsaris believed his success record outweighed the bad press. Still, he wanted certain damaging events kept out of the papers at any cost.

Some of his men made sure he was protected.

◆❖◆

In October, 1979, several months after Bundy's Chi Omega conviction, Tallahassee resident Rick Garzaniti made a claim for the reward money that had been offered for information leading to the arrest and conviction of the Chi Omega assailant. Ted Bundy had stolen Garzaniti's orange VW Bug and had driven it to Pensacola, where he was arrested attempting to flee the state. The *Democrat* received a copy of Garzaniti's claim, and it was reported that Garzaniti believed that God wanted Bundy to steal his VW so that he would be caught with it.

Joseph read the article about Garzaniti and believed he also had a claim to part of the reward money. By the deadline, there would be a total of four claims presented: Garzaniti's, Joseph's, David Lee's, and one other who chose to remain anonymous.

Joseph contacted the *Democrat* and was instructed how to file a claim. It needed to be written and submitted in person to the executive editor, Wyatt Matthews. The claims would then be reviewed by a panel that consisted of Matthews and several area Baptist ministers. Joseph was given the names of the ministers who would decide the outcome of the reward.

Joseph prepared his statement and drove to the *Democrat* offices to hand-deliver his claim to Matthews. The executive editor had a beautifully appointed office. His enormous desk, made of a solid hardwood, either mahogany or walnut, was highly polished and neat. A few newspapers were stacked on its edge.

Matthews remained seated at his desk when Joseph was shown to his office. He motioned for Joseph to sit on a couch. Matthews was a tall, thin man with conservatively cut hair. Joseph thought he looked like a banker. His eyes were direct and probing and he wore a stern expression as he watched Joseph. Matthews leaned back in his large, high-backed, brown leather executive chair and asked

Joseph what he wanted.

"Do you believe in God?" Joseph asked.

"Of course," Matthews snapped.

"Do you think it's possible God helped in capturing the killer?"

"Does this have anything to do with that Garzaniti boy, with his stolen car? Are you here to plead for him?" Matthews asked. "He's already placed a claim. The decision will be made very soon and there's nothing else I can do for him."

"No, no, sir, I'm not here on Garzaniti's behalf. I'm here on my own. Do you believe that God helped catch the killer?"

"Yes, I believe God helped us capture Bundy," Matthews said.

"Then do you think it's possible someone gave the sheriff's department information from spiritual sources that helped solve the case?"

"What do you mean?" Matthews said, his curiosity piqued.

"Do you believe that God wanted Bundy caught, so He had a person give the sheriff's department information about the killer? And they then used the information and it helped to catch the killer? Would you say that could be possible?" Joseph waited for a response.

"If God wanted that, yes. Anything God wants will happen." Matthews leaned forward on his elbows.

"Good. If I told you that's exactly what happened, would you check it out and help me?" Joseph was careful to maintain eye contact with Matthews.

Matthews looked around his office. He folded his hands, placed his index fingers on his chin, and leaned back on his chair again. "What are you saying? Are you saying that God told you to tell the police something?"

"Yes. That would be the easiest way to think of it. I worked with Lieutenant George Brand of the Leon County Sheriff's Department. I was thanked personally by Sheriff Ken Katsaris for my work in capturing Ted Bundy." Joseph squinted at the mention of Bundy's name. "Here's my letter claiming the reward money."

Matthews leaned forward and took the letter from Joseph. He opened the envelope and scanned it. Joseph had made two stipulations for the reward money. The first was that the reward was to be divided and given to the survivors and to the families of Margaret Bowman and Lisa Levy. The second condition was that his full name was never to appear in the paper or made public.

Joseph watched Matthews's eyes. After a few moments, Matthews put the letter down on his desk. "May I keep this?"

"Of course; I wrote it for you. But please remember, I don't want my name used in any news articles or in public. Is that alright with you?"

"I don't think there will be any problem with that," Matthews said. He exhaled sharply and raised his voice. "This is the biggest bunch of bullshit I've ever read! Who are you? Are you stoned on drugs or something?"

Joseph was floored. "No, sir, I'm not on drugs. I don't take drugs. I don't drink wine or liquor. Last month I took a special vow to God to not take drugs or alcohol to alter my consciousness. Call Lieutenant Brand at the Leon County Sheriff's Department. He'll confirm my whole story. He's the officer I worked with."

"Son, we have real issues to deal with here. I'll place your claim with the others. I wish you the best." Matthews picked up some papers on his desk. "Show yourself out. Good day."

Joseph rose to his feet. He was infuriated. "You're not even going to consider this, are you?"

"Oh, sure. But I think you need to see a doctor and get yourself straightened out. This is a stupid request." Matthews laughed. "We knew some nutty people would come out of the woodwork, but you get a high mark for creativity."

Impatiently, Matthews stood. "Now, excuse me. I have more important things to deal with than hippies who God talks to. I'm quite involved with the churches in this town, I'm a pillar of the religious community, and your story is ridiculous. *A vow to God.* Really? Good day."

Joseph took a step toward Matthews's desk. "You, being a pillar of the religious community, should know about the vow I've taken. It's in the Bible. It's called the 'Vow of a Nazarite.'"

"Yes, whatever you say."

Joseph stared at the editor for a moment, then turned and stepped out of the office. A security guard approached him as he glanced at the reporters in the newsroom.

"Boy! You with the long hair! Over here!" the guard called. "Mr. Matthews wanted me to make sure you didn't get lost in this building. It can be tricky."

Joseph fumed as he walked out to his car. He was frustrated and angry at the response of the editor.

When he got home, Joseph played his guitar for a while, but his mood darkened with the skies and he was unable to focus on music. He lay down and rested.

Joseph dreamed about a young blonde woman with a mole on her hip. When he woke up, he wished it wasn't a dream.

Over the next few days, Joseph had contacted the ministers who were on the panel to decide the reward disbursement. None of the four clergymen would consider Joseph's claim. As he waited for his toast to be ready, he glanced at a copy of the *Flambeau* that had been left on the counter by one of his roommates.

He looked inside for a telephone number. He called the newspaper and was told he needed to speak with Helen Baxter. He left a message for her.

On the afternoon of Wednesday, March 8th, 1989, Helen dropped her children with their father and drove from her apartment in Gainesville to Tallahassee. She had arranged to spend the next morning meeting with George Brand so that he could begin to tell the story he was unable to tell nearly 10 years earlier.

Helen spent the evening with her old friend Laurie Jones. She no longer worked for the *Flambeau*, but had taken a job with the Florida legislature. Laurie had lots of gossip to tell her friend. They enjoyed a meal at a local restaurant and then went dancing at some of their favorite spots, Tommy's Deep South Music Hall and Bullwinkle's.

The old friends danced, talked, and drank. Helen felt happier than she had in a long time. The places held so many good memories for her.

The next morning, she got up and pulled herself together to go meet George Brand. She drove over to the Doak Campbell Stadium at the edge of the FSU campus. She could not believe how large the stadium area had become. Coach Bobby Bowden had turned the FSU Seminole football team into a powerhouse, and they brought lots of revenue to the university and the town.

Brand, the self-proclaimed "King of Parking," had told her where to park when she arrived and how to find his office housed within the stadium. She was nervously excited to finally have an interview with the umquhile investigator.

Helen found his office and rapped gently against the open door. Brand looked up and stood. He greeted her with a hearty handshake.

"Hey there, I know you," he said. He had a bad head cold. "I'd recognize you anywhere. Long time ago, you worked for the mullet wrapper."

They both laughed. It was exactly how he'd greeted her the first time they met.

◆❖◆

Ken Katsaris was defeated by a wide margin in his 1980 reelection bid for Sheriff of Leon County. Former FDLE agent Eddie Boone assumed the leadership of the department and oversaw the construction of the new facilities on Thomasville Road. Katsaris still lives in Tallahassee and works as a consultant, trainer, and litigation consultant for law enforcement agencies.

During a February 1990 interview, Katsaris said his biggest mistake may have been his reluctance to allow the FDLE technicians to complete the forensics work on the Chi Omega murder scenes.

George Brand, a longtime friend and staunch supporter of Katsaris, lost his job with the sheriff's department after Boone took office. Brand was just shy of retirement and, with the termination, he lost his pension. Brand worked with the FSU Seminole Boosters as the manager of concessions. He also opened his own private security company. "I help keep the students safe," he said.

In late May, 1989, after Brand and Helen Baxter completed their third interview, Brand said he had something for her. "A souvenir, sort of." He unlocked a cabinet door and pulled out a file folder. Inside the folder was a sealed manila envelope.

He sat down at his desk and broke the seal. He pulled out a stack of photographs and glanced through them.

"How do you leave out of Tallahassee to hit I-10?" he asked absently.

"Oh, I usually take 90 west to 10," she said. "Why do you ask?"

"Well, take a look at these," he said and handed her the photos.

"What are these?"

"I'm giving these to you. They're photographs of Ted Bundy's handprints and a set of his fingerprints."

She was surprised "You're giving these to me?"

"Yes, Helen, I want you to have them. But I've got something I want you to do with them." Brand smiled and moved to the edge of his desk. "I want you to have a little fun with these."

"Okay, I'm game," she said.

"Have you ever noticed Madame Anna, the psychic and palm reader, up there on 90 West on the way to I-10?"

"I have. She's been in that little house for years, I guess. I used to see her sign when I was a student here, driving back and forth to Miami."

"Yep, that's the one. She's about as old as God, but she's pretty sharp." He lit a cigarette. "Stop in and take a couple of these handprints. Tell her I sent you. Ask her if she'll read the prints."

Helen studied the photographs and the originals of the prints.

"Really?" she said excitedly.

"Don't tell her who they belong to, though. Just see what she says and let me know."

◆❖◆

Helen spent the rest of the day going through newspaper archives and pulling news stories from microfilm at the library. Before she knew it, she had run out of time to spend in Tallahassee and needed to leave town. She had to get back to Gainesville and pick up her kids. She'd have to see Madam Anna on another visit.

Chapter 33: The Myth of the Fingerprints

On a day in early July 1989, Helen found herself bored at work. She pulled her briefcase out from under her desk and closed her office door. She thought she would continue to transcribe the tape-recorded interviews she'd done with George Brand.

As she brought out the recorder, she noticed the manila envelope. She had not gotten back to Tallahassee yet and wasn't certain when she would be able to return. She looked through the handprints and compared her hand to those of Bundy's. He had large hands.

She wondered what Madam Anna would have said and was disappointed she hadn't seen her, as Brand had suggested.

Helen reached into a drawer and pulled out a Gainesville telephone directory. She flipped to the Palm Readers section. There was a listing for one in Gainesville, so she dialed the number. It rang and played a prerecorded message: "The number you have dialed is no longer in service."

Helen hung up and redialed to make sure she had dialed correctly the first time. She got the same recording.

"Hmm." She wondered who else she could call. She looked up Psychics.

She scanned the five or six listings. She saw one that simply said Bernice, Psychic Readings and a phone number. The address was not printed, but the phone number was a local exchange.

Helen picked up the phone and dialed. Within two rings, a woman answered. She had a voice rough with cigarettes.

Helen identified herself and asked Bernice if she could read palms.

"Well, I wouldn't say that I'm an expert, but I'm willing to try."

"Do you think you can read someone's palm from a photograph?"

The woman coughed and cleared her throat. "I've certainly

never done that. What is this about?"

"It's nothing bad, I promise. I just have some photographs of someone's fingerprints and palms. I'd like to hear what you say about them."

"Is this a gag or something?"

"No, this is not a gag. I'm very serious."

Bernice agreed to try to read the handprints and they made an appointment for the following day, when Helen could leave work a little early. Bernice said she charged $25 for a psychic reading and told Helen to bring cash.

"I don't take checks from people I don't know."

Late the next afternoon, Helen pulled into a trailer park north of Gainesville on U.S. Highway 441. She circled the park, driving by the pool and tennis courts, until she reached Bernice's street. The address brought her to the penultimate trailer on the right. She pulled into the driveway and parked next to a red, older model Toyota sedan. Nervously, she ran her right hand through her hair and counted to five before she opened the car door. She wanted to appear calm.

The trailer was a single wide and looked to be the oldest one in the neatly manicured park. Bernice had blooming plants and cactus on her front porch, as well as a couple of outdoor chairs and a rocker. It seemed like a friendly place, albeit somewhat dogeared and worn.

She knocked on the glass portion of the screened door. She could already smell the years of cigarette smoke that adhered to the structure. *I'm glad I brought cigarettes.* Strangely, she found that by smoking she could better tolerate other smokers.

A small dog barked behind the door. She was about to knock again but figured the dog already alerted Bernice. At that moment, the inner door opened and an older woman with freshly dyed red hair greeted her.

"Are you Helen?" she asked as she pushed open the screen door. "Come in, don't mind the mess."

Just as Helen was about to step into the trailer, a sudden gust of wind blew the screen door out of her grasp. The door flew open and hit the side of the trailer, then slammed into her.

"Storm's coming," Bernice said. "Come in before you get blown away."

Bernice secured the doors and led Helen to the right, into the kitchen. Helen looked to the left, at the living room, which was neatly furnished but filled with dolls. The drapes were drawn against the late-afternoon sun.

"Hi Bernice, I'm Helen Baxter," she said.

She wiped her hand on her skirt and held it out to shake the woman's hand. She was perspiring heavily from nervousness. Bernice took her hand and held it for several seconds.

"Uh huh," she said when she released Helen's hand. They stood in the small kitchen. "I guess I figured as much. I am psychic, you know." She winked.

Both women laughed a bit uneasily. "Please sit," Bernice said, indicating a chair. "Can you get back there?"

"Oh, yes, that's fine," Helen said.

"I always sit here," Bernice said. "It's close to the phone and the coffee pot." She had been working on a crossword puzzle in a paperback book. She elbowed it to the edge of the table.

Helen slid into the chair between the table and the wall. She laid the manila envelope on the table. She had brought only four of the photographs, making sure not to bring ones that had Bundy's name on them.

"Coffee?" Bernice asked. "I just made a fresh pot."

"Sure, that'd be great," Helen said.

She looked around the kitchen. The table was covered with a freshly laundered green tablecloth and there was a deck of regular playing cards at Bernice's spot. There was also a clean ashtray, a pack of unfiltered Pall Mall reds, and a red plastic lighter. Helen noticed an image of Jesus on the bottom. "Jesus hates it when you smoke" chastised those who dared use it.

Helen chuckled. A small electric fan sat on the table by the window. Clean dishes were drying on a plastic rack. Counters and the bay windowsill were filled with ceramic angels, colored glass balls, stones, other knickknacks, and a house plant. A small dreamcatcher hung off the curtain rod. The lace curtains were stained yellow from years of tobacco.

Bernice set down two cups of coffee, both black, and sat down. Her mug said "I Love My Grandma." Helen smiled when she saw that. Bernice might be a psychic, but she was *definitely* a grandma.

"Cream? Sugar?" Bernice held up a cylinder of coffee whitener.

"Uh, no, just black, please."

Bernice's dog, a little gray poodle, freshly groomed with painted toenails and pink bows, was sniffing Helen's feet and legs. She shifted her legs away.

"Buffy, sit down. Don't bother her," Bernice commanded. "She smells your dog. You have one, don't you?"

"Yes, I do."

"Well, Helen, let me make sure I understand what you're seeking today." She eyed the envelope. "Is that what you brought for me to read?"

"Yes. I brought several photos." Helen picked up the envelope and began to open it.

"No, don't show me them yet," Bernice said and held out her hand. "Just let me hold them."

Helen handed her the envelope. Bernice closed her eyes, but quickly opened them and put the envelope on the table. She pushed it to the side, away from her.

"I'm going to do a reading on you first," Bernice said.

"Why? I don't want a reading done on me, I just want the photos read."

Helen wanted to make certain she wouldn't be charged for two readings. She could barely afford the $25 fee for one reading.

"That's okay, I'm only charging you for the handprints, but I'd like to do a reading on you first." Bernice took a drag and exhaled. "I always recommend that an inquirer keep a closed mouth about herself, but an open mind."

"Oh, okay. Which hand do you want to see?" Helen looked at her palms.

"Are you right-handed or left-handed?"

"Left-handed."

Bernice reached over and touched her left hand. Helen held it out. Bernice examined her palm and ran her nail down the lifeline.

"Oh, good, that's very good, you'll have a long, healthy life," she said as she lit an unfiltered cigarette. "Do you mind?"

"Smoking? No, I smoke too, sometimes."

Helen reached into her purse and pulled out a pack of cigarettes and a lighter. She lit one. Bernice reached over and turned on the fan. She held Helen's right hand and examined the lines, comparing them with the lines on her left hand.

"I see from your hands that you are a professional woman, you have a job that focuses on business and properties." Helen knew that one did not have to be a fortuneteller to figure that out. She was wearing a dress, stockings, and high heels: office attire.

"Yes."

"But that's not your true calling, am I right?"

"No, not really," Helen said. She did not want to betray anything about herself, so she tried to keep her face expressionless. She focused on the questions Bernice asked to keep extraneous thoughts out of her head.

"Are you married?" Bernice asked. Helen said nothing. "Because I see on your palm you will have two marriages. Is this your first one?"

"Yes."

Bernice continued to trace the lines on her palm. "Okay. I see that you are married, but that you're separated. Is that it?"

Helen nodded. This was an easy guess, as she no longer wore a wedding band.

"But you have children, yes? In this world?"

"Yes, yes I do. If you mean are they alive?" Helen was puzzled by this.

"Yes, that's what I mean. Sometimes people have children who have passed on, miscarriages and so on. I see three here. And three that have passed over." She quieted for a moment to see how Helen would react. "You'll be with them, too. They're waiting for you."

Helen had no idea what to think about this. *How could she have known that?* She felt a bit disoriented, a boat unmoored. Bernice had her complete attention.

"You won't have any more, you know," Bernice said. "Children."

Helen nodded.

The reading continued. She handed Helen the deck of cards.

"Go ahead and shuffle these. Either make a wish or tell the cards what you want to know. But don't tell me. When you're done, divide them into three stacks."

Helen picked up the cards and began to shuffle them. She laid the cards out as directed. Bernice picked up the three stacks and laid one on top of the next. She then began placing the cards on the table.

"I see that your father has passed, is that right?"

"Yes."

"But your mother is still here?"

"Yes, but not right here," Helen laughed. "Not in Gainesville, I mean." She almost added *Thank God.*

"Here are your three children. Two boys, one girl, correct?" Bernice touched three cards.

Helen nodded, but she was getting a jittery, nervous feeling and she didn't think it was from the coffee.

"You have an older sister, correct?"

"Yes."

"And she was, in some ways, like a mother to you?"

"Perhaps, yes, when I was a teenager. Now we barely speak."

The psychic nodded, as if this was not news to her. "There's a great deal of jealousy surrounding you."

Bernice continued to lay out the cards until she had placed them all on the table. She made nine piles in the Celtic Cross layout. Helen considered her statement as she examined the arrangement of cards in front of her. These weren't tarot cards, but regular playing cards.

Bernice stood up and got the coffee pot. She poured hot coffee into their cups.

"Your husband loves you, and your children, but... how can I say this? It's like he's sitting over here, on top of a hill, meditating about the world and only occasionally glancing at you and the kids. He's not a bad person, but he's not *interested*. Does that make sense?"

Helen's eyes filled with tears. She fought them back, refusing to become emotional. "That's a pretty good way of describing him," she said.

"You met because he wanted you to do something for him, is that correct?"

"Yes."

"And have you done what he wanted?"

"I'm trying to do it now." Helen pushed her hair away from her face and reached into her purse for a barrette. She wished she could pull off her stockings. She was feeling very warm and sweaty. The air conditioning in the trailer did not seem to be working; not well, anyway.

"Good," Bernice sighed. "Because the sooner you get it done, the sooner you can move on. You'll both be happier once you've finished whatever it is that you agreed to do."

"Okay."

"Did you bring something of his with you?" Bernice asked.

Helen wondered if she should show the woman what she'd brought. She took the envelope and pulled out a set of original handprints that Joseph had given her.

"Here. These are his."

Bernice studied the prints of both hands. "You want me to read another set, though. Other than these, right?"

"Yes, I do," Helen said. She pulled a cassette tape recorder out of her handbag and set it on the table. "Would you mind if I record this?"

Bernice glanced at the recorder. "No, not at all." She continued to study the handprints while Helen began recording.

"I think I see here what the problem is with your marriage," Bernice said. Helen held her breath. "His prints are on police forms, but this man has never been arrested. Did he get these made for you, before you came here?"

"Yes."

"He is extremely psychic. Did you know that?"

Helen nodded. "I do know that."

"He's your husband," Bernice continued, "but he's not the right partner for you. You already know this." She glanced at Helen. "You're in the process of divorcing."

Helen nodded again.

"This man is very gifted, I think. He's a musician and I think he'd be happy living by himself, just working on his music."

"That's very true," Helen said.

"He's very sensitive, psychically, and has traveled to the stars. This man could raise billions for the starving children of Africa, but come home and not notice that his own children need shoes."

Helen nodded mutely. The truth of Bernice's words was irrefutable.

Helen lit another cigarette and exhaled. She was practically chain-smoking and she knew she'd regret it later. She had brought a notepad and pen but had not taken any notes yet. She felt exposed by this woman, vulnerable, her soul laid bare.

Bernice picked up the playing cards and put them into a green velvet pouch. She gathered the coffee cups and emptied them in the sink and poured fresh coffee into them. Helen thanked Bernice as she accepted her freshened cup. She wiped tears from her face.

"I think I'm ready to look at the other prints," Bernice said as she settled in at the table. She picked up the envelope and felt a strong sense of revulsion. She wanted to take her lighter and ignite the envelope and let the contents burn. Instead, she lit a cigarette and cleared her throat.

She laid out the four 8"x10" black-and-white photographs. There were two of the right hand and two of the left. She examined all four, then picked up one of each and placed them back inside the envelope.

"These belong to a man diametrically opposite to your husband," Bernice said. "Do these belong to someone close to you?"

"No."

"Are you certain?" Bernice picked up a pencil. "Are you sure these don't belong to a man in your life? A boyfriend or a cousin, or someone you are related to?" She touched one of the photos with the pencil's eraser.

"No. I am not related to, or involved with, this man."

Helen sensed that Bernice was worried about the handprints. She reached over and touched the woman's hand. "No, these prints don't belong to someone close to me. I do not know him. Please tell me what you are seeing."

Bernice relaxed. "Okay, so overall, I'm picking up that this person is severely psychotic, like he needs to be removed from society; kept in a hospital, maybe. He should not be allowed around people. Women." She looked at Helen's blond hair. "Brunettes, especially."

Helen thought this was a good start.

Bernice ran the eraser down one of the lines on the right print. "This is his life line, and it's an unusual one. I don't think I've ever seen anything like this... but then, I'm not a palmist. But look."

Bernice showed Helen the life line. "It's very broad," the psychic said. "And it's very deep. There's feathering at the top, at the beginning, and then there's feathering again at the bottom. It's on both of his hands, but it's very prominent on his left hand. I don't know what this feathering means. Is he left-handed?"[25]

Helen shrugged. "I don't know." The room darkened as rainclouds covered the sun. The wind had become steady and Helen could hear tree branches scrape against the trailer's aluminum siding. She wanted to get up, to turn on a light, but she remained seated.

"Whoever he is, he's not a nice man," Bernice said. "He hurts people. He can be very cruel. Again, this person shouldn't be among us. He should be locked up somewhere. I think he is very, very sick."

"Do you think he's evil?"

"Whoever he is, and how you've come to have his handprints, worries me a great deal," Bernice said and lit another cigarette. "He would have no compunctions about beating a woman, or abusing a child, for that matter. Jesus, Helen, who is this?"

Helen ignored the question. "Do you think he is capable of killing someone?"

"Yes, this person is certainly capable of killing."

"Has he killed?"

"Yes. He has killed. Many times, I think."

Lightning slashed the sky. A loud and immediate blast of thunder shook the trailer. Helen held her breath. *This is a cliché if I've ever seen one. All we need is some organ music*, she thought as day turned to night.

"Is he evil?" Helen raised her voice over the sound of the rain pounding the trailer.

"Oh, God. He's worse than evil. He's also very, very psychic and used this ability to find his victims." Bernice turned the photos over. Her feeling of revulsion was so strong she thought she would throw up. "I can't look at these anymore."

Helen picked them up and put them back into the envelope. She slid the envelope into the opening of her handbag.

"Now," Bernice said. "Tell me who this is and how you got these

---

[25] He was left handed.

prints?"

"They belong to Ted Bundy," Helen said. "They were given to me."

"Turn off that recorder. Now!"

Helen turned off the machine. Bernice was pale and seemed to have aged at least 10 years.

"I've never been so frightened," Bernice told her. "I don't shock very easily, but I am very shocked at this, this *revelation.*" She closed her eyes. "My heart is pounding. I need to slow it down."

"I'm sorry, Bernice," Helen said. "I didn't want to tell you ahead of time who the prints belonged to. I wanted to see if you could pick up his energy."

"Boy, I'll say I could. When you told me his name, I felt a chill run through my body," Bernice said. "Not because of who the person was, but because I was so accurate in my reading. Maybe the feathering I saw in his life line is there because he was executed. I don't know why it was there at his birth, but maybe he's always been evil."

Bernice got up and shook two aspirin out of a bottle. She poured some water and swallowed the pills. "Jesus, you scared me half to death."

"I know," Helen said, "and I'm sorry that I frightened you. But your description of him was accurate. Uncanny, even."

"I don't think I could have done better if I'd had his résumé in front of me."

The women smoked and talked companionably for the better part of an hour as the late-afternoon storm died down outside. Helen explained how she had met Joseph, and the story he had told her about his involvement with the Bundy investigation in Tallahassee.

As she prepared to leave, Bernice asked her to come back again. "I haven't been so intrigued by a reading since... well, ever," she said.

"I will. I promise," Helen said as she hugged the woman.

Neither realized it at the time, but it would be over a year before they would speak again, when a serial killer would cross Helen's path for a second time.

Afterword

Jack Poitinger returned to law as a state prosecutor for the Second Judicial Circuit with six offices in North Florida. He denies that Joseph, or any psychic, helped catch the Chi Omega killer.

Steve Bodiford became a captain with the Leon County Sheriff's Department in the crime prevention division. Bodiford volunteered his expertise in multiple homicide investigations to the Gainesville Student Murders Task Force in 1990, but sources said he was rebuffed.

In August 1990, Helen tracked down David Lee, the Pensacola patrolman who arrested Ted Bundy—the man Bundy insisted would be promoted. Shortly after the Bundy arrest. Lee was invited to attend the FBI Academy in Quantico, Virginia, to receive special training. While this is considered an honor for police officers, he lost his job with the Pensacola Police Department upon his return. It seemed the department did not grant him sufficient leave time for the FBI training, and they considered him AWOL. Lee went through a difficult period of unemployment. Eventually, he was hired by the Florida Game and Freshwater Fish commission, where he became the supervisor of the investigators for the northern district of the state. The strangest aspect of Lee's story is that, until 1990, no one interviewed him about the arrest of one of America's most infamous serial killers.

It is ironic that nearly everyone directly connected with the infamous Bundy case is no longer actively involved in police investigations.

Shortly before Bundy was executed, Helen learned how Bundy's wife, Carol Ann Boone, became pregnant with his child. On one of Boone's visits to the prison, she gave Bundy an empty vial. Bundy went into the bathroom and filled it with his sperm. She took the vial from him, placed it inside her underwear, and walked out of the prison. She had the sperm frozen until she was ovulating, then had herself inseminated. The child, a girl, was born at a private midwifery center called Birthplace of Gainesville, Florida. Midwife and co-founder Nancy Redfern[26] claimed she felt Bundy's presence at the birth.

For years, Boone staunchly defended Bundy, insisting to everyone that he was not a killer and that he was innocent of all of the charges levied against him. The day before his execution, as Bundy sought to prolong his life, he confessed to a litany of murders he'd committed throughout the country. He had received three death sentences, one each for Margaret Bowman, Lisa Levy, and Kimberly Leach. His death warrant was issued for the murder of 12-year-old Leach, whose murder he refused to speak about. Learning of her husband's admissions, Boone left Gainesville with her daughter and teenaged son. She disappeared from the public eye.

The Independent Florida Flambeau, an excellent training ground for journalists, ceased publication in January 1998.

George Brand died in 2007 at the age of 67. He was a rare man and gifted story-teller. He loved, to the end, to talk about his work on the Chi Omega murders. He left behind some mighty big shoes.

---

[26] In addition to living in the same neighborhood as Carol Anne Boone, the author shared a second connection with Boone: the midwife, Nancy Redfern, also delivered the author's eldest child, at Birthplace, in Gainesville.

Exhibits

The following exhibits are photographs of Theodore Robert Bundy's fingerprints and handprints, given to the author by George C. Brand. The philosophy of palmistry tells us that the non-dominant hand holds the potential one is born with, and that the dominant hand portrays the life one has led.

Bundy was left handed. Notice the feathering near the start and end of his life lines that Bernice saw when reading his handprints.

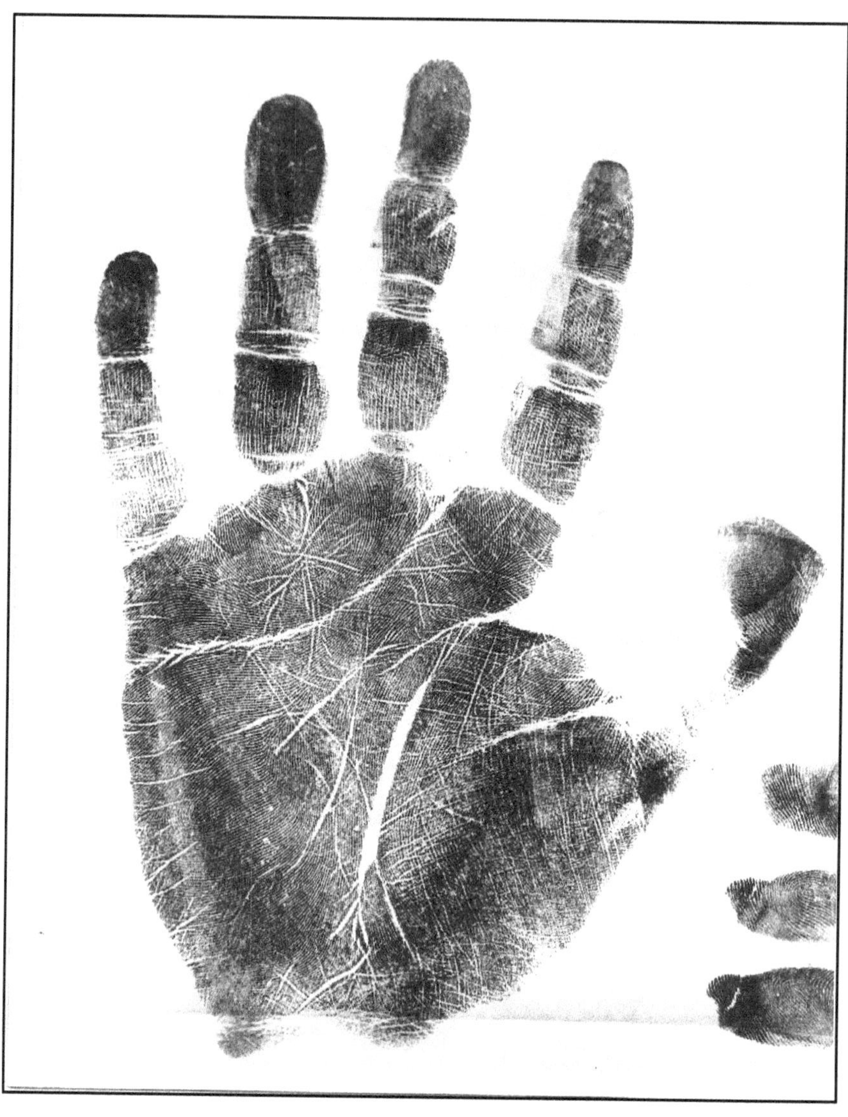

Exhibit 7: Bundy's left handprint (his dominant hand).

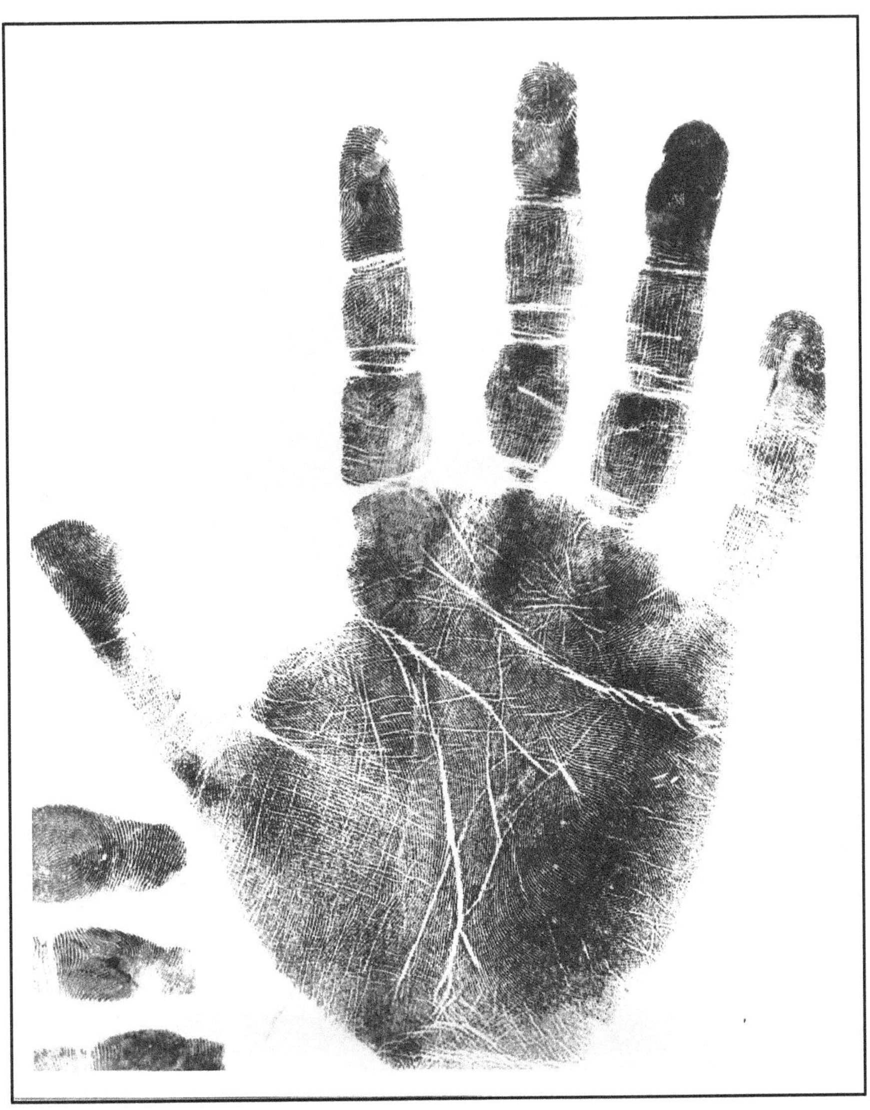

Exhibit 8: Bundy's right handprint.

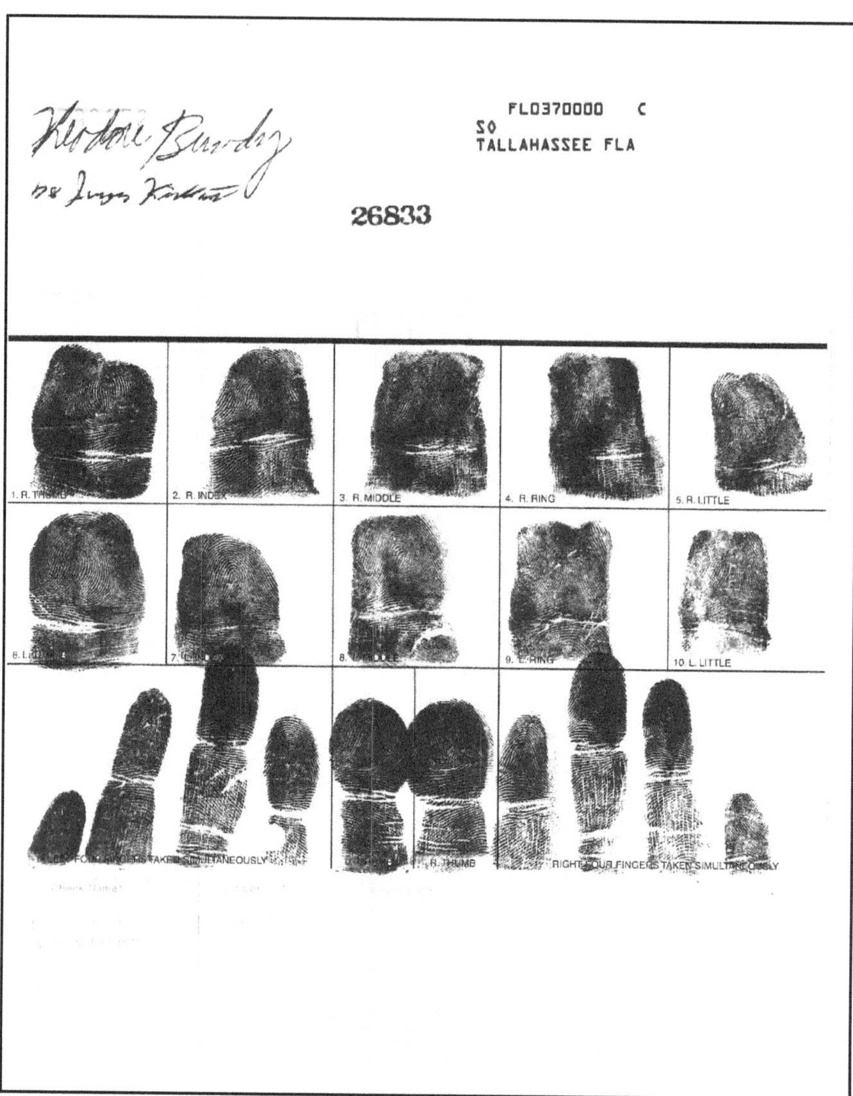

FL0370000 C
SO
TALLAHASSEE FLA

26833

1. R. THUMB
2. R. INDEX
3. R. MIDDLE
4. R. RING
5. R. LITTLE
10. L. LITTLE
R. THUMB
RIGHT FOUR FINGERS TAKEN SIMULTANEOUSLY

Exhibit 9: Bundy's fingerprints.

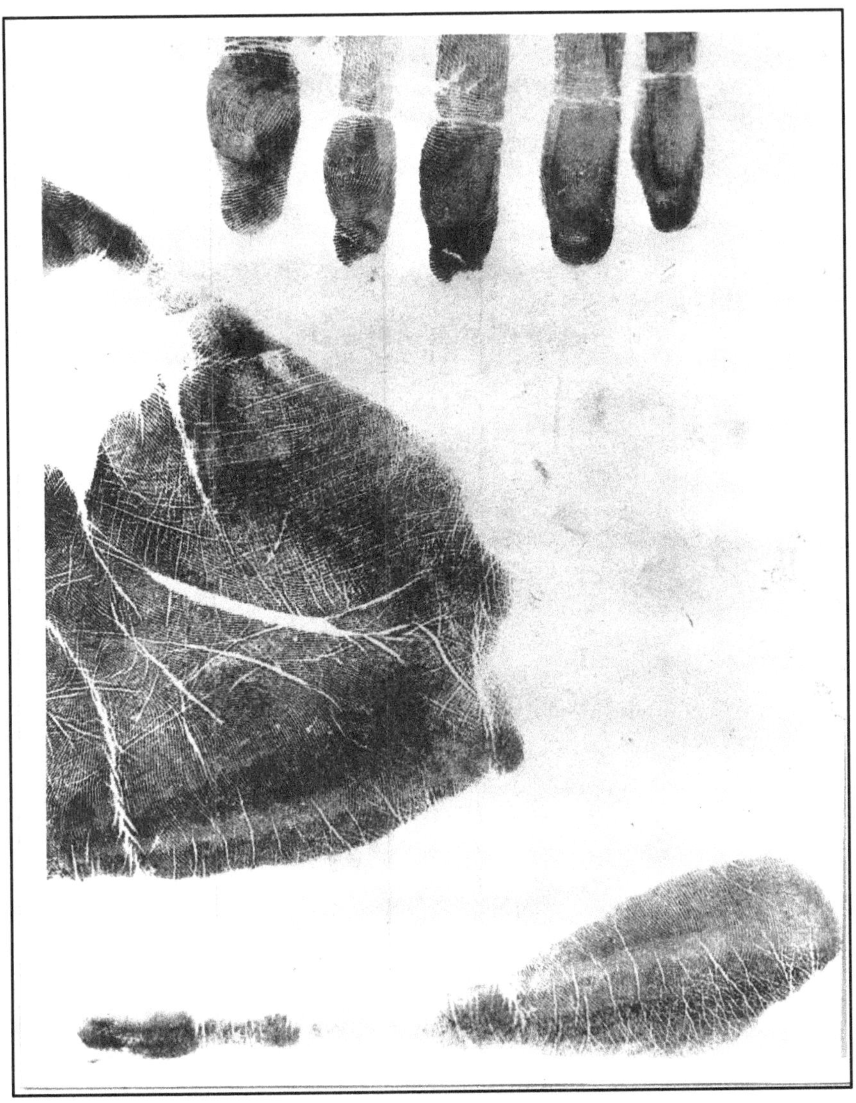

Exhibit 10: Bundy's left palm print.

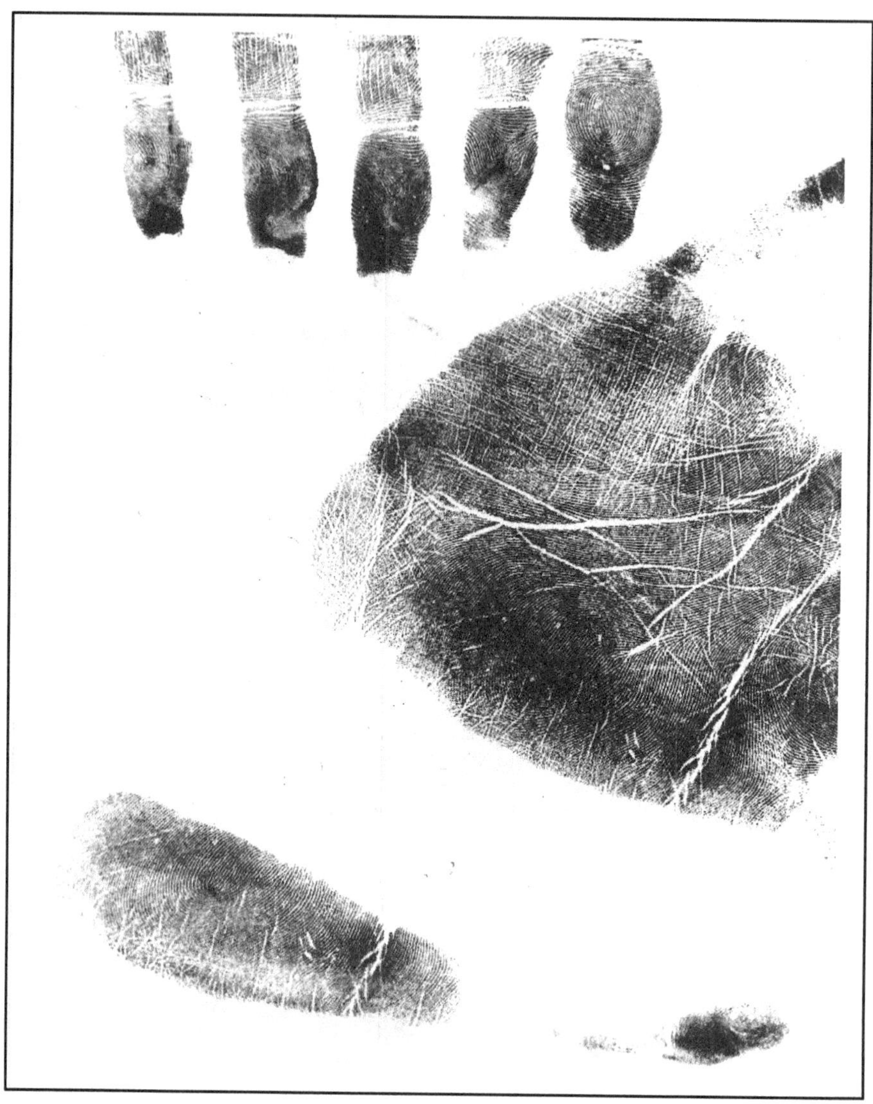

Exhibit 11: Bundy's right palm print.

Acknowledgements

Gratitude to R. David First for this story, and the journey, and to George Brand for keeping his promise to me. It's true to say this story changed the trajectory of my life. Much appreciation to David Lee for the afternoon interview at Camp Blanding, and telling the story of his arrest of Ted Bundy.

This book has taken many years, and has gone through several edits and rewrites. I thank editor Vince Font for the clarity he has given this narrative. At this point, any typographical errors are mine alone.

Happy trails to Bernice and Laurie Jones. Until we meet again.

Love and happiness to Peter Lehmann, my steadfast partner and traveling companion, who encouraged me to *finally* tell the story.

About the Author

Susan Waller Lehmann hails from Miami, Florida, and attended Florida State University. Perhaps because the temperate climate of the South attracts crazies, her life intersected with two serial killers, and, as a result, her first two books recount her stories of Ted Bundy in the aftermath of the 1978 Chi Omega murders, and Daniel Rolling during the 1990 Gainesville Student murders.

The non-fiction subjects she prefers to write about delve into her wide-ranging experiences as a journalist, private investigator, and death penalty mitigation expert. There ought to be a good story or two in there somewhere. What's that old saw? *Truth is stranger than fiction.*

Her formative years spent in the southeastern United States, she now lives with her husband and a well-loved feline in the beautiful northern Wasatch Mountains. She occasionally yearns for thunderstorms, trees, and the ocean. This emotional response does not extend to humidity, cockroaches or fleas.

Her husband is lobbying her to go camping. Unsuccessfully, so far.

About the Publisher

White Rhino Press is a small publishing house located in the northern mountains of Utah that specializes in bringing remarkable stories to the printed page.

Why a rhino? Due to poaching, the southern white rhino[27] is threatened with extinction, whereas the northern white rhino is considered to be extinct with only three remaining individuals alive in captivity. With a population of around 20,400, the southern white rhino survives in four countries: Kenya, Namibia, Zimbabwe, and South Africa.

Visit these countries and donate to a cause of your choice in order to protect these beautiful and irreplaceable beasts.

---

27 The word "white" originates from the Afrikaans word *"weit,"* and refers to the animal's wide mouth.

CPSIA information can be obtained
at www.ICGtesting.com
Printed in the USA
BVHW04*0713050718
520784BV00013B/219/P

9 780999 230015